...spitzen schaute und mit aller Kraft

...en kühlen Duft von Gras und Erde

...hemzigen zu ihm aufflog und dazwischen in lau...

...en Wolken der Duft der Vanillesträucher, fühlte er

...d konnte an nichts anderes denken. Ohne den Kopf

...ußte er, dass die alte Frau am *ihrem* Fenster saß, de...

...äude auf dem von der Sonne durchglühten Gesims...

...klopfende in den *das* blutlose, maskenhafte Gesicht e...

...grauenhafte Heimstätte für die ~~schmezgen~~ hilflo...

...ngen, die nicht absterben konnten. Ohne den Kopf z...

...fühlte er, wenn der Diener für Minuten von seinem Fens...

...und sich an einem Schrank zu schaffen ~~er~~ machte,

...aufzusehen erwartete er mit einer heimlichen Angst den

...er wiederkommen werde. Und er wusste, dass er wiede...

...werde. Während er ~~dachte~~ *mit beiden Armen,* biegsame Äste hinter sich zurück...

...m sich in der verwachsenen Ecke des Gartens zu verkr...

...lle Gedanken auf die Schönheit des Himmels drängte, der

...ücken von feuchtem Türkis von oben durch das dunkle

...von Zweigen und Ranken herunterfiel, bemächtigte sich se...

THE WHOLE
DIFFERENCE

THE WHOLE DIFFERENCE

SELECTED WRITINGS OF
HUGO VON HOFMANNSTHAL

EDITED BY J. D. McCLATCHY

PRINCETON UNIVERSITY PRESS · PRINCETON AND OXFORD

Introduction and poem translations copyright © 2008 by J. D. McClatchy, which include: "An Experience," "Stanzas in Terza Rima," "The Both of Them," "Ballad of the Outer Life," "We went along a way . . . ," "Three Epigrams," and "In Memory of the Actor Mitterwurzer"

Some material in this volume was reprinted from *Hugo von Hofmannsthal*, Bollingen XXXIII, copyright © 1980 by Princeton University Press

"The Tower" was reprinted from Alfred Schwartz's *Three Plays by Hugo von Hofmannsthal*, 1996, pp. 141–241, with the permission of Wayne State University Press. Copyright © 1966 by Wayne State University Press

Published by Princeton University Press, 41 William Street, Princeton, New Jersey 08540
In the United Kingdom: Princeton University Press, 6 Oxford Street, Woodstock, Oxfordshire OX20 1TW

Library of Congress Cataloging-in-Publication Data
Hofmannsthal, Hugo von, 1874–1929.
[Selections. English]
The whole difference: selected writings of Hugo von Hofmannsthal / edited by J. D. McClatchy.
—1st ed.
p. cm.
Includes bibliographical references.
ISBN 978-0-691-12909-9 (cloth)
1. Hofmannsthal, Hugo von, 1874–1929—Translations into English.
I. McClatchy, J. D., 1945–
II. Title.
PT2617.O47A2 2008
838'.91209—dc22   2007039181

British Library Cataloging-in-Publication Data is available

Frontispiece photo of Hugo von Hofmannsthal is from the *Opera News* archives.

Endpapers and part opener images from Hugo von Hofmannsthal. Pages from manuscript draft of "Das Märchen der 672. Nacht," 1895. Courtesy of the Frederick R. Koch Collection. Beinecke Rare Book and Manuscript Library, Yale University.

This book has been composed in New Baskerville with Trajan display

Printed on acid-free paper. ∞

press.princeton.edu

Printed in the United States of America

10 9 8 7 6 5 4 3 2 1

Das alles ist geheim, so viel geheim.
Und man ist dazu da, daß man's entragt.
Und in dem "Wie" da liegt der ganze Untershied—

It's all a mystery, so much is mysterious.
And we are here to endure it.
And in the How, there lies the whole difference—

Der Rosenkavalier, Act I

CONTENTS

Introduction · 1

POEMS

GHAZAL (1891) · 23
translated by Stephen Yenser

AN EXPERIENCE (1892) · 24
translated by J. D. McClatchy

STANZAS IN TERZA RIMA (1895) · 26
translated by J. D. McClatchy

THE BOTH OF THEM (1896) · 28
translated by J. D. McClatchy

BALLAD OF THE OUTER LIFE (1896) · 29
translated by J. D. McClatchy

WE WENT ALONG A WAY . . . (1897) · 30
translated by J. D. McClatchy

THREE EPIGRAMS (1898) · 32
translated by J. D. McClatchy

IN MEMORY OF THE
ACTOR MITTERWURZER (1898) · 33
translated by J. D. McClatchy

FICTION

THE TALE OF NIGHT SIX HUNDRED AND
SEVENTY-TWO (1895) • 39
translated by Michael Henry Heim

A TALE OF THE CAVALRY (1898) • 56
translated by Mary Hottinger

ESSAYS

THE LETTER OF LORD CHANDOS (1902) • 69
translated by Tania and James Stern

MOMENTS IN GREECE (1908–1914) • 80
translated by Tania and James Stern

A MEMORY OF BEAUTIFUL DAYS (1908) • 101
translated by Tania and James Stern

SHAKESPEARE'S KINGS AND NOBLEMEN (1905) • 109
translated by Tania and James Stern

BALZAC (1908) • 128
translated by Tania and James Stern

SEBASTIAN MELMOTH (1905) • 143
translated by Tania and James Stern

FROM THE *BOOK OF FRIENDS* (1922) • 147
translated by Tania and James Stern

LIBRETTI

THE CAVALIER OF THE ROSE, ACT I (1911) • 153
translated by Christopher Holme

PLAYS

THE DIFFICULT MAN:
A COMEDY IN THREE ACTS (1921) • 201
translated by Willa Muir

THE TOWER: A TRAGEDY
IN FIVE ACTS (SECOND VERSION, 1927) • 366
translated by Alfred Schwarz

Notes • 493

For Further Reading • 501

INTRODUCTION

No NOVELIST has better described the dissolution of the Hapsburg empire than Joseph Roth. Of course it did not collapse with a shudder at the death of the emperor and the end of the Great War, but had been rotting away for years, and the rot created its own luster, which Roth captured with an uncanny accuracy. He caught the rustling silks and sword hilts, the gutted nostalgia, the unwritten and impenetrable rules, the aimlessness and hollow laughter, the Prater and masquerades, the military maneuvers and opera boxes. He described it all as a dying candle, flickering, golden, consumed by the very liquid it had created.

> I lived in the cheerful, carefree company of young aristocrats whose company, second only to that of artists, I loved best under the old Empire. With them I shared a skeptical frivolity, a melancholy curiosity, a wicked insouciance, and the pride of the doomed, all signs of the disintegration which at that time we still did not see coming. Above the ebullient glasses from which we drank, invisible Death was already crossing his bony hands. We swore without malice and blasphemed without thought. Alone and old, distant and at the same time turning into stone, but still close to us all and omnipresent in the great and brilliant pattern of the Empire, lived and ruled the old Emperor,

Franz Joseph. . . . Our wit and our frivolity came from hearts that were heavy with the feeling that we were dedicated to death, from a foolish pleasure in everything which asserted life.

Imperial Vienna during the *fin de siècle*—the city of Klimt and Mahler, Freud and Schnitzler, Kokoschka and Schoenberg—gave birth to the modern world astride a luxuriant grave. If one word could characterize what happened during that time it would be the word Hugo von Hofmannsthal once said best described the heart of his own work: *Verwandlung*, transformation, a moment when nostalgia and necessity collide, when the past is turned inside out and becomes a future that both repudiates and resembles what it has replaced, when we forget in order to change, and change in order to remember.

The best writers in a convulsive era may embody the chaos of their time or diagnose it. Hofmannsthal did neither. One can find violent hysteria and pathological intensity in, say, his play *Elektra*; one can find collage and disjunctive narration, and other tricks of modernism, elsewhere in his output. But Hofmannsthal did not care to be relevant. "In our time," he once said, "too much fuss is made about our time." He cared only to be timeless. He set out—the rarest and riskiest of ambitions—to be a classic, and all along was what might be called a radical traditionalist. The powerful imagination, he knew, is conservative. He saw his world as an arena where *das Gleitende*—a gliding, swirling—held sway, and he eventually construed his art as one that tried not to fix but to blend. One critic has rightly said that he did so "not by imposing law, but by revealing the hidden forms in which the parts of life are bound to each other." This harmony was, in Hofmannsthal's own words, "the ceremony of the whole." He presided over it wearing a thin gold mask, from which shone a light that reflected in the meanest, darkest corners of life, and in the grandest.

• • •

It would be difficult to name another writer who made such an astonishing debut as Hofmannsthal. To be sure, Keats and Rimbaud achieved an early perfection, but no one ever dazzled the wider world at such a young age. At the age of sixteen, he began publishing essays under the name "Loris" (his school did not permit students to publish anything under their own names), and soon after, poems of a shimmering elegance. Then, one day, a slender, beardless seventeen-year-old youth in short pants showed up at the Café Griensteidl, the coffeehouse where the young literati of Vienna gathered, and in a piping voice introduced himself. The influential critic Hermann Bahr was a regular, and remembered seeing a youth with

> the profile of Dante, only a little softened and blurred, in more gentle, supple traits, as Watteau or Fragonard would have painted it, except for the nose with strong, rigid, motionless nostrils under the short, narrow brow, as if made of marble, so hard and decisive, topped by smooth bangs. Brown, merry, trusting eyes of a girl, in which there was something reflective, hopeful, and quizzical mixed in with a naïve coquetry, that kind that loves wry, sidelong glances; short, thick, shapeless lips, malicious and cruel, the bottom one turned inside out and hanging down so that one sees the gum. A fine, slender, pageboy body of gymnastic grace, flexible as a willow switch, and preferring to bend forward slightly in round lines, with the falling shoulders of those of sophisticated culture.

Bahr too had read Loris's essays and been struck with wonder, thinking him a middle-aged writer, unknown but extraordinarily refined and wise. He was startled when the young Hofmannsthal stood before him, becoming famous. The boy was soon invited by Arthur Schnitzler to his apartment to read one of his verse plays. "I had the feeling," Schnitzler recounted, "of having encountered a born genius for the first time in my life, and never again during my entire lifetime was I so overwhelmed." This was a time when the new German literature was making itself heard, the time of Gerhart Hauptmann, Stefan George, and Rainer Maria Rilke, of Stefan Zweig and Richard Beer-Hofmann. This was "Young Vienna" with its café society and its cosmopolitan manner, its rejection of a heavy-handed naturalism and its embrace of French symbolism. Hofmannsthal stunned them all. After that first reading, Schnitzler recalled,

> After a few minutes we riveted our attention on him, and exchanged astonished, almost frightened glances. We had never heard verses of such perfection, such faultless plasticity, such musical feeling, from any living being, nor had we thought them possible since Goethe. But more wondrous than this unique mastery of form (which has never since been achieved by anyone else in the German language) was his knowledge of the world, which could only have come from a magical intuition in a youth whose days were spent sitting on a school bench.

Zweig was likewise astounded by Hofmannsthal, "in whom our youth saw not only its highest ambitions but also absolute poetic perfection come into being, in the person of one of its own age."

Hugo von Hofmannsthal was born in Vienna on February 1, 1874. His father, also Hugo, was a successful bank director; his mother, Anna Maria Fohleutner, came from a wealthy Bavarian background. But the real source of the family's prosperity was his paternal grandfather, a businessman with interests in silk and potash. Decades before Hofmannsthal was born, his father's family had been ennobled and converted to Catholicism from Judaism, though a whiff of suspicion about his background lingered in the prominent salons he came to prefer, and even Hofmannsthal himself sometimes indulged casually in the anti-Semitism so common at that time. He studied law at the University of Vienna, but after his compulsory military service his interests turned to French literature and a possible academic career. Drawn to the clarity and elegance of French culture, he wrote a doctoral dissertation on the poets of the *Pléiade* and a post-doctoral dissertation on Victor Hugo, but by 1901 had decided to pursue the life of a writer himself. Literary friendships blossomed and travel added to his store of impressions, but this was also a time of intense reading, of early publication, and of productions of plays that met with little public success.

• • •

The reputation of Loris was such that the German poet Stefan George sought him out at the Griensteidl, trying to add another disciple to his circle of devotees, all of whom worshiped at the altar of symbolism. But George found that the young Hofmannsthal already knew the work of Swinburne and Pater, Baudelaire and Mallarmé, Maeterlinck and d'Annunzio, and would be less of a protégé than a precocious partisan. During the 1890s Hofmannsthal wrote poems and verse plays that constituted an extraordinary lyrical outpouring and a brief one, and for some readers indelibly fixed the image of his gifts they thought he later betrayed by seeking other means of expression. But for Hofmannsthal, unlike the hieratic George, Beauty *and* Truth, from the beginning, were joined in a sense of artistic purpose—aesthetic intensity and moral passion. The invisible links between disparate aspects of experience and the unity of all are common themes in a symbolist poem, as the mysterious source of its inspiration can be its occasion. Hofmannsthal's poems too—their music largely lost in English versions that stumble to mimic the rare delicacies of the original—work by suggestion and insinuation, their epiphanies shrouded in metaphysical mists. Still, he insisted that the source of lyrical inspiration lay in empathy. "If we wish to find ourselves," he later wrote, "we must not descend into our own inwardness; it is outside that we are to be found, outside." The self is a translucent metaphor given shape by things beyond it, and the language of poetry is meant continually to transform us. "And from all its transformations, all its adventures, from all the abysses and gardens, poetry will bring back nothing more than the quivering breath of human feelings."

During the same decade, Hofmannsthal wrote a series of short verse dramas, beginning in 1891 with *Gestern* (*Yesterday*), whose subject is the hedonistic musings of a Renaissance nobleman who is forced to confront his past. The dramatic force of the play is occluded, but its verse is gorgeous. The interplay of life and death, of pleasure and mortality is at the heart too of several similar playlets written during the following years: *Der Tod des Tizian* (*The Death of Titian*, 1882), *Der Tor und der Tod* (*Death and the Fool*, 1893), and *Alkestis* (1893). Many other plays followed during these years: *Die Frau im Fenster* (*The Woman in the Window*, 1897), *Das kleine Welttheater* (*The Little Theater of the World*, 1897), *Der weiße Fächer* (*The White Fan*, 1897), *Die Hochzeit der Sobeide* (*The Marriage of Sobeide*, 1897), *Der Kaiser und die Hexe* (*The Emperor and the Witch*, 1897), the "serious comedy" *Der Abenteurer und die Sängerin* (*The Adventurer and the Singer*, 1898), and the five-act "fairy-tale tragedy" *Das Bergwerk zu Falun* (*The Mine at Falun*, 1899). He later called them "speaking masks" or "operas without music." The reviews were rarely favorable. The critics listened only for the lyric note, and then used it to fault the dramatic structure. They still yearned for the miraculous Loris, and often held it against Hofmannsthal that he himself felt the need to move beyond his early reputation. Sadly, this became a model for much of the critical reaction to his work over the entire course of his career, a mix of adulation and condescension.

This remarkable decade of the 1890s was a time too when Hofmannsthal made important literary and personal connections. Alfred Walter Heymel and Rudolf Alexander Schröder, founders of the publishing house Insel Verlag, became important to him, as did the lawyer and patron Eberhard von Bodenhausen, and Countess Ottonie Degenfeld, at whose Chateau Neubeuern he was often welcomed. Gerhart Hauptmann, Rudolf Borchardt, and Count Harry Kessler became friends, along with the connoisseurs Helene and Alfred von Nostitz. On trips to Paris he befriended Auguste Rodin, Anatole France, and Maurice Maeterlinck. Though some people found him snobbish and irritable, his close friends thought him a generous, wise, and loyal man. His friend the painter Hans Schlesinger introduced Hofmannsthal to his sister Gertrude; after a five-year acquaintanceship Hugo and Gerty married in 1901, and he purchased a handsome *Schlösschen* in Rodaun, on the outskirts of Vienna. The marriage was close but never as intimate as several of his friendships. Though more recent commentators have generally concluded that Hofmannsthal was a repressed homosexual, the couple had three children: Christiane, born in 1902, Franz, a year later, and Raimund, in 1906.

• • •

The "Chandos crisis" hit in 1902. Though clearly a work of prose fiction, "The Letter of Lord Chandos" has always and rightly been read as an autobiographical confession, one that dramatizes its author's own "word-skepticism" and marks a decisive change of direction in his career. In the letter, Chandos writes to his friend Francis Bacon of "a peculiarity, a vice, a disease of my mind, if you like" that has rendered him incapable of writing. In the past he had "conceived the whole of existence as one great unit," a continuum in which the smallest detail of nature or thought, history or culture had its place. All that has shattered. Abstractions turn to dust in his mouth, descriptions distort rather than clarify, opinions only induce doubt. "For me everything disintegrated into parts, those parts again into parts; no longer would anything let itself be encompassed by one idea. Single words floated round me; they congealed into eyes which stared at me and into which I was forced to stare back—whirlpools which gave me vertigo and, reeling incessantly, led into the void." The mute creatures of the world appeal to him, but he feels himself condemned to silence. Hofmannsthal himself later described this as "the situation of a mystic without mysticism," and the allegory depicts his own impasse. He had arrived at the limits of aestheticism and symbolism, which has exhausted him and dried up his impulse to continue as a poet. A literature divorced from life, all incantation and allure, is a dead end. It is a crisis that had been building for some years. In 1896 he had written to Stefan George of the question "whether I have any right whatever to allow words with which we denote values and judgments to pass my lips." As Chandos writes, "To me, then, it is as though my body consists of nought but ciphers which give me the key to everything; or as if we could enter into a new and hopeful relationship with the whole of existence if only we begin to think with the heart." That relationship, in the years ahead, having abandoned his lyrical isolation, Hofmannsthal sought in the drama and opera, in a public art, in the social context that restores language to the community. He moved from the mystical to the moral. He sought now what he could see as the basis of, say, religious rituals—the enactment of *Elementarerfahrungen*, or fundamental human experiences.

He turned as well to the writing of fiction and essays. His early short stories are a prelude to the novel he launched in 1907, *Andreas*. Of all the projects left unfinished at the time of his death, this is to be most regretted. We have only eighty pages of the text—and a further fifty of notes—of what would have been one of the great examples of the tradition of the German Bildungsroman. His essays—they occupy nearly a third of his collected works—are in many ways the truest portrait of his mind. Their range is prodigious. There are literary portraits and studies. He writes on his travels. He writes on music and dance and painting, on his own work and that of the masters, on society and politics and culture. There is never a trace of strident ideology or of what he termed "the barrenness of concepts." He prefers the impression to the thesis; he appreciates rather than analyzes. The obligations underlying the essays are invariably ethical and social, the consideration of man and the achievements that confer on him some measure of immortality.

• • •

Like any true dramatist, Hofmannsthal was fascinated by the theater of ancient Greece, and during his career he translated or adapted work by Euripides, Sophocles, and Aristophanes. His two Sophocles plays, *Oedipus and the Sphinx* (1905) and *Oedipus, the King* (1907), are powerfully original versions of the most famous of classical dramas. It was Sophocles' *Elektra* that gave Hofmannsthal another of his triumphs. His version opened at Berlin's Kleines Theater on October 30, 1903, with Gertrud Eysolt in the leading role, in a production by Max Reinhardt. Soon after it opened, the composer Richard Strauss saw the play and immediately realized its potential for operatic treatment. Reinhardt's earlier production of Oscar Wilde's *Salome* had fired his imagination, and when he saw *Elektra* on the stage he was already at work on his opera *Salome*. Once that opera premiered in 1906, Strauss wrote to Hofmannsthal for permission to set his play. The playwright set about trimming and adding new material in accordance with the composer's needs, and to his delight, Strauss called Hofmannsthal "a born librettist." Their opera opened at the Königliches Opernhaus in Dresden on January 25, 1909, and was an immediate, if controversial, success around the world. Its complex psychologizing cannot disguise its raw brutality. Its single act hurtles through a series of confrontations towards the fatal dance of triumph at its conclusion, as Elektra celebrates her brother Orestes' murder of their mother Clytemnestra in revenge for her killing of their father Agamemnon. The text is a delirious rhapsody of anguish and violence; the music erupts with demonic force.

Thus began the twentieth century's greatest collaboration of composer and librettist. Their instinctive ability to work together was hardly matched by their personal dealings, however. Over the quarter-century of their correspondence, Hofmannsthal most often started his letters with "Dear Dr. Strauss," and always signed them just "Hofmannsthal." Their meetings were even more difficult. To his friend Countess Ottonie Degenfeld he wrote in a 1911 letter: "The twenty-four hours with the Strausses were a long, continuous, horrible nightmare. These boorish, half-insane, deathly strange people. Characters out of a dream—who are they?! How did I ever become involved with them?" Yet in another letter to her a year later: "Last night it was Strauss from eleven to midnight, and for the first time, I think I was able to *understand* him. . . . One must say he is truly a genius." Hofmannsthal's fastidiously elegant personality made it difficult for him to see beneath Strauss's vulgar, abrasive manner, but each man sensed that the other brought strengths to a project neither could manage alone. In any case, we have their sublime operas, and their unprecedented success has meant that Hofmannsthal is now most famous—or perhaps *only* famous—as a librettist. For that very reason, and because his libretti are performed regularly on every opera stage around the world, this side of his work is proportionately underrepresented in this volume. Only the first of *Der Rosenkavalier*'s three acts is included here as a resplendent example of Hofmannsthal's ability to create dramatic depths for his characters and musical opportunities for the composer.

The success of *Elektra* prompted discussions between the two men about their next project. Perhaps a comic opera based on Casanova's exploits? Or a mythological fable based on one of Hofmannsthal's favorite authors, Calderón? Maybe the French Revolution or Semiramis? But in February, 1909, he writes to Strauss: "I have spent three quiet afternoons here drafting the full and entirely original scenario for an opera, full of burlesque situations and characters, with lively action, pellucid almost like a pantomime." The opera was to be *Der Rosenkavalier* (*The Cavalier of the Rose*), one of the most nearly perfect works in the history of opera, its score sumptuous, and its libretto a literary masterpiece of refinement whose sophisticated humor yields to poignant depths. At its center, the Marschallin, Princess Werdenberg (whose given name, Maria Theresa, is that of the Empress of Austria during whose reign the opera's action is set), is a character of unending fascination who must renounce what she loves with the tender realization, "Easy is what we must be—holding and taking, holding and letting go." Hofmannsthal surrounds her with a gallery of foils, from her impetuous lover

Octavian to the oafish Baron Ochs to the vacuous beauty Sophie, in order to dramatize the fate of desire. "Molière's comedies, too," he wrote in a 1927 postscript to the opera, "rest not so much on the characters themselves as on the relations of the often very typical figures to one another." It is the tenuous fabric of relationships he explores so delicately. Though she isn't a leading character in the events that unfold in the opera, the Marschallin is its central presence because she is wiser than all the others, can see what they cannot—the evanescence of human things. From the start, Hofmannsthal had urged Strauss to avoid a Wagnerian bluster, and to think instead of "an old-fashioned Viennese waltz, half honey-sweet, half shameless." There is, of course, a certain measure of nostalgia at the heart of this comedy of manners, and coming as it did on the eve of the First World War, it has a valedictory air to it: one last look at a world of beguiling love and gentle loss. More to the point, maybe, is that the work's similarity to Mozart's *Nozze di Figaro* and Wagner's *Meistersinger* give *Der Rosenkavalier* a rare place among the most humane works of art ever conceived.

Der Rosenkavalier premiered in Dresden in January, 1911, and quickly made its way to opera houses around the world. For their next project, Hofmannsthal concocted a two-act opera, consisting, first, of a prologue in which a troupe of comedians and a traveling opera company are told to combine their efforts at the evening's fête, and then an "opera" in which the compromise—half high tragedy, half song-and-dance—is performed. *Ariadne auf Naxos,* which premiered in 1916, has transformation at its heart, not only in its mixing of genres but in the hearts of its main characters, where love dissolves misapprehensions and conquers death. What the opera is about, its librettist wrote, "is one of the straightforward and stupendous problems of life: fidelity; whether to hold fast to that which is lost, to cling to it even in death—or to live, to live on, to get on with it, to transform oneself."

There were three subsequent opera collaborations (though Hofmannsthal also wrote ballet scenarios for Strauss). In 1919, their *Die Frau ohne Schatten (The Woman without a Shadow)* premiered in Vienna. It was a story that had long preoccupied Hofmannsthal, and he also made a prose tale out of it. The score is Strauss at his most luxuriant, but critics have sometimes found the text murky. Hofmannsthal himself thought of this opera as their *Magic Flute*, to be put alongside *Der Rosenkavalier*'s take on the *Marriage of Figaro*. But it seems less like a fairy tale and more like a dream, with dark surrealist touches and psychic enigmas. As would seem appropriate for an opera opening in the wake of the Great War, it urges the blessings of child-bearing, though its subtle meditation on married love is what gives it force for later audiences. One writer has indeed best described it as a "parable of the survival of mankind." The emperor of the "South-Eastern Isles" will be turned to stone unless his empress gives him a child—which she cannot do because she lacks a shadow. In the company of her nurse, she descends to the world of humans and tries to bribe a dyer's wife to sell her shadow. What ensues—the tale of these two couples and their trials— drew from Hofmannsthal a symbolic poetry that combined his love of Goethe and of eastern fantasies. (His early story "The Tale of Night Six Hundred and Seventy-Two," though more naturalistic, is akin.) It took them a while to agree on a subject, but their next collaboration, *Die ägyptische Helena* (*The Egyptian Helen*), which did not premiere until 1928, is also about marriage, and an even stranger opera. It deals with an account from an alternative classical myth that Helen of Troy was not in fact abducted but was spirited safely away to Egypt awaiting Menelaus, while her phantom self cavorted in Troy. Hofmannsthal decided to give the story a further turn by having the sorceress Aithra cast a spell on Menelaus that causes him to think the guilty Helen innocent, and then to have him recognize and accept her. "Ewig eine, ewig neue!" (Ever the same, ever new!) Menelaus says of his wife. As before, the transforming power of memory and forgiveness is central to the opera. "Transformation is the life of life itself," Hofmannsthal wrote, "the real mystery of nature as a creative force. Permanence is numbness and death. Whoever wants to live must surpass himself, must transform himself: he has to forget. And yet all human merit is linked with permanence, unforgetfulness, constancy." But the material lacks clarity and lightness; there are elves and eunuchs and a character called The Omniscient Seashell. It is not the author at his best, nor has the opera gained a secure foothold in the international repertory. Their final collaboration, *Arabella*, is a sad story. The composer's final note to the librettist, sent on July 14, 1929, was in fact a telegram: "FIRST ACT EXCELLENT. MANY THANKS AND CONGRATULATIONS." The very next day, Hofmannsthal suddenly died. When the opera finally premiered in Dresden in 1933, Strauss had set acts II and III as Hofmannsthal had left them in draft. Those acts would undoubtedly have been tighter if Hofmannsthal's hand had gone over them again, but *Arabella* remains a transcendent opera, at once tender and wry, a witty take on romantic and sexual stereotypes and at the same time a heartbreaking excursion into the mysteries of love and fidelity. Hofmannsthal had cobbled his text together from a short story of his, "Lucidor," and a fragment, *Der Fiaker als Graf* (*The Cabbie as Count*), and again displayed his uncanny ability to remake familiar material in wholly original ways. In fact, Hofmannsthal's genius as an opera librettist consisted of his ability to plumb emotions while letting unspoken theatrical gestures— the presentation of a silver rose or of a glass of water—permit the music to carry the drama, and to make his characters out of a lyric poetry—unequaled on the opera stage before or since— suffused with exquisite detail and sweep.

• • •

As the Great War staggered to an end during the autumn of 1918, the Austro-Hungarian Empire had already cracked apart and the Hapsburg monarchy crumbled. The Austrian Republic that emerged was weak, and the devastations of social and economic failure only compounded the ravages of war. Indeed, all of Europe, in the bickering power-grab that the Paris Peace Conference became, was further torn apart. Vindictive winners and embittered losers alike brandished a treacherous jingoism, while the influenza pandemic killed off the weak who had some-how survived the war. The situation in Vienna was desperate. There was no food or fuel; looters with guns, escaped convicts, and starving prisoners of war roamed the freezing city streets. Women cut down the famed Vienna Woods for logs, and coffee was made from barley. If a family had jewelry it was sold on the black market, until inflation wiped out everyone's savings. Hofmannsthal (who had served in the army during the war in both military and diplomatic postings) and his family were hardly immune. In April, 1919, he wrote to a friend, "now even the horse meat, on which we have subsisted for the past year and a half, is no longer affordable and no longer available." Yet even in the midst of such suffering and humiliation, he was determined to salvage an ideal of European humanism. In 1877, a summer festival of music and drama was begun in Salzburg, but was discontinued because of the war. It was Hof-mannsthal's idea to restore it. He joined with Richard Strauss and the great stage director Max Reinhardt, along with scenic designer Alfred Roller and conductor Fritz Schalk, to establish a reborn Salzburg Festival, which opened on August 22, 1920 with a performance on the Domplatz of Hofmannsthal's *Jeder-mann*, his 1911 adaptation of the early-sixteenth-century En-glish morality play about faith and salvation, *Everyman*. The festi-val was meant to serve as a beacon to rally the cultural community shattered by nationalist conflict. Two years later, his play *Das Salzburger große Welttheater* (*The Salzburg Great Theater of the World*) again sought to use the traditions of cosmopolitan theatrical spectacle and indigenous moral inquiry—Goethe's *Faust* was his ideal—to make the old trope of the *theatrum mundi* (and Calderón's play *El Gran Teatro del Mundo*) a compelling vision of mankind's fate: "that the World erects a stage on which men enact the play of life in the roles allotted to them by God."

Earlier in his career, Hofmannsthal had turned to theater as the culmination of his aesthetic ambition to reach the widest possible audience, not for the sake of a vulgar popularity but because of his conviction that an all-encompassing art could counter the increasing fragmentation of civilization. The "lyrical dramas" he wrote as a young man were a halting first step, but could not leap from page to stage. The Chandos Letter's crisis concerning the limits of language can be seen in part as a frustration with a lyric mode too narrowly exquisite for anyone's good. "In action, in deeds," he wrote, "the enigmas of language are resolved." The theater—the arena of actors and masks, of confrontation and magic, of *change*—was the ultimate platform for "the mystery of voluptuous transformation." It is here that the self is "little more than a metaphor," and that words transcend themselves as gesture. In his 1911 essay "On Pantomime," he writes of the effect of the dancer or actor: "A pure gesture is like a pure thought that has been stripped even of the momentarily witty, the restrictedly individual, the grotesquely characteristic." The whole point of conventions is that every action has a precedent, every self-important assertion is an echo. In the theater we see ourselves as creatures beyond the confines of selfhood, and participate in a process that is instinctively communal.

It is no wonder that he was attracted to opera. Though he always claimed he was unmusical, he knew that "song is marvelous because it tames what otherwise is nothing but the organ of our self-seeking, the human voice." He was attracted as well to theater of various kinds. His verse plays are essentially dramatic monologues, closet dramas for reading, but he later began to try several different sorts of theater. "I want to dramatize everything that falls into my hand," he wrote to Schnitzler, "even the correspondence of Schiller and Goethe, or the *Linzer Tagepost.*" He translated Otway's *Venice Preserved*, adapted Molière and Calderón, and did brilliant versions of classic Greek plays. He tried symbolic fable in *The Mine at Falun*, and comedy in *Christina's Journey Home*. And amidst all of his experimentation he was criticized by the press (even his part in *Der Rosenkavalier* was derided by the first reviewers) for not conforming to the image they had of him as a delicate aesthete, an unworldling, and for having abandoned a higher calling. What they couldn't see is that he had embraced it.

In fact, one way Hofmannsthal occupied himself during the war—it was the instinct of a truly civilized man—was to work on a comedy. He began *Der Schwierige* in 1917. (The standard English translation of the title is *The Difficult Man*, though the French title, *L'Irrésolu*, may be a more accurate equivalent.) His portrait of the Man of Sensibility and of the fortunes of two hearts has all of the wit and tenderness a comedy of manners is meant to convey. His portrait of the Austrian aristocracy—its fatuity and nobility, indecisiveness and resignation—is as well an ironic commentary on the social and political state of affairs in a vanishing world. Comedy, like tragedy, depends upon choice. The "difficult" Hans Karl, because of the delicacy of his heart's motives, is a man who cannot choose. The comedy, then, is prompted by a set of exquisite scruples and two women whom he loves. Emotional fulfillment is an outgrowth of moral maturity, and nuance has the force of fate. The difficulty characters have in understanding each other is a part of their misunderstanding themselves. "Manners," Hofmannsthal once wrote, "are walls, disguised with mirrors." Hans Karl is the man who sees all and can say nothing. When in Act II he tells Helen about the famous circus clown Furlani, he could be describing himself as a Chaplinesque artist:

> He plays his role: the man who wants to understand everybody and help everybody and yet brings everything into the utmost confusion. He makes the silliest blunders, the gallery rocks with laughter, and yet he does it with such elegance, such discretion, that one realizes how much he respects himself and everything in the world. He makes a hash of everything; wherever he intervenes there's a complete mess, and yet one wants to cry out: "He's right, all the same!"

In the play, defying the usual path of comedy, the old order prevails, buttoned-up elegance upends brash youth. Still, this comedy, like most others, ends with a marriage, at once unexpected and inevitable, and the moral order puts uncertainty and impulsiveness to rights—though our lovers are absent. As so often, Hofmannsthal invokes convention in order to transfigure it. Of course, as he himself noted, *The Difficult Man* descends directly from "The Letter of Lord Chandos," and likewise addresses the dilemma of language's limitations. But the playwright's sparkling control makes of this *Konversationsstücke* an excursion into the language of the heart, like Jean Renoir's *Rules of the Game*, where we discover, as the characters do, all the depths that lie in the bright, fragile surface of things.

Like exploding bombs, the effects and import of the war more darkly resound through *Der Turm* (*The Tower*), the five-act play that preoccupied Hofmannsthal during his final years and, in his words, dramatized "the irruption of the forces of chaos into an order no longer upheld and supported by the power of the spirit." Once again, he took his inspiration from Calderón, this time from his celebrated play *La Vida es Sueño* (*Life Is a Dream*), first published in 1636, though any reader of both plays can see how far Hofmannsthal developed the material beyond its source. Set in the killing fields of seventeenth-century Poland, the story concerns its king, Basilius, who has imprisoned his son and heir, Sigismund, and kept him since birth living like a wild animal in a filthy tower dungeon, for fear of a prophecy that this son will rise up in rebellion against his father and destroy the kingdom. This tower, in the author's words, is "the hub of the world's injustice; here horrible injustice begets ceaselessly new monsters, as carrion breeds flies," but it is only the center of a world itself brutalized by anarchy, mob riot, corruption, and murder. And in the midst of chaos crouches the young man of Christ-like virtue and spiritual authority, chained in his cage.

A doctor, sent to minister to the now grown Sigismund in his misery, persuades the tower's governor, Julian, to release his prisoner and brings him to the king, who, frightened by the political unrest abroad in the land and wracked by his guilty conscience, decides the youth must either be freed or killed. When they meet, Sigismund's natural regality is evident, and to test it the king commands that he kill Julian; instead he strikes the king and declares himself ruler. He is subdued, though, and the king is revived. He orders Sigismund be returned to his prison, but that is delayed by the roar of peasants praying for the appearance of a "beggar king" who will lead them into a new age. The rebellious mob storms the tower, but Sigismund will not be tempted by the power Julian offers him. When he leaves the tower, he declares, he will leave in glory. The mob wants Julian killed and Sigismund as their leader, but he refuses, his gaze turned mysteriously inward. News comes of an army of orphan children on the march, led by a Children's King. Dreams, visions, gypsy poison, plots and counterplots all ensue. Sigismund, doing battle against the rebels, insists he will create a new order to transcend the bloody and debased world of the court, but collapses in death, poisoned but unafraid. The Children's King, proclaiming Sigismund's divinity, takes up his sword and marches into the future.

For all the mysticism and majesty of its poetic allegory, Hofmannsthal knew that the last act of the play was theatrically flawed, and he rewrote it. His second version—the version included in this volume—is darker, and eliminates the possibility of any future deliverance. It seems more than coincidental that in the same year this version of the play was published, *Mein Kampf* also appeared. The play moves starkly towards its terrible ending, and as he dies Sigismund whispers, "Bear witness, I was here, though no one has known me." Its eerie spiritual power undeniable, *The Tower* is an apocalyptic play enacted on a titanic stage and lit by flashes of lightning.

• • •

In the last years, though he traveled and wrote, Hofmannsthal complained of nervous exhaustion and depression, and suffered from hardening of the arteries. His dreams for a "conservative Revolution" and a culturally unified Europe were in tatters. On July 13, 1929, his eldest son Franz shot himself. The suicide shocked Hofmannsthal and his wife, and two days later, as they were dressing to leave home for the funeral and he had just put on his hat, he complained of feeling dizzy. His wife led him to a chair in his study and asked if he wanted her to loosen his collar. She could not understand his garbled reply and his face had gone aslant. She struggled to help him to the sofa, where he died of the stroke he had just suffered. He was only fifty-five years old. On July 18th, then, both son and father were buried. Hofmannsthal's friend Count Harry Kessler—with whom, years earlier, he had worked up the plot of *Der Rosenkavalier* and toured Greece—came to Rodaun for the funeral. By this time, though, thousands of other mourners had converged on the tiny town and, as Kessler wrote in his diary, "by now any vestige of funereal sobriety had been replaced by a feeling of participation, under sweltering conditions, in some sort of *Kermesse* spectacle. For a moment, as I scattered earth over it, I glimpsed the coffin in its vault. With that of the son who shot himself immediately below, it struck me how thin and frail it seemed. . . . With Hofmannsthal a whole chapter of German culture has been carried to the grave." He had asked to be buried in the habit of a Franciscan friar. It was an odd but appropriate gesture. The range and splendor of his work have rarely been equaled, yet he was humble before the tasks and traditions of his art. He had schooled himself to avoid life, and in the end embraced it. He was raised "early ripened and tender and sad," and grew to create work that shed both light and darkness. As his Marschallin muses, "It's all a mystery, so much is mysterious. And we are here to endure it. And in the How, there lies the whole difference—"

—*J. D. McClatchy*

POEMS

GHAZAL

In the cheapest mean violin the concord of the All is obscured.
In ecstasy's deepest groans, the sweet rejoicing they enthrall is obscured.

In the pathway's stone there lies the spark that would ignite the world;
The awful thunderbolt whose impact would appall is obscured.

In the dog-eared text there lies what all our research would discover:
One truth as luminous and clear as in a crystal ball is obscured.

Tease out the notes, transfix the truth, hurl the stone like Heracles!
Our vision of a ripe perfection ever since the Fall is obscured.

AN EXPERIENCE

At dusk a silvery fragrance filled the valley,
As when the moon is viewed through a veil of cloud.
But it was not yet night. In the darkening valley
That fragrance drifted through my shadowy thoughts
And silently I sank into the wavering,
Diaphanous sea, and left my life behind.
What wondrous flowers had bloomed there,
Cups of colors darkly glowing! And a thicket
Amidst which a flame like topaz rushed,
Now surging, now gleaming in its molten course.
All of it seemed filled with the deep swell
Of a mournful music. This much I knew,
Though I cannot understand it—I knew
That this was Death, transmuted into music,
Violently yearning, sweet, dark, burning,
Akin to deepest sadness.
                                        Yet how strange!
A nameless longing after life now wept
Inside my soul without a sound, wept
As one might weep who on a galleon
With giant gilded sails of an evening slides
Over the indigo waters past a town,
His native town. And there he spies again
The streets, hears the fountains plash, breathes
In the scent of lilacs, and sees himself again,

A child standing on the shore, wide-eyed,
Anxious and close to tears, and looks then through
An open window to see a light on in his room—
But the huge ship is bearing out to sea
Without a sound over the indigo waters
With its giant gilded unearthly sails.

STANZAS IN TERZA RIMA

I

On Mutability

On my cheek I still can feel their breath:
How can it be these days that seem so near
Are gone, forever gone, and lost to death?

This is a thought no mind can truly grasp,
A thing too terrifying for mere tears:
That all we want and are eludes our clasp.

And that, unchecked, even my own self has come
Across the years from a little child I find
As remote as the family dog and as dumb.

That I existed centuries ago, somewhere,
And ancestors, long to their graves confined,
Are yet as close to me as my own hair,

As much a part of me as my own hair.

II

These hours! Hours spent staring at the sea,
As if in its blue clarities we could somehow learn
About death, its simple rules and solemnity.

As little girls, whose great eyes seem to yearn,
When first they feel the evening chill their skin,
For what they do not know, still do not turn

Away, sensing how from each languorous limb
Into leaf and blade life rushes like a flood
While they feebly smile at the might have been,

Like martyrs shedding their otherworldly blood.

III

We are such stuff as dreams are made on: these,
These dreams that suddenly each night open our eyes
Like those of a child under the blossoming trees

Above whose crests the moon mounts the skies
On her pale gold course through the gathered night—
The way our own dreams loom so real and rise

Like a brightly laughing child, and to the sight
Appear as immense and still and far away
As the moon when the treetops edge her light.

Our inmost selves are subject to their sway,
Like strings held by ghostly hands that seem
To animate our lives, come what may.

And three are one: the man, the thing, the dream.

THE BOTH OF THEM

In her hand she carried the cup to him—
Her chin and mouth were like its rim.
Her coming was so light, so still,
That not a single drop was spilled.

So light, so firm as well his hand.
His prancing stallion fresh from pasture
At one indifferent, easy gesture
Stood tensely where he made it stand.

But when he bent to take from her hand
The cup she held up as his own,
For both of them it seemed too much
And both so trembled at the touch
Their fingers failed, and onto the sand
The glimmering wine splattered down.

BALLAD OF THE OUTER LIFE

And children with their deep-fixed gaze,
Who know nothing yet, grow up and die,
And all men go their separate ways.

And bitter fruit will ripen by and by
And at night dead birds fall to the ground
And for a few days rot where they lie.

And the wind blows, and we hear the sound
Of words and over and over repeat their sense
And feel a joy both weary and profound.

And roads run through the grass, a residence
Here or there with torches, ponds, trees,
And some are withered, or threaten violence.

Why are these built, each one ill at ease
With the rest, yet in the end all the same?
Why will neither tears nor laughter please?

What good is all of this to us, this game?
However great we grow, we are lonely still
And wander the world without an aim.

To learn merely this, we leave our homes?
And he says everything who just says "evening,"
A word from which the richest sadness spills

Like heavy honey from the hollow combs.

WE WENT ALONG A WAY ...

We went along a way with many bridges,
And three went on ahead, humming to themselves.
I mention this now to recall that moment.
You said then—pointing to the mountain
Crisscrossed with cloud-shadows and shadows
From the steep crags with their precarious trails—
You said: "If only we two were there alone!"
And the sound of your words seemed as foreign
As the scent of sandalwood or of myrrh.
—Even your face seemed strange as well.
It was as if a sudden drunken rapture
Took hold of me, as when the earth trembles
And precious ornaments are upended
And roll about and water gushes up
And one's view of everything is doubled:
For I was *here* and at the same time *there*,
You in my arms and all the rapture of it
Somehow mingled with all the rapture
This massive mountain with its gorges
Would offer one who like an eagle hovered
Over its heights, wings at their full span.
With you in my arms I was on that peak,
I knew all there was of its sublimity,
Its solitude, its never-trodden paths,
You in my arms and all the rapture of it . . .

And as today I woke in a summer-house
I saw on the cool wall a picture of the gods
Assembled in all their wondrous joy:
How light of foot, how nearly weightless
From the slatted roof of a vine-covered arbor
Through the blue sky they glided upwards,
Ethereal as flames, and with the sound
Of song and the echo of the bright lyre
They ascended. It struck me then
That I could touch the garment of one
Still close to earth, as might a friend,
A guest of theirs, of equal rank and fate:
I had our adventure still in mind.

THREE EPIGRAMS

The Art of Poetry

Art is frightening! From my own body I spin a web,
The very web that lets me make my way through air.

Mirror of the World

"Once before I inched this way," in the mouth of a sleeping king
Spoke the spotted worm.—"When?"—"In the poet's brain."

Knowledge

If I knew how this leaf had sprung from its sprig,
I would keep silent: there is knowledge enough.

IN MEMORY OF THE
ACTOR MITTERWURZER

He went out as suddenly as a candle.
We wore a pallor on our faces
Like the reflection of a lightning bolt.

He fell: and with him all the puppets fell
Into whose veins he had poured the blood
Of his being. Silently they died,
And where he lay, a heap of corpses lay
Haphazardly: the drunkard's knee
Up against the king's eye, Don Philippe
With Caliban the nightmare around his neck,
And all of them dead.

At last we knew whom death had taken from us:
The sorcerer, the high and mighty illusionist!
And we left our homes and gathered
To talk about what exactly he was.
But then, who was he, and who was he not?

From one mask he crept into another,
Sprang from the father's body to the son's,
Changed shapes as if they were merely clothes.

With swords, which he could brandish so quickly
That no one saw the glitter of their blades,

He cut himself into pieces: one was perhaps
Iago, while the other half of him
Might be a dreamer or some sweet fool.
For his whole body was a magic veil
Within whose folds all things seemed to dwell:
He could summon animals from himself,
The sheep, the lion, the devil of stupidity
Or the one of horror, this man and that
And you and me. Some sort of inward fate
Set his whole body shining, shimmering
Like coals aglow, and he lived in their midst
And looked out at us, who dwelt in houses,
With the eerie impenetrable stare
Of a salamander, the creature that lives in fire.
He was a savage king. Around his loins
He wore like strings of colored shells
The truths and lies we all of us live by.
Our own dreams flew past us in his eyes,
As flocks of wild birds are mirrored in a lake.

Here he could come, on this very spot
Where I now stand, and as in Triton's horn
The uproar of the ocean is contained,
So were in him the voices of life itself:
He became vast. He was the whole forest,
He was the countryside through which roads ran.
With eyes like children's we would sit
And gaze in wonder up at him, as from the slopes
Of a gigantic mountain: in his mouth
Was a bay, into which the sea surged.

There was in him something that could open
Many doors and fly through many rooms.
The force of Life itself was in him.
And over him now the power of Death!
It blew out his eyes whose inmost core
Was covered with some inscrutable code,

It strangled the throat with a thousand voices,
And killed the body whose every limb
Was laden with lives as yet unborn.

Here he stood. When will there be another like him?—
A spirit who peoples the maze of the human breast
With forms it comprehends, and unlocks
Anew for us such fearsome joys?
Those which he gave us we can no longer keep.
We hear his name and stare blankly
Down the abyss that swallowed them from sight.

FICTION

THE TALE OF NIGHT SIX HUNDRED
AND SEVENTY-TWO

I

A MERCHANT'S SON, a young man and very handsome who had
neither father nor mother, grew weary of society and social in-
tercourse soon after his twenty-fifth year. He closed off most of
the rooms in his house and let all his servants go, male and
female alike, excepting four, whose devotion and entire being
were pleasing to him. As he set no great store by his friends,
nor had he been captivated by the beauty of any woman such
that he should think it desirable or merely tolerable to have her
with him always, he lived an ever more solitary existence, which
appeared best suited to his disposition. Yet he was by no means
a recluse; on the contrary, he enjoyed strolling through the
streets or public gardens and observing people's faces. Nor did
he neglect the care of his body and fine hands or the decor of
his residence; indeed, the beauty of the carpets and fabrics and
silks, the carved and paneled walls, the metal sconces and ba-
sins, the glass and earthenware vessels had acquired a never
imagined significance. He gradually came to see how all the
shapes and colors in the world lived in his artifacts. In the intri-
cacies of the ornaments he discerned an enchanted image of
the intricate wonders of the world. He noted the shapes of ani-
mals and the shapes of flowers and the transition of flowers into

animals: dolphins, lions, and tulips, pearls and the acanthus; he
noted the conflict between the burden borne by columns and
the resistance offered by solid ground and the striving of all
waters to go upstream and then down; he noted the bliss of
motion and the sublimity of calm, dancing and death; he noted
the colors of flowers and trees, the colors of the hides of animals
and the faces of people, the color of precious stones, the color
of the stormy sea and of the sea calm and luminous; and, yes,
he noted the moon and the stars, the mystic globe, the mystic
rings, and the wings of the seraphim sprouting from them. He
was long intoxicated by this great, profound beauty, all his, and
his every day became fairer and less empty among these arti-
facts, which had ceased to be dead and lowly and were now a
great legacy, the divine work of all nations.

Yet he likewise felt the vanity of all these things as much as
their beauty, nor did the thought of death leave him for long:
it would visit him amidst laughing, boisterous crowds, often in
the night, often at table.

But as he suffered no malady, the thought was not baleful; it
rather had something ceremonious and scintillating to it and
was at its most powerful when he was intoxicated from thinking
fine thoughts or from the beauty of his youth and solitude. For
the merchant's son often derived great pride from the mirror,
from the lines of the poets, from his wealth and intelligence,
and grim proverbs did not press upon his soul. "Your feet will
take you to where you are to die," he would say, and saw him-
self, elegant, like a king lost on a hunt in an unfamiliar
wood under exotic trees, meet a strange and wondrous fate.
"Death will come when the house is done," he would say, and
saw Death plod across a bridge resting on the backs of wingèd
lions and leading to a palace, a house newly finished and filled
with life's spoils.

He believed he lived in perfect solitude, but his four servants
surrounded him like dogs, and though he spoke but little to
them he somehow felt they were constantly thinking of how best
to serve him. He also began to think about them occasionally.

The housekeeper was an old woman; her daughter, now dead, had nursed the merchant's son; all the rest of her children had died as well. She was very quiet, and her white face and white hands exuded the coolness of old age. But he liked her because she never left the house and because the memory of his own mother's voice and of his childhood, which he loved with great longing, accompanied her everywhere.

With his permission she had brought a distant relative into the house, a girl barely fifteen and very withdrawn. She was hard on herself and hard to understand. Once, in a sudden dark impulse of her raging soul, she had thrown herself out of a window into the courtyard, but her childlike body landed on a pile of garden soil accidentally deposited there and she merely broke a collarbone on a stone sticking out of the earth. When she had been taken to her bed, the merchant's son sent his doctor to see her, but that evening he went himself to see how she was faring. She kept her eyes shut, and for the first time he gave her a long, calm look and was amazed at the strange and precocious grace of her features except for the lips, which were very thin and had something unattractive and eerie about them. Suddenly she opened her eyes, gave him a cold and angry look, and, overcoming her pain, biting her lips in anger, turned to the wall, so that she lay on the side of her wound. At that moment her deadly pale face turned a greenish white and she lost consciousness, falling back into her previous position as if dead.

Long after she had recovered, the merchant's son did not address her when she passed him. He asked the old woman several times whether the girl did not like living there, but she always denied it. The only manservant he had decided to keep in his house was one he had met while dining at the house of the envoy maintained by the king of Persia in that city. The man had served him there and been so obliging and judicious and at the same time seemed so reserved and unassuming that the merchant's son took greater pleasure in observing him than in hearing the conversations of the guests. He was therefore only too glad when many months later the man accosted him in the street, greeted him with the same gravity he had shown that evening, and, without the slightest self-assertiveness, offered him his services. The merchant's son had recognized him at once by his somber, mulberry-colored face and his exquisite manners. He took him into his service there and then, dismissing two young servants still in his employ, and henceforth had all his meals served and other needs ministered to by this serious and sedate man alone. The man as good as never made use of the permission to leave the house in the evening hours. He showed a rare devotion to his master, whose wishes he anticipated and whose likes and dislikes he tacitly surmised, thereby augmenting his affections all the more.

Although his meals were served only by the male servant, he did have a female servant bring in the bowls of fruit and pastries, a young girl, though two or three years older than the housekeeper's relative. This girl was of the sort who, if seen from afar or by torchlight as a dancer on a stage, would hardly be regarded as beautiful because the delicacy of her features would be lost, but since he saw her close up and daily, he was taken with the incomparable beauty of her eyelids and lips, and the languid, joyless motion of her comely body was the enigmatic language of a wondrous world beyond his reach.

When the swelter of summer in town grew oppressive, the stifling heat drifting from house to house and the wind on sultry, muggy, full-moon nights blowing clouds of white dust through the empty streets, the merchant's son and his four servants removed to a country house he owned in the mountains in a narrow valley overhung by dark cliffs. There were many such country houses of the wealthy in the region. Waterfalls cascaded into the gorges from both sides, cooling the air. The moon was almost always behind the mountains, but great white clouds would climb behind the black walls, float solemnly across the darkly lit sky, and disappear on the other side. Here the merchant's son lived his customary life in a house whose walls of wood were constantly cooled by breezes from the gardens and the many waterfalls. In the afternoon, before the sun fell behind the mountains, he would sit in his garden, spending most of the time with a book that recorded the wars of a very great king of the past. Sometimes in the midst of a description of how thousands of the enemy kings' horsemen whooped and turned their chargers round or how their chariots hurtled down a steep riverbank he felt a sudden need to pause, sensing without looking up that the eyes of his four servants were upon him. He knew without lifting his head that they were watching him wordlessly, each from a different room. That is how well he knew them. He felt their lives more strongly, more vividly than he felt his own. He registered an occasional emotion or surprise vis-à-vis himself, but they inspired an enigmatic apprehension in him. With the clarity of a nightmare he sensed the lives of the two older servants moving hour by hour towards death in the slight yet inexorable modifications in the features and gestures he knew so well, sensed the two girls slipping into lives of airless, as it were, desolation. Like the horror and deadly pungency of a frightening dream forgotten upon wakening, the onerous quality of their lives, of which they themselves were unaware, weighed heavily upon him.

Sometimes he had to stand and walk about to keep his anxiety at bay, but looking down at the gaudy gravel before his feet and concentrating with all his might on the scent of the carnations wafting up to him in luminous puffs from the cool scent of grass and earth intermingled with the mild, cloyingly sweet clouds of heliotrope scent, he kept feeling their eyes on him and could think of nothing else. Without lifting his head, he knew that the old woman was sitting at her window, her bloodless hands on the sun-drenched ledge, her bloodless, masklike face an ever more ghastly abode for the helpless black eyes that could not die. Without lifting his head, he sensed when the manservant stepped back from the window for a few minutes and was busying himself at a cupboard; without looking up, he awaited in secret anxiety the moment of his return. While releasing the pliant boughs with both hands and letting them fall behind him so he could crawl to the most overgrown corner of the garden and direct all his thoughts to the beauty of the sky, which made its way through the dark network of branches and tendrils in small shiny snippets of moist turquoise from above, he was overpowered in his blood and mind by the awareness of the two girls' eyes fixed upon him, the older one's listless and mournful, with a vague, disquieting challenge, the younger one's with impatient or insolent vigilance he found even more disquieting. Yet he never thought they were looking directly at him as he walked about with his head down or knelt by a carnation to tie it with raffia or stooped to avoid a branch; no, he felt they were looking at his entire life, the depths of his being, his mysterious human inadequacy.

A terrible apprehension came over him, a deadly fear of life's inescapability. More terrible than their ceaseless observation of him was that they forced him to think about himself in a fruitless and highly exhausting manner. And the garden was far too small for him to escape them. Yet when he was close to them, his fear would expire so completely that he nearly forgot what had gone before. Then he managed to ignore them or watch their familiar movements with composure, they being so familiar that he felt a constant, all but physical empathy with their lives.

The young girl crossed his path but rarely, on the stairs or in the entrance hall, though the other three were often in the same room with him. Once he caught sight of the older one in a tilted mirror. She was walking through a higher adjacent room, but in the mirror she appeared to be coming towards him out of the depths. Though perfectly erect, she moved slowly and with difficulty: she was carrying a gaunt, heavy, dark-bronze Indian deity under each arm, the figures' ornamented feet resting in the hollows of her hands. The dark goddesses reached from her hips to her temples and leaned their dead weight against her soft, living shoulders, while their dark heads with evil snake mouths, three wild eyes in the foreheads, and eerie jewelry in the cold, hard hair moved next to her breathing cheeks, grazing her fair temples in time with her slow gait. However, it was not so much the goddesses' weight and solemnity that seemed a burden to her as the beauty of her own head with its heavy jewelry of dark, vivid gold, two great arching coils on either side of her clear brow, like an Amazon queen. He was taken by her great beauty, though he knew as well that to hold her in his arms would mean nothing to him; he knew that in the end his servant's beauty filled him with longing rather than desire, so he did not rest his gaze upon her for long but left the room, in fact, went outside, walking in the narrow shadow between houses and garden in a strange state of unrest. He ended up on the riverbank, where the gardeners and florists lived, and searched long, much as he knew it was in vain, for a flower whose shape and fragrance or a spice whose breath on the air might put him in tranquil possession of that sweet charm which lay in his servant's disturbing, unnerving beauty. And as he vainly scoured the stifling greenhouses with longing in his eyes and bent over the long beds outside in the growing darkness, the words of the poet kept running through his head, unbidden, indeed, increasingly tormenting and contrary to his will: "In the stems of swaying carnations, in the fragrance of ripe grain thou didst arouse my longing, but when I found thee, thou wert not she whom I sought but the sisters of your soul."

II

In these days it came to pass that he received a rather disturbing letter. The letter bore no signature. Its author vaguely accused the manservant of the merchant's son of having committed some abominable crime in the house of his former master, the Persian envoy. This unknown person seemed to harbor an unbridled hatred towards the servant and made many threats; he even used an impolite, almost threatening tone with the merchant's son. But it was impossible to fathom of what the crime alluded to consisted, or what purpose the letter might have served its author, who neither gave his name nor made demands. He read the letter several times and confessed to himself that he felt great anxiety at the thought of losing his manservant in so repugnant a manner. The more he reflected, the more agitated he grew and the less he could bear the thought of losing one of those people to whom habit and other secret forces had so completely conjoined him.

He paced to and fro, so inflamed by his irate agitation that he flung off his tunic and belt and kicked them. He felt that his innermost possession had been maligned and threatened and he was being forced to flee his very person and deny what was dear to him. He pitied himself and felt—as is usual at such moments—like a child. He imagined his four servants torn from his house, and it seemed as if the entire content of his life were being noiselessly extracted from him—all the bittersweet memories, all the half-unconscious expectations, the things that cannot be put into words—the better to be cast off and disregarded like a clump of algae and seaweed. For the first time he grasped something that had always aroused his anger as a child: the anxious love with which his father clung to what he had acquired, the riches of his vaulted warehouse, these beautiful, insensitive children of his seeking and caring, the mysterious offspring of the vague but deepest desires of his life. He realized that the great king of the past would have had to die had he been deprived of the lands he had traversed and conquered from the sea in the west to the sea in the east and had dreamed of ruling even though they were so infinitely large that he had no power over them and received no more tribute from them than the thought that he had conquered them and he and he alone was their king.

He resolved to do everything possible to settle this matter, which so plagued him. Without saying a word about the letter to the servant, he set out alone for the city. There he decided first of all to visit the house inhabited by the Persian king's envoy in the vague hope of finding a clue there.

When he arrived, however, it was late afternoon and no one was at home, neither the envoy nor any of the young people in his entourage. He did see the cook and an old, petty scribe sitting in the gateway in the cool semi-darkness, but they were so ugly and gave such curt, sullen replies to his questions that he turned his back on them impatiently and made up his mind to return the next day at a better time.

Since his own house was closed—he had left no servant behind in the city—he needed to find lodging for the night like a stranger. Curious, like a stranger, he walked through the familiar streets, finally coming to the bank of a small river that was all but dry at that time of year. From there, lost in thought, he followed a shabby street, home to a good many prostitutes. Not paying much attention to his path, he turned right into a completely deserted, deathly still cul-de-sac that ended in a towering flight of steep steps. He paused on the steps, gazing back over his path. He could look into the courtyards of the small houses; here and there he saw red curtains in the windows and ugly, dusty flowers; the broad, dry riverbed was funereal in its sadness. He kept climbing and at the top entered a neighborhood he could not recall having seen before. And yet an intersection of low streets suddenly assumed a dreamlike familiarity. Walking on, he came to a jeweler's shop. It was very shabby, in keeping with that part of town, its window full of the kind of worthless baubles one buys from pawnbrokers and receivers of stolen goods. The merchant's son, who was well versed in precious stones, was hard put to find a fairly decent one among them.

All at once his gaze fell on an old-fashioned setting of thin gold and beryl, which for some reason reminded him of the old woman. He had probably seen her once wearing a similar ornament from her younger years. The pale, rather melancholy stone also struck him as oddly appropriate to her age and appearance, and the old-fashioned setting had the same sadness. So he entered the low-ceilinged shop to buy it. The jeweler was overjoyed to see so well dressed a customer and wanted to show him his more valuable stones, the ones he did not put in the window. As a courtesy to the old man he let him bring out many things, but he had no desire to buy anything more, nor would he have had use for such gifts given his solitary existence. In the end he grew impatient and at the same time ill at ease, for he wanted to get away and yet spare the old man's feelings. He decided to buy another small item, then make a quick exit. Casting a faraway glance over the jeweler's shoulder, he noticed a small silver hand mirror, half-clouded. And suddenly the image of the girl with the iron goddesses' dark heads came to him from another, inner mirror and for a moment he felt that much of her charm lay in the submissive, childlike grace with which her shoulders and neck bore the beauty of the head, the head of a young queen. And for a moment he thought it would be lovely to see a thin gold chain on that neck, ringing it many times round, childlike yet like a coat of mail as well. And he asked to see such chains. The old man opened a door and asked him to step into another room, a low sitting room, where, however, a great deal of jewelry was displayed in glass cases and on open shelves. There he soon found a chain to his liking and asked the jeweler to tell him the price of the two pieces. The old man asked him first to examine the unusual fittings of some old-fashioned saddles—they had inlays of semi-precious stones—but he replied that as a merchant's son he had had nothing to do with horses, indeed did not even know how to ride and took no pleasure in saddles, new or old, whereupon he paid for his purchases with a gold piece and several silver coins and showed a certain impatience to leave the shop. While the old man, not saying another word, took out some fine tissue paper and wrapped the chain and the beryl piece separately, the merchant's son happened to go over to the only window, low and barred, and look outside. He saw a very well-tended kitchen garden with two greenhouses and a high wall at the far end. He felt an immediate desire to see those greenhouses and asked the jeweler whether he could tell him the way to them. The jeweler handed him his two packages and took him through an adjoining room into the courtyard, which was connected to the neighboring garden by means of a small gate. There the jeweler paused and rapped on the grille with an iron knocker. As the garden remained quite still and no one stirred in the house, he urged the merchant's son to examine the hot-houses on his own. Should anyone bother him, he could refer to him, the jeweler, for he knew the garden's owner well. Then he opened the gate for him by reaching through the grille.

The merchant's son went in immediately and followed the wall to the closer greenhouse, which he entered to find so rich a collection of rare and curious narcissi and anemones and such strange and totally unfamiliar foliage that he stood there for a long while transfixed. When he finally glanced up, he noticed that without his being aware of it the sun had sunk entirely behind the houses. He no longer wished to remain in a strange, unattended garden; he wished only to have a look through the panes of the second greenhouse and then be on his way. But as he moved slowly in the direction of the glass walls, looking intently ahead, he gave a sudden, violent start and drew back. For there in the glass was a human face peering out at him. After a moment he regained his composure and realized it was a child, a little girl, four at most, her white dress and pale face pressing against the glass. But when he looked closer, he gave another start with an unpleasant feeling of horror at the back of the neck and a clutch in the throat and deeper in the chest. For the child, who, motionless, was glaring at him maliciously, bore an inconceivable resemblance to the fifteen-year-old girl he had in his house. Everything was the same: the light eyebrows, the fine, quivering nostrils, the thin lips, even the way she slightly raised one shoulder. Everything was the same, except that in the child it came together in a way that terrified him. He did not know what made him feel that nameless fear; all he knew was that he could not bear to turn around knowing that the face would be staring at him through the glass.

In his anxiety he swiftly made for the door of the greenhouse, intending to enter. The door was shut, bolted from the outside. He quickly bent over the bolt, which was quite far down, and gave it such a shove that he gave a joint of his little finger a painful sprain; then he went up to the child, almost at a run.

The child moved towards him and braced herself against his knee without a word, trying to drag him out with her weak little hands. It was all he could do not to kick her. But his fear subsided now that they were close. He leaned over the child's face, which was quite pale, the eyes flickering with fury and hatred, the tiny teeth in the lower jaw biting into the upper lip with sinister rage. His fear vanished for an instant when he stroked the girl's short, fine hair, but he immediately recalled the hair of the girl in his house, which he had once touched when she lay in her bed, deathly pale and with closed eyes, and another shudder ran down his spine and he drew back his hands. She had given up trying to drag him away. She took a few steps back and stared straight ahead. He found the sight of the weak, doll-like body in its white dress and the contemptuous, gruesome, pale face almost impossible to bear. He was so overcome with horror that he felt a throb in his temples and throat when his hand touched something cold in his pocket. It was a few silver coins. He took them out, leaned down, and gave them, glistening and tingling, to the child. The child took them and dropped them at his feet; they disappeared into a crack in the boarded floor. Then she turned her back and walked slowly off.

He stood motionless for a while, his heart pounding with dread at the possibility of her returning and watching him through the glass from the outside. He would have liked to depart immediately, but it was better to give the child time to leave the garden. By now the greenhouse was growing dark and the shapes of the plants had begun to look strange. Black, wildly menacing dwarves emerged from the semi-darkness at a distance, and from behind them came a white shimmer, as if the child were standing there. A row of wax flowers in earthenware pots stood on a board. To distract himself and stall for time, he counted the blossoms, which were so stiff as to look less like living plants than masks, malicious masks, their eyeholes grown over. When he had finished, he went to the door to leave. The door would not open: the child had bolted it from the outside. He wanted to shout but feared his own voice. He beat his fists against the glass. The garden and the house remained deathly still. All he could hear was the rustle of something in the bushes. He told himself it was leaves shaken loose by the moist air and now falling. Still, he stopped pounding and peered through the tangle of shoots and branches. Suddenly he saw something like a rectangle of dark lines on the twilit rear wall. He crept towards it, past caring that he was trampling the earthenware pots and that the tall slender stalks and swishing fan-shaped crowns were caving in phantom-like above and below him. The rectangle of dark lines was the contour of a door, which yielded to his push. Fresh air blew over his face; behind him he heard the rustle of broken stalks and battered leaves rising slowly as after a storm.

He stood in a narrow walled passageway with the open sky above; the walls on either side were little higher than a man. But after a stretch of about fifteen paces the passageway ended in another wall, and he thought he was trapped yet again. Advancing hesitantly, he came to an opening in the right-hand wall the width of a man. There was a plank running from it through the air to a platform, which was closed on the side facing him by a low iron grille and on the other two sides by the backs of high residential buildings. At the point where the plank came to rest on the edge of the platform like a gangplank the grille had a small door.

So pressing was the desire of the merchant's son for release from the realm of his fear that he immediately placed first one then the other foot on the plank and, fixing his gaze firmly on the far side, set across it. Unfortunately he could not help perceiving that he was suspended over a walled chasm many stories deep, and in the soles of his feet and the bend of his knees he felt fear and helplessness, in the vertiginous state of his entire body—the nearness of death. He knelt and closed his eyes; his groping arms, reaching out, made contact with the bars of the grille. He clenched them firmly, but they gave way: with a soft creak that sliced through his body like the breath of death the door he was clutching began to open towards him, towards the abyss. And in his deep fatigue and great despondency he had a presentiment of the smooth iron bars wresting themselves from his fingers, which seemed to him the fingers of a child, and of himself hurtling down, smashed to pieces at the foot of the wall. But the slight motion of the door came to a halt before his feet could lose their hold on the plank, and with a bound he heaved his trembling body through the opening onto the hard floor.

He felt no joy. Not looking around and with a numb feeling of something akin to hatred for the senselessness of his torture, he entered one of the houses and went down the neglected stairs and out into a street that was ugly and ordinary. But he was now very sad and tired and could think of nothing worthy of any joy whatever. Everything seemed to have fallen away from him, and he walked down that street and the next and next completely empty and forsaken by life. He had taken the direction that he knew would bring him back to the part of town where the wealthy lived and where he could find shelter for the night. Oh how he craved a bed! With childlike longing he recalled the beauty of his own wide bed; he thought too of the beds that the great king of the past had had made for himself and his companions when celebrating their weddings to the daughters of subservient kings: a bed of gold for himself and of silver for the others, carried by griffins and wingèd bulls.

Eventually he came to the low houses where the soldiers lived. He did not notice them. Two soldiers with yellowish faces and sad eyes sitting at a barred window called out something to him. Only then did he lift his head and breathe in the musty odor coming from the room, a particularly oppressive odor. He did not understand what they wanted of him. But because they had aroused him from his blinkered advance, he now looked into the courtyard as he passed the gate. The courtyard was very large and sad and in the twilight appeared larger and sadder still. There were also very few people in it, and the surrounding buildings were low and of a dirty yellow, which made it look even larger and more deserted. In one area about twenty horses had been tethered in a straight line with a soldier in dirty twill stable clothes kneeling in front of each washing its hooves. Many others in similar twill attire were coming two by two out of a gate in the distance. They walked slowly, shuffling their feet and carrying heavy sacks on their backs. Not until they came closer did he see that the open sacks they were trudging along with in silence contained bread. He watched them disappear slowly through another gate, passing on as if bearing an ugly, ominous burden, carrying their bread in sacks like the ones that clothed the sadness of their bodies.

Then he went up to the men who were kneeling in front of the horses and washing their hooves. They too looked alike and resembled the ones at the window and the ones carrying bread. They must have come from neighboring villages. They too spoke scarcely a word to one another. It being very hard for them to hold down the horses' forefeet, their heads swayed and their tired, yellowish faces rose and fell as in a strong wind. Most of the horses' heads were ugly, and their pulled-back ears and raised upper lips, which laid bare the upper canines, gave them a malicious look. Most also had nasty rolling eyes and an odd way of forcing the air impatiently and contemptuously through twisted nostrils. The last horse in the row was particularly strong and ugly. With its large teeth it was trying to bite the shoulder of the man kneeling before it drying the hoof he had washed. The man had such hollow cheeks and so deathly sad an expression in his eyes that the merchant's son was overcome with deep, bitter sympathy. He wanted to cheer up the poor man for a moment with a gift and reached into his pocket for some silver coins. Not finding any, he recalled that he had attempted to give the last of them to the child in the greenhouse and that she had scattered them at his feet with a malign look. He would find a gold coin, for he had put seven or eight by for the journey.

At that moment the horse turned its head and fixed him with ominously pressed-back ears and rolling eyes made all the more nasty and wild by a star running across the ugly head and level with the eyes. At this ugly sight a long forgotten human face came to him in a flash. Had he made the effort to bring this person's features to mind, he would have failed, yet there they were. The memory that came with the face was not so clear, however. He knew only that he had been twelve years old at the time, a time somehow connected with the memory of the smell of sweet, warm, shelled almonds. And he knew it was the deformed face of a poor little ugly man whom he had seen only once in his father's shop. And that the man's face was deformed by fear because he was being threatened by people for possessing a large gold piece and refusing to say where he had come by it.

As the face dissolved, his finger was still searching in the folds of his clothing, but then, restrained by a sudden vague thought, he withdrew the hand hesitantly and threw the beryl ornament wrapped in tissue paper beneath the horse's feet. He bent down; the horse kicked him in the groin with all its strength, and he fell to the side on his back. He groaned loudly; his knees shot up, and his heels started beating the ground. A few of the soldiers stood and lifted him by the shoulders and under the knees. He smelled the odor of their clothing—the same damp, dreary odor that had come out of the room and onto the street earlier—and tried to recall where he had inhaled it a long time, ever so long a time before, and while so doing he lost consciousness. They carried him up a low staircase, through a long, semi-dark passageway into one of their rooms, and laid him on a low iron bed. Then they looked through his clothes, took the chain and the seven gold pieces, and finally, out of pity for his constant groaning, went for one of their surgeons.

Some time later he opened his eyes and became aware of his excruciating pain. But what frightened and worried him even more was being alone in that dreary room. With great effort he turned his eyes in their aching sockets to the wall and saw a board with three slices of the bread he had seen being carried across the courtyard.

There was nothing else in the room but hard, low beds and the smell of the dry reeds the beds were stuffed with and that other damp, dreary smell.

For a while he could think of nothing but his pain and the suffocating fear of death compared to which the pain was a relief. Then he was able to forget his fear of death for a moment and reflect on how it had all come about.

Then he felt another fear, a stinging, less overwhelming fear, one he had felt before but now felt as something overcome. And he clenched his fists and cursed his servants, who had driven him to his death: the manservant, who had sent him into the city, the old woman into the jeweler's shop, the girl into the back room, and the child, using her insidious replica, into the greenhouse, whence he saw himself reeling over gruesome stairs and bridges to sink under the horse's hoof. Then he fell back in great, dull fear. Then he whimpered like a child, not with pain but with grief, and his teeth chattered.

With great bitterness he looked back upon his life and renounced everything once dear to him. He hated his premature death so much that he hated his life for having brought him to it. These wild ravings consumed the last of his strength. He felt giddy and fell again for a time into a reeling, uneasy sleep. Then he awoke and tried to cry out, because he was still alone, but his voice failed him. In the end he brought up bile, then blood, and died with deformed features, the lips so torn that the teeth and gums were exposed, lending him a strange, evil expression.

A TALE OF THE CAVALRY

ON JULY 22, 1848, before six o'clock in the morning, the second squadron of Wallmoden cuirassiers, a troop of cavalry a hundred and seven strong under Captain Baron Rofrano, left the Casino San Alessandro and took the road to Milan. The wide, sunny landscape lay in untroubled peace; from distant mountain peaks, morning clouds rose like steady plumes of smoke into the radiant sky. Not a breath of air stirred the corn. Here and there, between clumps of trees fresh-bathed in the morning air, there was a bright gleam of a house or a church. Hardly had the troop left the foremost outposts of its own army about a mile behind them when they caught sight of a glint of weapons in the cornfields, and the vanguard reported enemy infantry. The squadron drew up for the attack by the side of the highroad; over their heads cannonballs flew, whizzing with a strangely loud, mewing noise; they attacked across country, driving before them like quails a troop of men irregularly armed. They belonged to the Manara Legion, and wore strange headgear. The prisoners were sent back in charge of a corporal and eight men. Outside a beautiful villa approached by an avenue of ancient cypresses, the vanguard reported suspicious figures. Anton Lerch, the sergeant, dismounted, took twelve men armed with carbines, whom he posted at the windows, and captured eighteen students of the Pisan Legion, well-bred, handsome young men with white hands and long hair. Half an hour later the squadron stopped a wayfarer in the Bergamasque costume whose very guilelessness and insignificance aroused suspicion. Sewn into the lining of his coat he was carrying detailed plans of the greatest importance relating to the formation of irregular corps in the Giudicaria and their liaison with the Piedmontese army. About ten o'clock, a herd of cows fell into the squadron's hands. Immediately afterwards, they encountered a strong enemy detachment which fired on the vanguard from a cemetery wall. The front line, under Lieutenant Count Trautsohn, vaulted over the low wall and laid about them among the graves on the enemy, most of whom escaped in wild confusion into the church and through the vestry door into a dense thicket. The twenty-seven new prisoners reported themselves as Neapolitan irregulars under Papal officers. The squadron had lost one man. Corporal Wotrubek, with two men, Dragoons Holl and Haindl, riding round the thicket, captured a light howitzer drawn by two farm-horses by knocking the guard senseless, taking the horses by the bridles, and turning them round. Corporal Wotrubek was sent back to headquarters, slightly wounded, to report these skirmishes and the other successes of the day, the prisoners were also sent back, while the howitzer was taken on by the squadron which, deducting the escort, now numbered seventy-eight men.

Since the prisoners declared with one voice that the city of Milan had been abandoned by the enemy troops, regular and irregular, and stripped of artillery and ammunition, the captain could not deny himself and his men the pleasure of riding into the great, beautiful, defenseless city. Amidst the ringing of noonday bells, under the march trumpeted into the steely, glittering sky by the four buglers, to rattle against a thousand windows and re-echo on seventy-eight cuirasses and seventy-eight upright, naked swords, with streets to right and left swarming like a broken anthill with gaping faces, watching pallid, cursing figures slipping into house doors, drowsy windows flung wide open by the bare arms of unknown beauty, past Santa Babila, San Fedele, San Carlo, past the famous white marble cathedral, San Satiro, San Giorgio, San Lorenzo, San Eustorgio, their ancient bronze doors all opening wide on silvery saints and brocade-clad women with shining eyes, on candlelight and fumes of incense, on the alert for shots from a thousand attics, dark archways, and low shop stalls, yet seeing at every turn mere half-grown girls and boys with flashing teeth and black hair, looking down on it all from their trotting horses, their eyes glittering in masks of blood-spattered dust, in at the Porta Venezia, out at the Porta Ticinese—thus the splendid squadron rode through Milan.

Not far from the Porta Ticinese, on a rampart set with fine plane trees, it seemed to Sergeant Anton Lerch that he saw, at the ground-floor window of a new, bright yellow house, a woman's face he knew. Curious to know more, he turned in his saddle; a slight stiffness in his horse's gait made him suspect a stone in one of its foreshoes, and as he was riding in the rear of the squadron, and could break file without disturbance, he made up his mind to dismount, even going so far as to back his horse into the entry of the house. Hardly had he raised the second white-socked hoof of his bay to inspect the shoe when a door leading straight into the front of the entry actually opened to show a woman, sensual-looking and still not quite past her youth, in a somewhat disheveled bedgown, and behind her a sunny room with a few pots of basil and red pelargonium in the windows, while his sharp eyes caught in a pier glass the reflection of the other side of the room, which was filled with a large white bed and a papered door, through which a stout, clean-shaven, elderly man was just withdrawing.

As there struggled back into the sergeant's mind the woman's name and a great many other things besides—that she was the widow or divorced wife of a Croat paymaster, that, nine or ten years before, he had on occasion spent the evening or half the night in Vienna with her and her accredited lover of the moment—he tried to distinguish, under her present stoutness, the full yet slender figure of those days. But standing there, she gave him a fawning Slav smile which sent the blood pulsing into his thick neck and under his eyes, and he was daunted by a certain archness in the way she spoke to him, by her bedgown and the furniture in the room behind. At the very moment, however, when with heavy eyes he was watching a big fly crawl over the woman's comb, when he had no thought in mind but of his hand on the warm, cool neck, brushing it away, the memory of the skirmishes and other lucky chances of the day came flooding back upon him, and he pressed her head forward with a heavy hand, saying: "Vuic"—he had not pronounced her name for ten years at least, and had completely forgotten her first name—"a week from now we shall occupy the town and these shall be my quarters," and he pointed to the half-open door of the room. Meanwhile he heard door after door slam in the house, felt his horse urging him to be gone, first by a dumb dragging at the bridle, then by loud neighing after the others. He mounted and trotted off after the squadron with no answer from Vuic save an evasive laugh and a toss of the head. But the word, once spoken, made him feel its power within him. Riding beside the main column of the squadron, his bay a little jaded, under the heavy, metallic glow of the sky, half-blinded by the cloud of dust that moved with the riders, the sergeant, in his imagination, slowly took possession of the room with the mahogany furniture and the pots of basil, and at the same time entered into a life of peace still irradiated by war, an atmosphere of comfort and pleasant brutality with no officer to give him orders, a slippered life with the hilt of his saber sticking through the left-hand pocket of his dressing gown. And the stout, clean-shaven man who had vanished through the papered door, something between a priest and a pensioned footman, played an important part in it all, more important, even, than the fine, broad bed and Vuic's white skin. The clean-shaven man was now a somewhat servile companion who told court gossip and brought presents of tobacco and capons, now he was hard-pressed and had to pay blackmail, was involved in many intrigues, was in the confidence of the Piedmontese, was the Pope's cook, procurer, owner of suspect houses with gloomy pavilions for political meetings, and swelled up into a huge, bloated figure from which, if it were tapped in twenty places, gold, not blood, would pour.

There were no further surprises for the squadron that afternoon, and there was nothing to check the sergeant's musings. But there had awakened in him a craving for strokes of luck, for prize moneys, for ducats suddenly falling into his pockets. And the thorn which festered in his flesh, round which all wishes and desires clustered, was the anticipation of his first entrance into the room with the mahogany furniture.

When the squadron, its horses fed and half-rested, attempted towards evening to advance by a detour on Lodi and the Adda bridge, where there was every prospect of an encounter with the enemy, a village lying in a dark hollow off the high road with a half-ruined church spire looked enticing and suspicious enough to attract the sergeant's attention. Beckoning to two dragoons, Holl and Scarmolin, he broke away from the squadron's route with them, and, so inflamed was his imagination that it swelled to the hope of surprising in the village some ill-defended enemy general, or of winning some other great prize. Having arrived at the wretched and seemingly deserted place, he ordered Scarmolin to reconnoiter the houses from the outside to the left, Holl to the right, while he himself, pistol in hand, set off at the gallop through the village. Soon, feeling under his feet hard flagstones which were coated with some slippery kind of grease, he had to put his horse to the walk. Deathly silence reigned in the village—not a child, not a bird, not a breath of air. To right and left there stood foul hovels, the mortar scaling from their walls, with obscene drawings in charcoal here and there on the bare bricks. Between the naked doorposts the sergeant caught sight from time to time of a dirty, half-naked figure lounging on a bed or hobbling through the room as if on broken hips. His horse advanced painfully, pushing its haunches leadenly forward. As he turned and bent to look at its hind shoe, shuffling footsteps issued from a house; he sat upright, and a woman whose face he could not see passed close in front of his mount. She was only half-dressed, her rag-

ged, filthy gown of flowered silk, half-torn off her shoulders,
trailed in the gutter, there were dirty slippers on her feet. She
passed so close in front of his horse that the breath from its
nostrils stirred the bunch of greasy curls that hung down her
bare neck under an old straw hat, yet she made no move to
hurry, nor did she make way for the rider. From a doorstep to
the left, two rats, bleeding in their death-agony, rolled into the
middle of the street, the under one screaming so desperately
that the sergeant's horse stopped, staring at the ground, its
head averted and its breathing audible. A pressure on its flank
sent it forward again, the woman having disappeared in an
entry before the sergeant could see her face. A dog ran out
busily with upraised head, dropped a bone in the middle of the
street and set about burying it between the paving stones. It was
a dirty white bitch with trailing teats; she scraped with fiendish
intentness, then took the bone between her teeth and carried
it away. As she began to dig again, three dogs ran up, two of
them mere puppies with soft bones and loose skin; unable to
bark or bite, they pulled at each others' muzzles with blunt
teeth. The dog which had come with them was a pale yellow
greyhound; its body so bloated that it could only drag itself
along on its four skinny legs. The body was taut as a drum, so
that its head looked far too small; there was a dreadful look of
pain and fear in it restless little eyes. Two other dogs ran up at
once, one thin and white, with black furrows running from its
reddened eyes, and hideous in its avidity, the other a vile dachs-
hund with long legs. This dog raised its head towards the ser-
geant and looked at him. It must have been very old. Its eyes
were fathomlessly weary and sad. But the bitch ran to and fro in
silly haste before the rider, the two puppies snapped soundlessly
with their muzzles round the horse's fetlocks, and the grey-
hound dragged its hideous body close in front of the horse's
hoofs. The bay could not advance a step. But when, having
drawn his pistol to shoot one of the dogs, it misfired, the ser-
geant spurred his horse on both flanks and thundered away
over the paving stones. After a few bounds he was brought up

short by a cow which a lad was dragging to the shambles at the end of a tight-stretched rope. But the cow, shrinking from the smell of blood and the fresh hide of a calf nailed to the door-post, planted its hooves firm on the ground, drew the reddish haze of the sunset in through dilated nostrils and, before the lad could drag her across the road with stick and rope, tore away with piteous eyes a mouthful of the hay which the sergeant had tied on the front of his saddle.

He had now left the last house of the village behind him and, riding between two low and crumbling walls, could see his way ahead on the farther side of an old single-span bridge over an apparently dry ditch. He felt in his horse's step such an unutter-able heaviness that every foot of the walls to right and left, and even every single one of the centipedes and wood lice which housed in them, passed toilsomely before his eyes, and it seemed to him that he had spent eternity riding through the hideous village. But as, at the same time, he heard a great rasp-ing breath from his horse's chest without at once realizing what it was, he looked above and beside him, and then ahead to see whence it came, and in doing so became aware, on the farther side of the bridge and at the same distance from it as himself, of a man of his own regiment, a sergeant riding a bay with white-socked forefeet. But as he knew that there was no other horse of the kind in the whole squadron but the one on which he was at that moment mounted, and as he still could not recognize the face of the other rider, he impatiently spurred his horse into a very lively trot, whereupon the other mended his pace in exactly the same way till there was only a stone's throw between them. And now, as the two horses, each from its own side, placed the same white-socked forefoot on the bridge, the ser-geant, recognizing with starting eyes his own wraith, reined in his horse aghast, and stretched his right hand with stiffened fingers towards the being, while the wraith, also reining in its horse and raising its right hand, was suddenly there no longer; Holl and Scarmolin appeared from the dry ditch to left and right quite unperturbed, while loud and near at hand the bugles of the squadron sounded the attack.

Taking a rise in the ground at full speed, the sergeant saw the squadron already galloping towards a thicket from which enemy cavalry, armed with pikes, were pouring, and as he gathered the four loose reins in his left hand and wound the hand strap round his right, he saw the fourth rank leave the squadron and slacken its pace, was already on the thundering earth, now in the thick smell of dust, now in the midst of the enemy, struck at a blue arm wielding a pike, saw close at hand the captain's face with starting eyes and savagely bared teeth, was suddenly wedged in among enemy faces and foreign colors, dived below whirling blades, lunged at the next man's neck and unseated him, saw Scarmolin beside him, laughing, hew off the fingers of a man's bridle hand and strike deep into the horse's neck, felt the thick of battle slacken, and was suddenly alone on the bank of a brook behind an enemy officer on an iron-gray horse. The officer put his horse to the jump across the brook, the horse refused. The officer pulled it round, turning towards the sergeant a young, very pale face and the mouth of a pistol, then a saber was driven into his mouth with the full force of a galloping horse in its tiny point. The sergeant snatched back his saber, and at the very spot where the fingers of the fallen rider had opened, laid hold of the snaffle of the iron-gray, which, light and airy as a fawn, lifted its hoofs across its dying master.

As the sergeant rode back with his splendid prize, the sun, setting in a thick mist, cast a vast crimson haze over the fields. Even on untrodden ground there seemed to lie whole pools of blood. A crimson glow lay on white uniforms and laughing faces, cuirasses and saddle cloths sparkled and shone, and three little fig trees on which the men had wiped the grooves in their sabers glowed deepest of all. The captain came to a halt by the blood-stained trees, beside the bugler of the squadron, who raised his crimson-dripping bugle to his lips and blew. The sergeant rode from line to line and saw that the squadron had not lost a man, but had taken nine horses. He rode up to the captain to report, the iron-gray still beside him, capering with upraised head and wide nostrils, like the young, vain, beautiful horse it was. The captain hardly listened to the report. He made a sign to Lieutenant Count Trautsohn, who at once dismounted, unharnessed the captured light howitzer, ordered the gun to be dragged away by a detachment of six men and sunk in a swamp formed by the brook, having driven away the now useless draught-horses with a blow from the flat of his saber, and silently resumed his place at the head of the first rank. During this time, the squadron, drawn up in two ranks, was not really restless, yet there was a strange feeling in the air; the elation of four successful skirmishes in one day found vent in outbursts of suppressed laughter and smothered shouts to each other. Even the horses were restless, especially those flanking the prizes. What with all these windfalls, the parade-ground seemed too small to hold them; in the pride of victory, the men felt they must scatter, swarm in upon a new enemy, fling themselves upon him, and carry off yet more horses.

At that moment Captain Baron Rofrano rose up to the front rank of his squadron and, raising his big eyelids from his rather sleepy blue eyes, gave, audibly but without raising his voice, the command "Release led horses." The squadron stood still as death. Only the iron-gray beside the sergeant stretched its neck, almost touching with its nostrils the forehead of the captain's mount. The captain sheathed his saber, drew a pistol from its holster and, wiping a little dust from its shining barrel with the back of his bridle hand, repeated the command, raising his voice slightly and beginning to count, "One . . . two . . ." When he had counted "two," he fixed his veiled eyes on the sergeant, who sat motionless in his saddle, staring him full in the face. While Anton Lerch's steady, unflinching gaze, flashing now and then an oppressed, doglike look, seemed to express a kind of servile trust born of many years of service, his mind was almost unaware of the huge tension of the moment, but was flooded with visions of an alien ease, and from depths in him unknown to himself there rose a bestial anger against the man before him who was taking away his horse, a dreadful rage against the face, the voice, the bearing, the whole being of the man, such as can only arise, in some mysterious fashion, through years of close companionship. Whether something of the same sort was going on in the captain's mind too, or whether he felt the silently spreading danger of critical situations coming to a head in this moment of mute insubordination, we cannot know. Raising his arm with a negligent, almost graceful gesture, he counted "three" with a contemptuous curl of his upper lip, the shot cracked, and the sergeant, hit in the forehead, reeled, his body across his horse's neck, then fell between the iron-gray and the bay. He had not reached the ground, however, before all the other noncommissioned officers and men had driven off their captured horses with a twist of the rein or a kick, and the captain quietly putting away his pistol, was able to rally his squadron, still twitching from the lightning stroke, against the enemy, who seemed to be gathering in the distant, shadowy dusk. The enemy, however, did not engage the new attack, and not long after, the squadron arrived unmolested at the southern outposts of its own army.

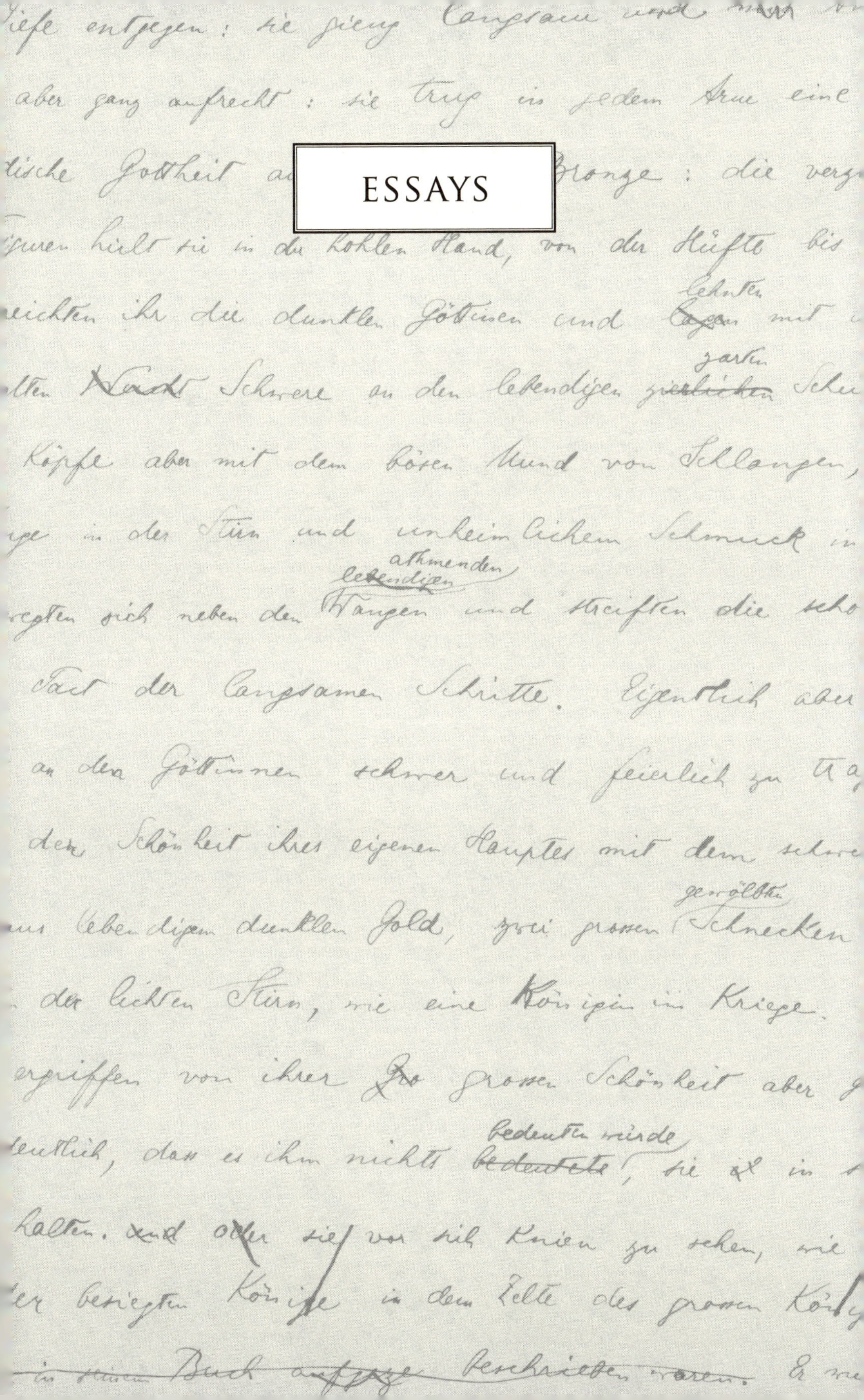

ESSAYS

THE LETTER OF LORD CHANDOS

This is the letter Philip, Lord Chandos, younger son of the Earl of Bath, wrote to Francis Bacon, later Baron Verulam, Viscount St. Albans, apologizing for his complete abandonment of literary activity.

IT IS KIND OF YOU, my esteemed friend, to condone my two years of silence and to write to me thus. It is more than kind of you to give to your solicitude about me, to your perplexity at what appears to you as mental stagnation, the expression of lightness and jest which only great men, convinced of the perilousness of life yet not discouraged by it, can master.

You conclude with the aphorism of Hippocrates, "Qui gravi morbo correpti dolores non sentiunt, iis mens aegrotat" (Those who do not perceive that they are wasted by serious illness are sick in mind), and suggest that I am in need of medicine not only to conquer my malady, but even more, to sharpen my senses for the condition of my inner self. I would fain give you an answer such as you deserve, fain reveal myself to you entirely, but I do not know how to set about it. Hardly do I know whether I am still the same person to whom your precious letter is addressed. Was it I who, now six-and-twenty, at nineteen wrote *The New Paris, The Dream of Daphne, Epithalamium*, those pastorals reeling under the splendor of their words—plays which a divine Queen and several overindulgent lords and gentlemen are gracious enough still to remember? And again, was it I who, at three-and-twenty, beneath the stone arcades of the great Venetian piazza, found in myself that structure of Latin prose whose plan and order delighted me more than did the monuments of Palladio and Sansovino rising out of the sea? And could I, if otherwise I am still the same person, have lost from my inner inscrutable self all traces and scars of this creation of my most intensive thinking—lost them so completely that in your letter now lying before me the title of my short treatise stares at me strange and cold? I could not even comprehend, at first, what the familiar picture meant, but had to study it word by word, as though these Latin terms thus strung together were meeting my eye for the first time. But I am, after all, that person, and there is rhetoric in these questions—rhetoric which is good for women or for the House of Commons, whose power, however, so overrated by our time, is not sufficient to penetrate into the core of things. But it is my inner self that I feel bound to reveal to you—a peculiarity, a vice, a disease of my mind, if you like— if you are to understand that an abyss equally unbridgeable separates me from the literary works lying seemingly ahead of me as from those behind me: the latter having become so strange to me that I hesitate to call them my property.

I know not whether to admire more the urgency of your benevolence or the unbelievable sharpness of your memory, when you recall to me the various little projects I entertained during those days of rare enthusiasm which we shared together. True, I did plan to describe the first years of the reign of our glorious sovereign, the late Henry VIII. The papers bequeathed to me by my grandfather, the Duke of Exeter, concerning his negotiations with France and Portugal, offered me some foundation. And out of Sallust, in those happy, stimulating days, there flowed into me as though through never-congested conduits the realization of form—that deep, true, inner form which can be sensed only beyond the domain of rhetorical tricks: that form of which one can no longer say that it organizes subject matter, for it penetrates it, dissolves it, creating at once both dream and reality, an interplay of eternal forces, something as marvelous as music or algebra. This was my most treasured plan.

But what is man that he should make plans!

I also toyed with other schemes. These, too, your kind letter conjures up. Each one, bloated with a drop of my blood, dances before me like a weary gnat against a somber wall whereon the bright sun of halcyon days no longer lies.

I wanted to decipher the fables, the mythical tales bequeathed to us by the Ancients, in which painters and sculptors found an endless and thoughtless pleasure—decipher them as the hieroglyphs of a secret, inexhaustible wisdom whose breath I sometimes seemed to feel as though from behind a veil.

I well remember this plan. It was founded on I know not what sensual and spiritual desire: as the hunted hart craves water, so I craved to enter these naked, glistening bodies, these sirens and dryads, this Narcissus and Proteus, Perseus and Actaeon. I longed to disappear in them and talk out of them with tongues. And I longed for more. I planned to start an *Apophthegmata*, like that composed by Julius Caesar: you will remember that Cicero mentions it in a letter. In it I thought of setting side by side the most memorable sayings which—while associating with the learned men and witty women of our time, with unusual people from among the simple folk or with erudite and distinguished personages—I had managed to collect during my travels. With these I meant to combine the brilliant maxims and reflections from classical and Italian works, and anything else of intellectual adornment that appealed to me in books, in manuscripts or conversations; the arrangement, moreover, of particularly beautiful festivals and pageants, strange crimes and cases of madness, descriptions of the greatest and most characteristic architectural monuments in the Netherlands, in France and Italy; and many other things. The whole work was to have been entitled *Nosce te ipsum*.

To sum up: In those days I, in a state of continuous intoxication, conceived the whole of existence as one great unit: the spiritual and physical worlds seemed to form no contrast, as little as did courtly and bestial conduct, art and barbarism, solitude and society; in everything I felt the presence of Nature, in the aberrations of insanity as much as in the utmost refinement of the Spanish ceremonial; in the boorishness of young peasants no less than in the most delicate of allegories; and in all expressions of Nature I felt myself. When in my hunting lodge I drank the warm foaming milk which an unkempt wench had drained into a wooden pail from the udder of a beautiful gentle-eyed cow, the sensation was no different from that which I experienced when, seated on a bench built into the window of my study, my mind absorbed the sweet and foaming nourishment from a book. The one was like the other: neither was superior to the other, whether in dreamlike celestial quality or in physical intensity—and thus it prevailed through the whole expanse of life in all directions; everywhere I was in the center of it, never suspecting mere appearance: at other times I divined that all was allegory and that each creature was a key to all the others; and I felt myself the one capable of seizing each by the handle and unlocking as many of the others as were ready to yield. This explains the title which I had intended to give to this encyclopedic book.

To a person susceptible to such ideas, it might appear a well-designed plan of divine Providence that my mind should fall from such a state of inflated arrogance into this extreme of despondency and feebleness which is now the permanent condition of my inner self. Such religious ideas, however, have no power over me: they belong to the cobwebs through which my thoughts dart out into the void, while the thoughts of so many others are caught there and come to rest. To me the mysteries of faith have been condensed into a lofty allegory which arches itself over the fields of my life like a radiant rainbow, ever remote, ever prepared to recede should it occur to me to rush towards it and wrap myself into the folds of its mantle.

But, my dear friend, worldly ideas also evade me in a like manner. How shall I try to describe to you these strange spiritual

torments, this rebounding of the fruit branches above my out-
stretched hands, this recession of the murmuring stream from
my thirsting lips?

My case, in short, is this: I have lost completely the ability to
think or to speak of anything coherently.

At first I grew by degrees incapable of discussing a loftier or
more general subject in terms of which everyone, fluently and
without hesitation, is wont to avail himself. I experienced an
inexplicable distaste for so much as uttering the words *spirit*,
soul, or *body*. I found it impossible to express an opinion on the
affairs at Court, the events in Parliament, or whatever you wish.
This was not motivated by any form of personal deference (for
you know that my candor borders on imprudence), but because
the abstract terms of which the tongue must avail itself as a
matter of course in order to voice a judgment—these terms
crumbled in my mouth like moldy fungi. Thus, one day, while
reprimanding my four-year-old daughter, Katherina Pompilia,
for a childish lie of which she had been guilty and demon-
strating to her the necessity of always being truthful, the ideas
streaming into my mind suddenly took on such iridescent color-
ing, so flowed over into one another, that I reeled off the sen-
tence as best I could, as if suddenly overcome by illness. Actu-
ally, I did feel myself growing pale, and with a violent pressure
on my forehead I left the child to herself, slammed the door
behind me, and began to recover to some extent only after a
brief gallop over the lonely pasture.

Gradually, however, these attacks of anguish spread like a cor-
roding rust. Even in familiar and humdrum conversation all
the opinions which are generally expressed with ease and sleep-
walking assurance became so doubtful that I had to cease alto-
gether taking part in such talk. It filled me with an inexplicable
anger, which I could conceal only with effort, to hear such
things as: This affair has turned out well or ill for this or that
person; Sheriff N. is a bad, Parson T. a good man; Farmer M. is
to be pitied, his sons are wasters; another is to be envied because
his daughters are thrifty; one family is rising in the world, an-

other is on the downward path. All this seemed as indemonstrable, as mendacious and hollow as could be. My mind compelled me to view all things occurring in such conversations from an uncanny closeness. As once, through a magnifying glass, I had seen a piece of skin on my little finger look like a field full of holes and furrows, so I now perceived human beings and their actions. I no longer succeeded in comprehending them with the simplifying eye of habit. For me everything disintegrated into parts, those parts again into parts; no longer would anything let itself be encompassed by one idea. Single words floated round me; they congealed into eyes which stared at me and into which I was forced to stare back—whirlpools which gave me vertigo and, reeling incessantly, led into the void.

I tried to rescue myself from this plight by seeking refuge in the spiritual world of the Ancients. Plato I avoided, for I dreaded the perilousness of his imagination. Of them all, I intended to concentrate on Seneca and Cicero. Through the harmony of their clearly defined and orderly ideas I hoped to regain my health. But I was unable to find my way to them. These ideas, I understood them well: I saw their wonderful interplay rise before me like magnificent fountains upon which played golden balls. I could hover around them and watch how they played, one with the other; but they were concerned only with each other, and the most profound, most personal quality of my thinking remained excluded from this magic circle. In their company I was overcome by a terrible sense of loneliness; I felt like someone locked in a garden surrounded by eyeless statues. So once more I escaped into the open.

Since that time I have been leading an existence which I fear you can hardly imagine, so lacking in spirit and thought is its flow: an existence which, it is true, differs little from that of my neighbors, my relations, and most of the landowning nobility of this kingdom, and which is not utterly bereft of gay and stimulating moments. It is not easy for me to indicate wherein these good moments subsist; once again words desert me. For it is, indeed, something entirely unnamed, even barely nameable

which, at such moments, reveals itself to me, filling like a vessel
any casual object of my daily surroundings with an overflowing
flood of higher life. I cannot expect you to understand me with-
out examples, and I must plead your indulgence for their absur-
dity. A pitcher, a harrow abandoned in a field, a dog in the sun,
a neglected cemetery, a cripple, a peasant's hut—all these can
become the vessel of my revelation. Each of these objects and
a thousand others similar, over which the eye usually glides with
a natural indifference, can suddenly, at any moment (which I
am utterly powerless to evoke), assume for me a character so
exalted and moving that words seem too poor to describe it.
Even the distinct image of an absent object, in fact, can acquire
the mysterious function of being filled to the brim with this
silent but suddenly rising flood of divine sensation. Recently,
for instance, I had given the order for a copious supply of rat
poison to be scattered in the milk cellars of one of my dairy
farms. Towards evening I had gone off for a ride and, as you
can imagine, thought no more about it. As I was trotting along
over the freshly-ploughed land, nothing more alarming in sight
than a scared covey of quail and, in the distance, the great sun
sinking over the undulating fields, there suddenly loomed up
before me the vision of that cellar, resounding with the death
struggle of a mob of rats. I felt everything within me: the cool,
musty air of the cellar filled with the sweet and pungent reek of
poison, and the yelling of the death cries breaking against the
moldering walls; the vain convulsions of those convoluted bod-
ies as they tear about in confusion and despair; their frenzied
search for escape, and the grimace of icy rage when a couple
collide with one another at a blocked-up crevice. But why seek
again for words which I have forsworn! You remember, my
friend, the wonderful description in Livy of the hours preced-
ing the destruction of Alba Longa: when the crowds stray aim-
lessly through the streets which they are to see no more . . .
when they bid farewell to the stones beneath their feet. I assure
you, my friend, I carried this vision within me, and the vision of
burning Carthage, too; but there was more, something more

divine, more bestial; and it was the Present, the fullest, most exalted Present. There was a mother, surrounded by her young in their agony of death; but her gaze was cast neither towards the dying nor upon the merciless walls of stone, but into the void, or through the void into Infinity, accompanying this gaze with a gnashing of teeth!—A slave struck with helpless terror standing near the petrifying Niobe must have experienced what I experienced when, within me, the soul of this animal bared its teeth to its monstrous fate.

Forgive this description, but do not think that it was pity I felt. For if you did, my example would have been poorly chosen. It was far more and far less than pity: an immense sympathy, a flowing over into these creatures, or a feeling that an aura of life and death, of dream and wakefulness, had flowed for a moment into them—but whence? For what had it to do with pity, or with any comprehensible concatenation of human thought when, on another evening, on finding beneath a nut tree a half-filled pitcher which a gardener boy had left there, and the pitcher and the water in it, darkened by the shadow of the tree, and a beetle swimming on the surface from shore to shore—when this combination of trifles sent through me such a shudder at the presence of the Infinite, a shudder running from the roots of my hair to the marrow of my heels? What was it that made me want to break into words which, I know, were I to find them, would force to their knees those cherubim in whom I do not believe? What made me turn silently away from this place? Even now, after weeks, catching sight of that nut tree, I pass it by with a shy sidelong glance, for I am loath to dispel the memory of the miracle hovering there round the trunk, loath to scare away the celestial shudders that still linger about the shrubbery in this neighborhood! In these moments an insignificant creature—a dog, a rat, a beetle, a crippled apple tree, a lane winding over the hill, a moss-covered stone, mean more to me than the most beautiful, abandoned mistress of the happiest night. These mute and, on occasion, inanimate creatures rise towards me with such an abundance, such a presence of love, that my enchanted eye can find nothing in sight void of life. Everything that exists, everything I can remember, everything touched upon by my confused thoughts, has a meaning. Even my own heaviness, the general torpor of my brain, seems to acquire a meaning; I experience in and around me a blissful, never-ending interplay, and among the objects playing against one another there is not one into which I cannot flow. To me, then, it is as though my body consists of nought but ciphers which give me the key to everything; or as if we could enter into a new and hopeful relationship with the whole of existence if only we begin to think with the heart. As soon, however, as this strange enchantment falls from me, I find myself confused; wherein this harmony transcending me and the entire world consisted, and how it made itself known to me, I could present in sensible words as little as I could say anything precise about the inner movements of my intestines or a congestion of my blood.

Apart from these strange occurrences, which, incidentally, I hardly know whether to ascribe to the mind or the body, I live a life of barely believable vacuity, and have difficulties in concealing from my wife this inner stagnation, and from my servants the indifference wherewith I contemplate the affairs of my estates. The good and strict education which I owe to my late father and the early habit of leaving no hour of the day unused are the only things, it seems to me, which help me maintain towards the outer world the stability and the dignified appearance appropriate to my class and my person.

I am rebuilding a wing of my house and am capable of conversing occasionally with the architect concerning the progress of his work; I administer my estates, and my tenants and employees may find me, perhaps, somewhat more taciturn but no less benevolent than of yore. None of them, standing with doffed cap before the door of his house while I ride by of an evening, will have any idea that my glance, which he is wont respectfully to catch, glides with longing over the rickety boards under which he searches for earthworms for fishing bait; that it plunges through the latticed window into the stuffy chamber where, in a corner, the low bed with its checkered linen seems forever to be waiting for someone to die or another to be born; that my eye lingers long upon the ugly puppies or upon a cat stealing stealthily among the flower pots; and that it seeks among all the poor and clumsy objects of a peasant's life for the one whose insignificant form, whose unnoticed being, whose mute existence, can become the source of that mysterious, wordless, and boundless ecstasy. For my unnamed blissful feeling is sooner brought about by a distant lonely shepherd's fire than by the vision of a starry sky, sooner by the chirping of the last dying cricket when the autumn wind chases wintry clouds across the deserted fields than by the majestic booming of an organ. And in my mind I compare myself from time to time with the orator Crassus, of whom it is reported that he grew so excessively enamored of a tame lamprey—a dumb, apathetic, red-eyed fish in his ornamental pond—that it became the talk of the town; and when one day in the Senate Domitius reproached him for having shed tears over the death of this fish, attempting thereby to make him appear a fool, Crassus answered, "Thus have I done over the death of my fish as you have over the death of neither your first nor your second wife."

I know not how oft this Crassus with his lamprey enters my mind as a mirrored image of my Self, reflected across the abyss of centuries. But not on account of the answer he gave Domitius. The answer brought the laughs on his side, and the whole affair turned into a jest. I, however, am deeply affected by the affair, which would have remained the same even had Domitius shed bitter tears of sorrow over his wives. For there would still have been Crassus, shedding tears over his lamprey. And about this figure, utterly ridiculous and contemptible in the midst of a world-governing senate discussing the most serious subjects, I feel compelled by a mysterious power to reflect in a manner which, the moment I attempt to express it in words, strikes me as supremely foolish.

Now and then at night the image of this Crassus is in my brain, like a splinter round which everything festers, throbs, and boils. It is then that I feel as though I myself were about to ferment, to effervesce, to foam and to sparkle. And the whole thing is a kind of feverish thinking, but thinking in a medium more immediate, more liquid, more glowing than words. It, too, forms whirlpools, but of a sort that do not seem to lead, as the whirlpools of language, into the abyss, but into myself and into the deepest womb of peace.

I have troubled you excessively, my dear friend, with this extended description of an inexplicable condition which is wont, as a rule, to remain locked up in me.

You were kind enough to express your dissatisfaction that no book written by me reaches you any more, "to compensate for the loss of our relationship." Reading that, I felt, with a certainty not entirely bereft of a feeling of sorrow, that neither in the coming year nor in the following nor in all the years of this my life shall I write a book, whether in English or in Latin: and this for an odd and embarrassing reason which I must leave to the boundless superiority of your mind to place in the realm of physical and spiritual values spread out harmoniously before your unprejudiced eye: to wit, because the language in which I might be able not only to write but to think is neither Latin nor English, neither Italian nor Spanish, but a language none of whose words is known to me, a language in which inanimate things speak to me and wherein I may one day have to justify myself before an unknown judge.

Fain had I the power to compress in this, presumably my last, letter to Francis Bacon all the love and gratitude, all the unmeasured admiration, which I harbor in my heart for the greatest benefactor of my mind, for the foremost Englishman of my day, and which I shall harbor therein until death break it asunder.

This 22 August, A.D. 1603

PHI. CHANDOS

MOMENTS IN GREECE

I

THE MONASTERY OF ST. LUKE

WE HAD BEEN riding that day from nine to ten hours. As the sun stood high overhead, we had lain down to rest in front of a small rest place near a well of pure water and a huge, beautiful plane tree. Later, lying prone on the ground, we had again quenched our thirst, with the mules, from a thread of running water. At first our road was cut into a slope of Parnassus, then into a primeval petrified riverbed, then into a depression between two cone-shaped mountains; finally it passed through the green cornfields of a fertile plateau. Some stretches were silent with the silence of millenniums—nothing but a lizard rustling across the road and a sparrow hawk circling high in the air; others were alive with the life of flocks of sheep. Then came the barking of the wolflike dogs, which bared their teeth so near to the mules that we had to drive them off with stones. Sheep, heavy with wool, stood massed together in the shadow of a rock, trembling from their heated breathing. Two black rams butted one another with their horns. A handsome young shepherd carried a small lamb over his shoulders. On a flat stony landscape rested the motionless shadow of a cloud. In a strangely formed hollow, wherein lay thousands of single great boulders among which grew thousands of small, pungently aromatic shrubs, a large tortoise dragged itself across the road. Then, towards evening, a village showed itself in the distance, but we passed it by. At the side of our road was a cistern, the spring caught in its depths. Near the fountain stood two cypresses. Women hauled up the clear water and brought it to our animals to drink. Across the evening sky sailed tiny clouds, in twos and threes. Sheep bells sounded from near and far. The mules moved on faster, drawing in the air drifting towards us from the valley. A perfume of acacias, of strawberries and thyme, was wafted over the road. We felt that the bluish mountains were closing in on us and that this valley was the end of the road. We rode on between two hedges of wild roses. A small bird, no larger than the little patch of shade beneath one of the roses, flew ahead of us; the hedge on the left, on the valley side, ended, and we looked down and across, as though from a balcony. Down to the bottom of the small, bow-shaped valley and on the opposite slope, halfway up the mountain, stood groups of fruit trees among dark cypresses. Between the trees grew flowering hedges. Sheep moved in and out of them, and birds sang in the branches. Beneath our road ran other roads. These, one could see, had been laid out for pleasure, not for wanderers or shepherds. They wound along in gentle curves, always at the same height above the valley. In the center of the slope stood a single stone pine, a lone, regal tree—the only really large tree in the whole valley. It could have been as old as the hills, but the grace with which it rose and held its three crowns in delicate curves towards the sky suggested something of eternal youth. Low walls now bordered the road to right and left, with orchards behind them. A black goat stood with its forelegs propped against an ancient olive tree, as though wanting to climb it. An old man, pruning knife in hand, waded up to his waist in blossoming briar roses. One had the feeling that the monastery was quite near, not more than a hundred yards or even less, and we were surprised not to see it. In the wall on the left was a small open door; in the doorway leaned a monk. The long black gown, the high black headgear, the casual way he stood there, gazing towards us in this paradisal solitude—all this gave him the air of a magician. He was young, with a long, light red beard, its cut reminiscent of Byzantine portraits, an eagle nose, restless, almost intrusive blue eyes. He greeted us with a bow and a spreading of both arms, in which there was something forced. We dismounted, and he led the way. Crossing a small garden enclosed by walls, we entered a room, where he left us alone. The room had the minimum of furniture. Under a Byzantine image of the Holy Virgin burned a perpetual flame; opposite the entrance an open door led onto a balcony. We stepped out to find that we were in the center of the monastery, which was built into the mountain. Our room, which, from the garden side, was on the ground floor, lay here two stories high above the cloisters. The church, with the reflection of the evening sun on its thousand-year-old reddish walls and cupolas, closed off one side; the other three sides were formed by houses similar to that in which we were standing, with the same kind of small wooden balconies as that on which we were leaning. The houses were irregular, of different colors, and the little balconies were light blue, yellowish, or pale green. From the house which formed the corner a loggia, like a drawbridge, led to the church. Parts of the building looked immeasurably ancient, others no older than a generation. Everything breathed peace and a scent-sweetened serenity. From below, a fountain murmured. On a bench sat two older monks with ebony-black beards. Opposite them, on a second-floor balcony, leaned another of uncertain age, his head on his hand. Small clouds sailed across the sky. The two monks rose and went into the church. Two others came down a staircase. They also wore the long black gowns, but the black caps on their heads were not so high, and their faces were beardless. Their gait had the same indefinable rhythm: as far removed from haste as from slowness. They disappeared simultaneously through the church door, not so much like men entering a house as sails vanishing beyond a rock, or as great unobserved animals stalking through the forest and disappearing behind trees. Inside the church faint voices began chanting psalms, following an age-old melody. The voices rose and fell; there was in them something end-less, as remote from lamentation as from desire, something solemn which might have been sounding from eternity and continue to sound far into eternity. Above the yard from an open window a voice followed the melody, from cadence to cadence; a woman's voice. This sounded so strange it seemed like an hallucination. But it started again, and a female voice it was. And yet it wasn't. The echo-like quality, the utterly faithful following of this solemn, hardly any longer human sound, this will-less, almost unconscious voice, did not seem to issue from the breast of woman. It sounded as if mystery itself were singing, something insubstantial. Now it was silent. From the church, with the soft, dark, tremulous men's voices, there came forth an aroma of wax, mingled with honey and incense, like the fra-grance of the chant itself. Now the feminine voice began again, following the phrases of the singing. But other similar voices from the same open window, not far from my balcony, joined in, *mezza voce* and not seriously, as though in mockery; the beautiful voice broke off; and now I realized that they were the voices of boys. Immediately their heads appeared at the window. There was one among them, gentle and beautiful, like a girl, whose fair hair fell over his shoulders to his waist. Other choirboys, standing down in the courtyard, called up. "The brother!" they shouted. "His brother! The shepherd! The shepherd!"

Later I happened to be there when the brothers took leave of one another. The young shepherd stood in the light of the sinking sun, dark, slender, and warrior-like, against a back-ground of sheep and dogs. In his strong bronzed hand he held the small hand of the boy with long hair. A monk in black robe, a handsome, beardless, twenty-year-old novice, with a smile which, round his young mouth and smooth cheeks, was thoughtless and vain, but in the neighborhood of his dark eyes submissive and knowing, stepped into the half-open door. He did not call to the boy, just waved. The gesture of his raised hand was without impatience. Rather than the commander, he was the transmitter of a command, the messenger. Onto a small balcony above the doorway stepped an older monk; he placed his elbows on the banister, his head in his hand, and calmly watched how the command was transmitted and carried out. The novice gave him a barely perceptible nod, a smile a trifle more bright and submissive. The beautiful boy let go the brother's hand and ran back to the novice. The shepherd turned and promptly, with long calm strides, walked downhill, into the country. The sheep, as though part of him, were already moving, surging down the road, hemmed in by the dogs. In the church the singing grew louder. During the service at this evening hour everyone was on his knees in the twilit chapel, or lying stretched out on the stone floor, or standing deep in meditation in the high pews, his face on crossed arms over the Holy Book. In the sublime composure of their chanting trembled an ardor subdued by ancient laws. The perpetual lamps swung gently in the incense- and honey-laden air. The ceremony performed here was the same as had been performed for a thousand years, evening after evening in the same spot at the same hour. What torrent of water is so venerable as to roar over the same course for ten times one hundred years? What ancient olive tree has been whispering in the wind with the same crest for ten times one hundred years? There is nothing like it save the eternal sea down in the bays and the everlasting summit of the snow-shimmering Parnassus under the everlasting stars.

The stars were taking fire over the darkening walls of the valley. The evening star was of a rare brilliance; if there were water somewhere—no more than a spring or a pool, perhaps, between two fig trees—a shaft of its light would perforce lie there as from the moon. Under it now, here and there in the human sphere, on the near, heavy, earthly horizon, more bright stars were blazing: these were the shepherds' fires, high and low on the slopes of the dark mountains which enclosed the bow-shaped valley. Near each fire lay a lonely man with his animals. In a wide circle round the monastery, in which perpetual lamps were burning, the wealth of the monastery was spread out. The dogs began to bark, to be answered by dogs. There were more than thirty fires; the mountain slopes were alive with sleeping men. Here and there a lamb bleated from its interrupted slumber. Owlets called; the chatter of the cicadas grew loud; yet the calm, eternal night prevailed.

There, where the evening star stands, Parnassus radiates invisibly behind dark mountains. There, in the mountain's flank, lies Delphi. Under the Temple of the Gods, where once the holy city lay, there stands today a thousand-year-old olive grove, ruins of columns between the tree trunks. And these thousand-year-old trees are too young, these Ancients are too young, they do not hark back, never have they seen Delphi and the House of the Gods. You gaze down into their centuries as into a cistern, and down there in dream-depths lies the Unreachable. But here it is near. Under these stars, in this valley, where sheep and shepherds sleep, here it is near, as nowhere else. The same soil, the same breezes, the same life, the same repose. An Unnameable is present, neither denuded nor veiled, neither tangible nor evasive: enough, it is near. Here is Delphi and the Delphic Plain, sanctuary and shepherds; here is the Arcadia of many dreams, yet it is no dream. Slowly our feet carry us back into the monastery. Huge dogs growl quite close to us. On the balcony over the doorway leans a figure. Another, a servant, steps forth sideways from the hedge—there, where the dogs are growling.

"Athanasios!" calls the monk from the balcony. "Athanasios!" He speaks rather than calls the word, calm and gently commanding. "Athanasios, what's going on there?"

"It's the guests, the two strangers, walking around."

"Good. Keep an eye on the dogs."

These words are few. The dialogue between the priest and the serving man is short. But its tone is from the time of the patriarchs. It is composed of few links. Unchallenged self-confidence of priestly rule, a gentle tone of uncontradicted authority, hospitality practiced quietly and as a matter of course, the house, the sanctuary guarded by many dogs. Nevertheless, this insignificant incident, these few words exchanged in the night, have in them a rhythm hailing from eternity. It reaches back whither the age-old olive trees do not reach. Homer is still un-born, and words such as these, spoken in these tones, pass from priest to servant, from lip to lip. Should there fall from a distant star a trivial but living object—the petal of a flower, a chip from the bark of a tree—it would nevertheless be a message that would shudder through us. That was how this dialogue sounded. The hour, the air, and the place are all-important.

II
THE WANDERER

THE SLEEP of monks is short. Soon after midnight they rang the bells, prayed, sang; before sunrise they began again. With hardly two hours of half slumber behind us, we were all the more awake. We strode very fast along the narrow path in single file, the mules, with the guides in the saddle, in our rear. In the cool of the morning the road led back along the slope above the lovely valley, across the same plain between two barren mountains; then, in the dried-out bed of a mountain torrent, it turned down sideways, split in one direction towards Daulis, in the other towards Chaeronea in Boeotia; to this point the jour-ney was supposed to take seven hours, with a vein of good water halfway which never gave out and which was known to shep-herds near and far.

Our conversation continued until our meeting with the lonely wanderer; thus it lasted without interruption from two and a half to three hours, with not the slightest effort or con-scious intention of keeping it up, and was one of the strangest and most beautiful conversations that I can remember.

There were two of us, and while talking it seemed as if each were following only his own memories, many of which we shared. Sometimes one of us recalled the figure of a friend whom the other had never seen, but of whom he had heard a great deal. Yet the deep and timeless solitude which enveloped us, the incorporeal sublimity of our surroundings—that we were descending from the foot of Parnassus to Chaeronea, from the Delphic Plain towards Thebes, the road of Oedipus—the radiant clarity of the morning hour after a night without deep heavy sleep, all this so strengthened our imagination that every word pronounced by the one carried away the mind of the other so that he believed himself capable of touching with his hands what hovered in the other's thoughts.

Our friends rose before us and, by bringing themselves, brought with them the purest essence of our existence. Their expressions were serious and of almost frightening clarity. While they were standing before us and looking at us, the smallest circumstances and things, through which our union with them had come to pass, were present. A twitching, a softening glance, a moistening of the inner hand in an agitated hour, a perplexed faltering, a gliding away, an estrangement, again a drawing near—all these very small delicate things were in us, and with the strangest vividness; yet we hardly knew whether what we remembered were the stirrings of our own inner selves or those of the others whose faces were looking at us; only that it was lived life and life that somewhere continued to live on, because everything appeared to be the present, and the mountains in this soundless, bluish life of the air were not more real than the visions that accompanied us.

With a single name carelessly dropped by one of us, we could conjure up new ones. Figure after figure rises up, satisfying us with its appearance, accompanies us, and vanishes again; others, evocative, have already been waiting to occupy the empty place. They illuminate a circle of lived life, then fall behind, as it were, on the road, while we walk on and on—as though it were upon our walking that the continuance of this enchantment depended—and the little group of men and mules remained many hundreds of yards in our rear. Those who are still alive and breathe in this light come to us as well as those who no longer exist. During these minutes our vision is pure; the mysterious power, Life, flares up in us—the revealer of the unrevealable. We see their faces, we believe we hear the sound of their voices uttering seemingly trifling short sentences, yet it is as if they contained the whole individual; and their faces are more than faces: the same quality as from the sound of their broken sentences surges up in them, comes nearer and nearer towards us, seems to be caught and confirmed in their features, in the inexpressible of their expressions, yet not quite at rest. It is a never-ending desire, possibility, readiness, something suffered and still to be suffered. Each of these faces is a destiny, is unique, the most singular that can be, and at the same time infinite, a wandering on to an immeasurably distant destination. It seems to exist only while it is looking at us, as though it were living merely for the sake of our responsive glance. We see the faces, but the faces are not everything; in the faces we see the destinies, but even the destinies are not everything. In each one that greets us is something still more distant, a being beyond both, which touches us. We are like two spirits that fondly remember having taken part in the banquets of mortal men.

Many visions of boys and men had come and gone, when there appeared still another. We saw him, who had suffered so unspeakably, emerge before he vanished from us for good. I say "our friend," though the meetings were few; he crossed our path, once, in a passionate discussion, tearing himself open without restraint, laying bare heaven and hell, a parting like brothers, then again strangeness, icelike strangeness. But his letters—one word cold and majestic, another word as though bleeding—his diary, the few incomparable poems (all from a single year of his life, the nineteenth) which he hates, despises, and tears to pieces wherever he finds them, spitting on them, stamping his feet on the scraps; the story of his last cruel weeks and his dying, noted down by his sister—thus is his picture engraved on our souls. He is poor and suffers, but who could dare to offer him help, this boy lonely beyond words? What man would even dare to approach him who, with superhuman strength, bends himself like a bow, to let off from the string the most merciless arrow, who thrusts from himself every helping hand, hides in the underworld of great cities, answers all advances with sneers, recoils from any mention of his talents, his genius, like the convict from the red-hot iron, turns up unexpectedly, now here, now there, flings a letter to his family from Macedonia, from the Caucasus, from Abyssinia, whose hopes bear the sound of threats, whose dry accounts bristle with boundless revolt and self-inflicted sentence of death; who believes he is struggling for money, money, and more money, but who is really struggling with his own demon for something gigantic, which cannot be named? And now we see him being carried down from the Abyssinian mountains, down a lonely, rocky path, in the silent air: an eternal Present, as here; it's as if they are carrying him towards us. He lies on a litter, his face covered by a black shawl, the diseased knee huge as a pumpkin, rising up under the blanket; the beautiful emaciated hand, the hand loved by his sisters, now and again tears the shawl from his face, to give the dark-colored people who bear him orders about the road; they had intended to descend diagonally across the slope, while he insists on a steep, fast descent, across country. Indescribable rebellion, defiance of death up to the whites of his eyes, the mouth distorted with suffering, yet refusing to complain.

None of our day visions had been so powerful as this last. What more could come? We slackened our pace, neither of us speaking. The morning sun shone almost threateningly on this solemn, foreign landscape. Gone was the natural sensation of the Present, wherein men and animals feel at ease. Strange destinies, normally invisible currents, struck some strong chord in us and revealed themselves. We would have been pleased at the sight of a flock of sheep, would have welcomed a bird in the air. Then in the distance a human being came towards us. The man walked fast. He was alone, and in these parts it is rare for someone to walk alone. The shepherd walks with his flock; he who is no shepherd rides; this man walked. He seemed to be bareheaded. In these regions, because of the sun's power, no one goes around without covering his head; so it must be an optical delusion. He came nearer, and was bareheaded. His hair was black, the whole face surrounded by a black, disheveled beard; he swayed while walking. In his hand he carried a rough stick on which he leaned. The sun sparkled on the rocky boulders and we were under the impression that he had naked feet. This was impossible; the paths uphill and down are stony rubble, sharp as knives; even the poorest beggar here protects his feet at least with wooden shoes. The man came nearer, and he had bare feet. Rags, remnants of the kind of trousers worn by people in towns, hung round his emaciated legs. Here no one, meeting another wanderer in the solitude of the mountains, passes him by without a word. With head turned askew he tried to sidle by us ten steps off our path, without greeting. We called out to him the Greek phrase commonly used for salutation. He answered without stopping and his words were German. At this, my friend barred his way with a brief speech, a question as to whence he had come and whither he was going. Meanwhile I stood three paces away, saw congealed blood on his feet, a deep bloody wound on his strong hand. Broad shoulders, a powerful neck; the face between thirty and forty, nearer forty perhaps, suffering, made even yellower by the blackness of the beard. The eyes unsteady, flickering, savage as the look of a shy, tortured animal. He mentioned his name: Franz Hofer, from Lauffen on the Salzach, bookbinder's apprentice. Age: twenty-one. Destination: Patras. From here Patras was a five-day journey for a robust man with a knowledge of the country, mountains between, a deserted plain, a sea bay. When not leaning on his stick, his body shook, his lips trembled. He'd had the fever for three months. This was why he was making for home. From Alexandria in Egypt as far as the port of Piraeus, a ship's stoker let him lie in the coal bunker; but the ship had moved on to Constantinople, which was why he now had to go on foot to Trieste. How was he going to find the way? This he had on him. From under his belt he produced a scrap of paper on which were written, in pencil by now almost obliterated, the names of places. He pointed at one: thither he had to go today. The place lay in the neighborhood of Delphi, an eight-hour walk from where we were stand-ing, provided one knew the way and how to decipher the few signs on the deserted landscape. Did he know the language of the country? Not a word: the people didn't understand you if you spoke German or Italian, damn it! When had he last eaten? Yesterday noon a piece of bread, and today a drink of water from a well back there. This was the spring to which we were walking, halfway to Chaeronea in Boeotia.

Meanwhile our men, with the mules, had caught us up, and stood about and stared in astonishment at the wanderer. We handed him some wine in a little cup; his hand shook wildly and spilled more than half; then we gave him bread and cheese, and his mouth trembled so that he could hardly get the morsels into it. We bade him sit down; he said he had no time, that he still had a long way to go today. At this, something mad came into his eyes. We told him we'd give him some money and in-quired whether one of us had better write to his hometown, so that his kin should know that he was ill and how matters stood with him. This, he said, we should do under no condition; he would not tolerate it; it would be a damned nuisance; it was no one's business at home how matters stood with him. Where-upon he turned and began to walk off, leaning on his stick. We followed him and insisted that he mount one of the mules and return with us; that we would bring him to Athens, to the port of Piraeus, and there put money in his hand for the journey to Trieste and beyond. Our guides, who understood our inten-tions, had already brought up a harnessed mule and started to lift him into the saddle. He, however, stepped back, his stick raised: travel back all the way he had just taken so many days to come! He'd be damned if he would! This no one should dare force him to do. One could see now, as he stood there with his stick raised against us (though with a noticeably trembling arm), what a big strong man he was, what unruliness was in him, and how he could be the bully of the whole village and the feared one, and how all this in him had been debased into a beastlike frightened being, who would this day and the next still drag himself along, but before nightfall die a miserable lonely death. Were we to abandon him now, he would not leave these mountains alive. We told the guides to move away, while just the two of us approached him. We made it clear we didn't want to leave him in the lurch, that he himself should tell us what he wanted from us; whatever it was, we would do it. "That's where I want to go," he said, and pointed in the direction whence we had come. In this case, we told him, he should mount a mule and have himself strapped into the saddle; we would send along with him two of the guides with their mules, who would bring him this very day to a village on the slope of Parnassus, whence he could see the bay on the far end of which lay Patras; and they would find quarters for him and buy him the customary native footwear. There he should take care of himself, allow the wounds on his feet to heal and remain quiet for six or even ten days. Then we would join him again and take him with us to Patras.

He grasped the front and rear ends, where the saddle is raised; with an effort hoisted himself up and with the help of the guides (who called him "the foreign Mr. Beggar") he was bound fast, with decorum and reverence, sidesaddle, the position in which women at home sit a horse. Then the mule set off uphill, the bound man swaying along, while we also mounted and let ourselves be carried, riding silently, downhill towards Chaeronea.

The eager, advancing footfalls of the mules seemed strange, and it was in a strange atmosphere that we reached that brook, running swift and clear between the rocks, that the mules were unharnessed, that the men were lying on the ground beside the mules, drinking, and that we, higher up among the shrubs, let ourselves down, like them, to drink. A few hours ago he, the shipwrecked, the wandering naked human life, had also lain here, while all round the whole world lay in wait like one single enemy. I felt, while drinking here now, as if the water were flowing from his heart into mine. His face looked at me, as hitherto those other faces had looked at me; I almost lost myself to his face, and as if to save myself from his embrace, I said to myself, "Who is this? A strange man!" Then alongside this face were the others, looking at me and exerting their power over me, and there were many more. Nothing in me at this moment knew whether they were strangers among strangers, whose faces were turned towards me, or whether at some time somewhere I had said to each of them, "My friend!" and had heard, "My friend!" Without any transition something rose up, a vision, distant, something submerged, aquiver with exquisite anxiety, a boy watching the faces of soldiers pass, company after company, countless numbers, tired dusty faces, always in fours, each a single individual and none whose face the boy had not absorbed into himself, forever groping mutely from one to the other, touching each one, counting to himself, "This one, this one, this one!" while tears were rising in his throat.

A something remained circling somewhere above this, nothing but a wondering, a belonging nowhere, a penetrating aloneness, a searching question: "Who am I?" Then, in the moment of most anxious wondering, I once more came to, the boy sank into me, the water flowed by under my face, bathing one cheek, the propped-up arms supported my body, and I raised myself and it was nothing more than the rising of one who, with his lips lying upon the flowing water, had taken a long draught.

But this hour, and then the next, as far as Chaeronea, and the following hours during which we boarded the train and were carried through Boeotia and Attica until the train ran into the station at Athens, I beheld a landscape which had no name. The mountains called to one another; the clefts were more alive than a face; each little fold on the distant flank of a hill lived; all this was as near to me as the palm of my hand. It was something that I shall never see again. It was the guest gift of all the lonely wanderers who had crossed our path.

Everything alive, every landscape, reveals itself once, and in its entirety: but only to a heart deeply moved.

III
THE STATUES

THE FOLLOWING evening, as I climbed up to the Acropolis, the Wanderer was far away from me. Strange had it been to meet, in the Phocaean mountains, that fever-stricken man from Lauffen on the Salzach. Strangely unreal the way he had walked in silence towards his death and how nothing could persuade him to take again the road by which he had come.

But I was not tempted to think any more about it. "Passed," said I involuntarily, and lifted my foot over the fragments of ruin that lay around here by the hundreds. Only now did I notice that the sun was setting behind the Parthenon and that I was the only person still up here. There was something solemn about the streaming forth of the shadows, as though the last of life still in them were pouring itself in an evening libation onto this hill, where even the stones were decaying with age. Unintentionally, my eye chose one of those columns. There was an unspeakable severity and tenderness in the way it stood there; I felt that as I breathed, its contour rose and fell. But in the evening light, clearer than dissolved gold, the consuming whiff of mortality also played around it.

Magnificently self-composed, nevertheless, it stood there. I wanted to walk over to it; I felt the urge to walk around it; the side turned away from me, facing the setting sun, this held the promise of real life.

But before I took the first step I already stopped short. A touch of despondency blew over me, a sense of disappointment overcame me beforehand. That morning returned, the endless wandering from one thing to another. The fatigue of the road, step by step, over stones and fragments of stones; there were the excavations in the Agora, there was the Pnyx, there was the Orator's Hill, there the Tribune; there the traces of their houses, their winepresses, there were their tombs on the Eleusinian road. This was Athens. Athens? So this was Greece, this antiquity. A sense of disappointment overwhelmed me. I sat down on one of the stones that lay on the ground and seemed to be waiting for eternal night.

These Greeks, I asked within myself, where are they? I tried to remember, but I remembered only memories. Names came floating near, figures; they merged into one another as though I had dissolved them into a greenish smoke wherein they appeared distorted.

Because they had passed long ago I hated them, and also because they had passed so fast. Their few centuries, the wretched span of time, on the other side of the enormous abyss; their history, that tangle of fabrication, untruth, empty talk, deceit; and the eternal boasting in it all, the eternal anxiety, the lightning disappearance. All was gone, even while it still believed it existed! And over it, floating, the eternal fata morgana of their poetry; and their deities themselves, what uncertain phantoms flitting by: there stood Chronos and the Titans, ghastly and grand, already they were gone, overthrown by their own children and forgotten; then those others come near, the Olympians: who believed in them? They, too, were gone, dissolved in a colored mist. Gods, eternal gods? Milesian fables, a decoration painted on the wall of a wanton's house.

Where is this world, I called out, and what do I know of it? Where do I seize it? Where do I believe it? Where do I surrender myself to it entirely? Here! Or nowhere. Here is the air and here is the place. Does nothing penetrate me? As I lie here, is it here that it will be denied me forever? Will nothing be mine but this sense of the ghastly, this fearful shadowy premonition?

The sun must have sunk lower, the shadows lengthened, when a glance met mine—deep and equivocal as that of a passerby. He walked on and was already half-turned away from me, also contemptuous of this town, his hometown. His glance revealed me to myself, and revealed him: it was Plato. Around the lips of the inventor of myths, the despiser of gods, hovered arrogance and spook-like dreams. In a magnificent, spotless garment carelessly brushing the ground, he walked along, the non-citizen, the regal man; he floated past, like ghosts who walk with locked feet. Contemptuously he touched time and place, he seemed to hail from the East and to disappear towards the West.

After the phantom had vanished, everything seemed sober and sad. Doubly desecrated, both the hill with its ruins and my guilt lay clear as the day. It is your own weakness, I called to myself, you are unable to revive all this. It is you yourself who tremble with transience, you who steep all about you in the terrible bath of time. When you wanted to walk around the column, you wanted merely to chase the just departed moment!— Aimlessly I stood up. I am going to read, said I to myself. I took the book from my pocket, the *Philoctetes* of Sophocles, and began to read. Clear and transparent, verse after verse stood before me, melodious and dreadful the wailings of the lonely man rose into the air. I felt the whole burden of this sorrow and at the same time the incomparable tenderness and purity of the Sophoclean line. But between me and everything that greenish veil moved again, and I was seized by that consuming suspicion. These gods, their sayings, these men, their deeds, everything appeared to me strange beyond measure—treacherous, vain. These figures, they seemed, while talking before me, to change their faces. They act, cheat—do they cheat themselves? This son of Achilles, does he believe what he says? Sometimes it appears as though Odysseus had ensnarled his unsuspecting mind with intrigue, at other times as though he were his willing, knowing accomplice. What does it mean when he suddenly revolts against him and promises Philoctetes a safe return home? He has no ship in which to take him home. What is going on in him? They threaten to take the bow away from the sick man; yet they know, they must know that without Philoctetes himself the town cannot fall. Do they realize that what they do is in vain, in vain this sly talk, and do they not admit it to themselves? All this was strange beyond measure and inaccessible. I could not read any further. I laid the book down. A wind rose, sped over the hill, and turned the pages of the book lying near me on the ground. All of a sudden the air smelled simultaneously of strawberries and acacias, of ripening wheat, of the dust on the roads, and of the open sea. I felt the enchantment of this aroma in which the whole landscape seemed to be caught; this landscape round which hung the air of millenniums. But I wanted no part of it. I bent down, put the book in my pocket, and turned to walk away.

Impossible antiquity, said I to myself, aimless searchings. — The harshness of these words pleased me. — Nothing of all this exists. Here, where I had hoped to touch it with my hands, here it is gone, here more than anywhere else. A demonic irony hovers round these ruins which in their decay still retain their secret.

I raised my foot to leave the ghostly place of the Nonexistent and proceed to the little museum which is built of insignificant masonry against the slope. There, I thought to myself, laid out in showcases, are treasures found in the rubble of the graves: they have resisted, at least for the moment, the power of time; they express only themselves and are of incomparable beauty. A goblet resembles the roundness of a breast or the shoulder of a goddess. A golden snake that once encircled an arm evokes that arm. So I shall go there. It is vain to try and struggle for the unattainable.

I quickly crossed over into the dark hall of the museum. The next room was even darker for possessing but one small window. I entered a third room.

There were statues, of women, in long garments. They stood around me in a semicircle; I drew the curtain across the door and was alone with them.

At that moment something happened to me: an indescribable shock. It came not from outside but from some immeasurable distance of an inner abyss: it was like lightning: the room, as it was, rectangular with whitewashed walls and the statues that stood there, became for an instant filled with a light utterly different from that which was really there: the eyes of the statues were all at once turned towards me and an unspeakable smile occurred in their faces. At the same time I knew: I am not seeing this for the first time—in some other world I have stood before these, have had some kind of communion with them, and ever since then everything in me has been waiting for just this shock, and so dreadfully I had to be shaken thus within my innermost self in order to become again what I had been. — I say "since then" and "at that time," but nothing of the limitation of time could penetrate the entrancement wherein I had lost myself. It was unbounded, and what it contained occurred outside of time. Somewhere a ceremony was taking place, a battle, a glorious sacrificial offering: that was the meaning of this tumult in the air, of the expanding and shrinking of the room, the meaning of this unspeakable exaltation in me, of this effervescing sociability, alternating with this mysterious anxiety and despondency: for I am the priest who will perform the ceremony—I, too, perhaps the victim that will be offered: all this presses towards decision, it ends with the crossing of a threshold, with a landing—with this standing here, I amidst these statues. And now already all this dies down into their faces turning back into stone, it expires and is gone; nothing remains but the death-sigh of despondency. Statues stand about me, five of them, only now am I aware of their number, strange they stand before me, heavy and stonelike, with slanting eyes. Their figures are enormous; built—animal-like, divine—out of overpowering forms; their faces are strange; pouting lips, raised eyebrows, mighty cheeks, a chin round which life flows; are these still human features? Nothing about them alludes to the world in which I breathe and move. Am I not standing before the strangest of the strange? Does not the eternal dread of chaos stare at me here from five virginal faces?

Yet, my God, how real they are! They have a breathtaking sensual presence. Erected like a temple, each body rises from feet of majestic strength. Their solemnity has nothing of masks: the face receives its meaning from the body. They are nubile women, brides, priestesses. In their faces is the severity of expectation, the elect strength and sublimity of their race, an awareness of their own rank. They participate in things that are above any common conception.

How beautiful they are! Their bodies are more convincing to me than my own. In this material there is a tension, so powerful that it creates in me a tautness, too. Never before have I seen anything like these proportions and this surface. Did not the universe, for a fleeting moment, open up to me?

From where else rose in me this foreboding of a departure, this rhythmical expansion of atmosphere, whence this whole portentous restiveness, this soundless tumult, which threatens me or which I can command? — It is, I answer myself, unerringly like a dreamer, it is the secret of infinity in these garments. He who would truly be a match for them must approach them by means other than the eye, with greater reverence yet with more daring. And still, it is the eye that would have to bid him, beholding, absorbing, but then drooping, growing dim as with one overwhelmed.

My eye did not droop, but a figure sank down over the knees of the priestess, someone rested his forehead on the foot of a statue. I know not whether I thought this or if it happened. There is a sleep in wakefulness, a sleep of but a few breaths that holds in itself a greater power of transformation, and is more closely related to death than the long deep slumber of the nights.

• • •

ONCE more I return to myself. Maybe, I tell myself, it is from these statues that my soul received its direction, maybe it is something else of which these statues standing about me are messengers. For it is strange that again I do not really embrace them as something present, but that I call them to me from somewhere with continuous wonder, with a feeling anxiously sweet, like memory. It would be unthinkable to want to cling to their surface. This surface actually is not there—it grows by a continuous coming from inexhaustible depths. They are there and are unattainable. So, too, am I. By this we communicate.

And while I feel myself becoming stronger and under this one word "Eternal" forever losing more and more of myself, vibrating like a column of heated air above a conflagration, I ask myself, slowly fading like the lamp in bright daylight: If the Unattainable feeds on my innermost being and the Eternal builds out of me its eternity, what then still stands between me and the Deity?

A MEMORY OF BEAUTIFUL DAYS

As we arrived the sun still stood quite high, but I asked at once to be steered into the dark narrow streets. While we glided soundlessly along, Ferdinand and his sister sat close to one another, their eyes passing over the ancient walls whose red and gray reflection we divided, over the portals whose thresholds lay washed by the water, over the stony, moist, shimmering crests and the powerfully barred windows. We passed under small bridges, their damp arches close above our heads, bridges over which little old women and bent old men limped along and from which naked children lowered themselves sideways in order to bathe. In front of a small quiet square I asked the man to stop. Steps led up to a church. In the walls stood many stone statues that seemed to step forth from niches into the evening light . . . Brother and sister wished to remain but I pulled them along behind me through even narrower alleys that had, instead of water, a stone floor, finally beneath a damp dark archway out into the great Square that lay there like a hall of pleasure, with the sky, of an indescribable color, forming a roof: for the naked blueness, vaulted, carried no cloud, yet the air was as though saturated with dissolved gold, and, like a sediment from the air, a hint of twilight-red hung on the palaces that formed the sides of the great Square. Brother and sister, seeing this for the first time, were as though in a dream. Katherina gazed to her right, towards the Palazzo Sansovino, towards those pillars, balconies, loggias, whereof the shadows and the radiance of the evening fashioned something unreal—the mute beginning of a feast to which day and night were invited; to her left she saw the older Palazzo, whose red wall seemed to be alive, the fantastic tower with the blue clock; she saw before her the fabulous church, the cupolas, the bronze horses high up, the openwork shrines of stone in which stood sculptures, the golden gates, the interior mysteriously shining forth, and again and again she kept asking, "Is this true? Can this be true?"

Ferdinand continued to hasten ahead. "Can there be more?" he asked. "Does this go on?"

Now he stopped and saw the open sea and gondolas and sails and pillared portals, new cupolas on the other side, and beyond the islands the triumph of the evening on clouds like faraway mountains of gold. Now, as he turned to call us, he noticed behind him the bulk of the campanile rising straight as an arrow so that the luminous arch above seemed to fall away from it.

"I'm going up there!" called Ferdinand, who rarely left a tower, be it that even of a village church, unclimbed.

But Katherina took him vehemently by the hand so that he had to turn round, and with both hands pointing in front of her she didn't stop but continued to walk ahead towards the water, in which a stream of golden fire seemed to pour out a deep blue glitteringly metallic substance. Ferdinand remained beside her; now they were close to the edge; the men in the gondolas, in the blinding dreamlike light looking completely black, waved at them; one of them rowed nearer, they lowered themselves down into his black boat and glided out into the fiery street. Many gondolas were out there, and between them dark sailboats cut their way through; everything was laden with life, everywhere faces wanting to move towards one another and the paths crossing one another were like magic signs on a fiery tablet, and in the air flew small dark birds whose paths were also similar magic signs.

Standing there on the bridge, leaning over the smooth ancient stone and watching a couple of barges steering towards each other, I found myself thinking of lips and how they find their long lost way, easily and as though in a dream, back to beloved lips. Although I could feel the painful sweetness of the thought, I was swimming too lightly on the surface of my thinking, I could not dive down to discover of whom I had been thinking in my innermost soul; the thought came like the glance from a mask and I had a notion that it was the eye of Katherina, whose mouth I had never yet kissed. Now everything was on fire, behind the islands the clouds seemed to dissolve in golden smoke, the wingèd lion glowing on his globe of gold: it struck me that it was the sun not only of this moment but of bygone years—yes, of many centuries. Sensing that I could never again lose this light, I turned round and came back. Girls brushed past me, one pushing the other and pulling her black shawl down from behind; whereupon I caught sight of the nape of her neck between the black hair and the black shawl, which she immediately pulled up again: but the gleam of this tender neck was the shining forth of light that existed everywhere and everywhere was being covered up. The half-grown girls with the shawls had promptly disappeared again, like bats in the crack of a wall; an old man passed by, and in the depths of his eyes, the eyes of a sad old bird, shone a spark of light. Without meaning it, for I felt too well to mean anything, I walked round in a circle and, stepping once more through the archway back into the great Square, wandered along under the arcades. But the golden light of the fire was no longer in the air; only in the illuminated shops that were everywhere and under the dusky arcades lay things that gleamed: there was a jeweler's shop with rubies, emeralds, pearls, small ones on strings and large ones each of which wore round it a luster like the moon. I halted before the booth of a dealer in antiques, where lay old silken materials shot with gold and silver flowers: everywhere in these silks was the life of light and I know not what memories of beautiful figures from whom these stiff wrappings had slipped off during nights of festivity. Opposite, in a small shop, sparkled blue and green butterflies and shells, above all nautilus shells that are mother of pearl and have the shape of a ram's horn. I stood before each shop, walking to and fro from one to the other of these creations whence the life of light vanishes not even at night, and I was filled with desire to fashion something like them with my own hands, to produce something out of the fermenting bliss in me and to cast it out. As the moist fiery air of an island shore forms a sparkling butterfly, as the sea with its demonic light buried beneath its might forms the pearl and the nautilus and casts them out, so I longed to give shape to something that sparkled with the inner joy of living and cast it behind me, when the impetuous and enchanting cascade of existence carried me along.

Although aware of the dark powers, I still did not know what it was that I should create. So I returned to the inn and realized that I had not yet seen my room. As I mounted the dark staircase a young woman passed me. She was very tall, and wore a light-colored evening dress and pearls round her bare neck. She was one of those English women who resemble antique statues. Wonderful the youthful glow of her almost severe face and the arch of her winglike eyebrows! Passing me on her way down, she looked at me neither cursorily nor overlong, neither shyly nor too self-assuredly, but quite calmly. Her glance was one with her beauty, charged with a poise that lay precisely between the grace of a young girl and the all-too-conscious splendor of a great lady. In a masquerade she could have played Diana being surprised by Actaeon, but one would have said, "She is too young." She waited downstairs and looked up (this I felt rather than saw), and now her husband or friend passed me—also a young, very tall, handsome person with dark hair and a mouth that at some future date would look like the mouth on the bust of a Roman emperor, a Nero.

I LAY on the bed, still half-dressed, and heard through the paper-covered door the voices of the couple in the neighboring room. Down below something murmured softly, probably the well in the street—no, this was no village street, it was the sea lapping against the marble steps of the house. From afar came

the sound of singing; by now they must have arrived at the is-
lands on the other side, their gondolas hung with Chinese lan-
terns; perhaps they had landed and hung their Chinese lanterns
in the branches of the convent garden and sat close to one an-
other in the grass amidst five thousand blossoming lilies and
shrubs of rosemary, and begun to sing. The voices sounded like
high-flying birds, so high that they still held the light that had
plunged beyond the world—would hold it until it began every-
where to live again. Now the singing died down, but of a sudden
it rose once more to the surface, quite near, sounding deeper,
fuller, like the soulful sound of a bird it was, so near to human
speech, more human than speech, saturated with dark gushing
life, not overloud yet still quite close to me. There behind the
paper-covered door it was: it was no singing, it was the low, deep
laugh of that tall, handsome woman: oh, how utterly herself she
was in this laughter, her beautiful proud body, her commanding
shoulders! Now she was speaking: she spoke to him who was her
husband or her friend. I could not understand what they said.
Was she refusing him what he whisperingly begged? She might
yield, she might refuse, she might do anything. There was such
a swelling sense of her own self in the sound of her low laughter.
Now a door opened in the next room and steps sounded out-
side in the corridor. Then everything was still. So she was alone.
At this moment it seemed more wonderful to be wrapped about
by solitude, alone and next to her, than with her. It was like a
domination over her out of the darkness. It was Zeus to whom
it had not yet occurred that he could throw Amphitryon's body
round his divine limbs like a cloak and appear to her, who
would be doubtful and doubt her doubts and with these doubts
transform her face like a wave. But the darkness tried to pull
me into it, into a black boat that glided along over black water.
Light existed no longer anywhere but here near this woman.
My thinking must not fall entirely into darkness, else I too shall
sleep: like a sparrow hawk it had to circle about the Luminous,
above reality, above myself and this sleeping woman. Rapture
of the stranger who comes and goes ... (thus my thinking

nourished itself on the Luminous and continued to circle) . . .
to possess the rights of the master and still remain a stranger
. . . Thus he must feel who today is not allowed to sleep next to
his belovèd. So it has to be. Coming and going. Abroad and at
home. To return. At times Zeus returned to Alcmene. Our
deepest desire aims at transformation. From this enchanting
truth, thought burned as bright as a blazing torch. No, four
blazing torches, one over each bedpost. It is the old sinister
torch cart; now the horses pull hard, it drags me into the night.
I must lie, lie still, as one asleep, for it goes mountainwards, up
into the mountains over stone bridges, across raging streams,
all the way up into the old village. Here the stream flows quiet
and deep between the old houses. I must hurry: for I must catch
the fish before the break of dawn. In the dark, where the mill-
race flows deepest and swiftest, above the weir, there in the dark
lies the huge old fish which has swallowed the light. Stab him I
must with the trident so that I can take the light out of his belly
with my hands. The light he has swallowed is the voice of the
beautiful woman, not the voice wherewith she speaks but her
most secret laughter with which she surrenders herself. I must
search for the trident further upstream, among the juniper
bushes. The junipers are small but they are powerful when they
grow close together: they are faithful, that is their strength.
Should I fall among them, I shall never again transform myself.
I merely want to thrust my hand between them to seize the tri-
dent when something quivers—that's Katherina's never-kissed
mouth! So I stand again, and dare not. But I no longer need
what I was seeking, for it is almost morning. I hear bells and the
sounds of an organ. No doubt Kathi has already gone down-
stairs and is praying in St. Mark's—offering up a lip-prayer like
a child, then dreaming to herself without words in the golden
church.

IT WAS a slumber and continually a new waking, merging into
new dreams, a possessing and losing. I beheld my childhood
afar, like a deep mountain lake, and walked into it as into a

house. It was a self-possessing and a self-not-possessing, a hav-
ing-all and having-nought. Morning air of childhood mingling
with premonition of being dead, the globe of the world floated
past in a blue fixed light, while a dead man sank deeper and
deeper into the dark, and then it was a fruit that rolled towards
me, but my hand was too cold and rigid to seize it: now I myself
as a child leapt from under the bed on which I had lain with
cold rigid hands, and tried to snatch it. From each dream vision
sprang forth harmonies as from an Aeolian harp, a reflection
of flames fell on the white quilt, and the early sea wind rose and
moved the white paper on the little table. Gone was the slum-
ber, gaily the naked feet touched the stone floor, and from the
water pitcher leapt forth water of its own will like a living
nymph. The night had poured its power into everything, every-
thing looked more knowing, nowhere was there any dream but
everywhere Love and the Present. The white pages gleamed in
full morning light, they were asking to be covered with words,
they wanted my secret in order to give me back a thousand se-
crets in return. Close to them lay the beautiful big orange that
I had put there the evening before; I peeled it and hastily ate
it. It seemed as though a ship were weighing its anchors and I
had to leave in a hurry for a foreign world. A magic formula
pressed and quivered in me, but I could not remember the first
word. I possessed nothing but the transparent colorful shadows
of my dreams and half-dreams. When, filled with impatience, I
tried to pull them towards me, they retreated, and it seemed as
though the walls and the peculiarly shaped old-fashioned furni-
ture of the inn's room had absorbed them. The whole room
still looked knowing, but mocking and void. Yet the moment the
shadows reappeared there, and while my heart pressed against
them and I let my wish—which was directed towards fidelity and
infidelity, towards departure and remaining, towards here and
there—play against them like a magic wand, I felt how I could
draw forth from the naked floor real characters, and how they
shone and cast physical shadows, how my wish moved them
against one another, how they were actually there for my sake

and still took notice only of one another, how my wish had formed for them youth and age and all masks and fulfilled itself in them, and how they were yet detached from me and lusted one for the other and each for itself. I could move away from them, could let a curtain fall in front of their existence and raise it again. Yet all the time, as the slanting rays of the sun beyond a voluptuous thundercloud fall on a livid-green garden land-scape, I saw how the splendor of the air, of the water and the fire, streamed into them as it were from above in slanting, spectral rays, so that they were, for my mysteriously favored eye, si-multaneously human beings and sparkling incarnations of the elements.

SHAKESPEARE'S KINGS
AND NOBLEMEN

Address to the Shakespeare Society, Weimar, 1905

I THINK I KNOW why you called me here to speak before you. It was certainly not the desire to learn something new; you certainly could not expect my handful of observations to add a substantial weight to the load of knowledge about Shakespeare with which your warehouses are overcrowded and your ships overburdened to the point of sinking. None of the obscurities (insofar as there are any left for you) could expect an illumination from me; none of the findings that you have received from preceding generations and will hand on, purified and deepened, to the generations to come, could want confirmation from my lips. But perhaps you feel a trifle oppressed, even overawed, at so much accumulated wealth; perhaps you sometimes feel stupefied by the immense flood of tradition in whose tumultuous roar the voice of Herder mingles with that of Sarah Siddons. And an inner voice—was it memory or intuition?—told you that beyond the pure passion of understanding, a less rational, less pure, more heterogeneous instrument is still needed to work the true magic. So you stepped out of the silent study of the scholar into the forest of life, and as the magician reaches for the mandrake you reached for someone alive; you reached for me and set me down in this circle. Accustomed to dissect the marvelous phenomenon into its elements and to dwell with your thoughts in the streaming rays of its divided light, you sometimes desire to call in from outside a living person at whose soul Shakespeare, as an undivided Whole, knocks like Fate demanding to be admitted, and for whose eyes this undivided light illuminates the depths and summits of existence. In your memory, which harbors an almost boundless tradition, there stirs an old saying occasionally obscured but never quite forgotten: the true readers of Shakespeare and also those in whom Shakespeare is truly alive are those who carry within them a stage.

"The gift of imaginary performance . . . this very specific creativeness: to produce within oneself action as it is on paper as the most personal experience." For this reason—and the words with which I try to convey it are from one out of your midst—let me believe that you called me here; for this reason, and because, to continue quoting Karl Werder, "Shakespeare's work is action, not mere description. Whoever wants simply to be told stories misunderstands him. Whoever only listens while reading him reads him only half and therefore mishears him. Shakespeare needs to be played, because only then can we hear and see what he does not and cannot say. If he were to say what would be necessary to make uncreative readers understand him without seeing him acted, then he would cease to be Shakespeare."

When I ponder these words and realize that with you they are a tradition—a tradition as unlikely to be lost as anything essential and intelligent ever said by a scholar in your field; and when at the same time I remember a paragraph from Otto Ludwig's essays whose first line runs: "Shakespeare wrote his plays from the core of dramatic art," then it is fully transparent to me what persuaded you to call me here: you presumed I know how to read Shakespeare with imagination. It is with the reader of Shakespeare that you are concerned, with the reader from whom you can assume and demand this "very specific creativeness"; and I feel that if I am not to dissipate your indulgence I must speak to you only of what is a pleasure and a passion, a conscious talent, an imagination, an innate art perhaps, like playing the flute or dancing, a shattering but silent inner orgy—the reading of Shakespeare.

I am speaking not of those who read Shakespeare like the Bible or some other true or great book; not of those who lower their faces, tired and wilted by life, over this deep mirror in order to realize that "life has always been like this," and who "cleanse the stuff'd bosom of that perilous stuff"; not of those whose heart is filled with "the ignominy that weighs upon the poor man's shoulder," with "the law's delay, the insolence of office," and all the other terribly real evils of Hamlet's monologue. I am speaking not of those who turn to the wisest of all books, seeking solace when before their outraged eyes the course of the world looks hopelessly out of joint—although it seems to me that it is on them that the marrow of Shakespeare's work continually renews itself. But the readers about whom I wish to speak are those on whom the skin also feeds, retaining forever the brilliant bloom of youth. These are the readers whose passion sees each of Shakespeare's works as a Whole. Those others, driven to Shakespeare by tragic experience, offer their soul—cruelly bent by the pain and harshness of life, like the body of a musical instrument—as the sensitive sounding board for the fall from grandeur, the degradation of the good, self-destruction of the noble, and the ghastly fate of the tender spirit exposed to life. Those of whom I wish to speak are the sounding board, however, not for this alone, but also for a thousand more delicate, more hidden, more sensual, more symbolic things—which, with their intertwining diversity, form the mysterious unit whose passionate servants they are. For them it is not only the great destinies, the sudden turning points of Fate, the tremendous tragedies, that exist. The scene, for instance, where Lear's daughters enter the castle at the approach of rough weather: the heavy door groans to a close behind them and the old man stands there, his white hair exposed to the drenching rain, his heart to the sinister night and the frenzy of his impotent rage. Or the scene in the gloom of the castle yard when Macbeth and his wife, their glances locked in complicity, exchange muttered words. Or that in which Othello steps from the door into the yard, from another door onto the rampart, Iago always one pace behind him, words pouring from his mouth like corrosive poison, a devouring, inextinguishable fire-poison eating through the bone into the marrow, Othello listening all the time and protesting, his tongue twisting in his mouth like that of an animal about to be slaughtered, his rolling bloodshot eyes as helpless as a tortured steer's; and Iago, his fangs always in the other's entrails, dragging him, the dog the steer, through rooms and corridors, doors and courts, letting go only in the final death struggle. . . . Although nothing created by human beings can be compared with these scenes, it is not for them alone that the readers about whom I wish to speak lose themselves in a world built by a genius. For them there are innumerable encounters during which the soul does not have to hide fearfully in the dark and cry out to itself: *Guarda e passa!*

These dramas are not exclusively filled with events whose aspect is of the same order of things as the maelstrom, the surging sinister sea, the landslide, or the human face frozen in death. Not everything in them emanates the dread loneliness that hovers round the monstrous fates as it does round the summits of icy mountains. At times in one of these dramas the human destinies, the dark and shining, yes, even the torments and degradation and bitterness of the death hour, are so well woven into a Whole that their being side by side, their merging and disappearing into one another, creates something like a deeply moving, solemn, and woeful music. In *Henry VIII* Wolsey's fall and his calm acceptance of it, the clear sound of his great, resigned words, and again the dying of Queen Katharine, this fading away of a gentle, suffering voice, the festive music surrounding the King and the new Queen, all merge inextricably into a melodious Whole, which, in its heroic elements and the recurrent theme, is reminiscent of a Beethoven sonata. In the romantic plays, in *The Tempest,* in *Cymbeline, Measure for Measure,*

As You Like It, and in *The Winter's Tale,* the Whole is interwoven by this music. Or rather everything joins into it, everything surrenders to this music, everything which is placed side by side, everything breathing at the other, mingling love and hatred in their breath, everything that glides past the other, that delights or terrifies, all that is sublime and all that is ridiculous—yes, all that is there and not there, insofar as in each work of art those things which do not appear in them also play a part by spreading their shadows round the Whole. Only the combination of all this can produce the unutterably sweet music of the Whole. And it is precisely of the reader who can hear this music that I wish to speak to you—because he is the person who reads Shakespeare with all his heart, with all his soul, with all his strength. And of him in whom this passion dwells let me speak to you as of a figure, as Milton in his verse speaks of L'Allegro and Il Penseroso, or as La Bruyère speaks of the Distracted and the Ambitious. I feel that such plays as *Cymbeline, The Tempest,* and the others possess the power to produce again and again in the imagination of the creative reader an inner stage on which their magic can live and their music be heard as a Whole.

In the same way the figures of Lear and Shylock, of Macbeth and Juliet, overpower the body of the great actor in order to live and die in it—for there is no doubt that Shakespeare's reader and Shakespeare's actor are closely related. The difference is that round the actor a single figure wraps itself like a skin, whereas in the reader all figures want to live simultaneously. The former is beckoned aside by a phantom: "Give me all your blood to drink," while the latter is surrounded by a host of phantoms. I do believe that with this mysterious awakening of a "specific creativeness" on a day unlike other days, under a wind and weather unlike other wind and weather, the figure will demand to be played by the actor (who is powerless to refuse) and the drama demand of the reader: "Today you read me, and I live in you." I don't believe that the reader who "carries within him a stage" could have read *Romeo and Juliet* on the day he was destined to read *The Tempest.* Perhaps he reached out for *Romeo and Juliet*; he leafed through it, but the play left him cold. It didn't tempt him. The lines of verse whereon his eye fell today seemed to him indifferent, not like eyes, not like the calyx of a flower through which one can peer into its depths. The stage directions for the acts and scenes did not seem like little hidden doors in a mysterious wall, not like narrow clearings which open and lead into the dusky heart of the forest. So he laid the volume down and was about to go off without Shakespeare when his eye fell on this title: *The Tempest*. And in a flash he knew: "I can, after all, create life. Today I am able to revive within myself Prospero and Miranda, Ariel and Caliban, more effectively than water can revive wilted flowers. Today or never am I the island on which all this has happened. Today or never I carry within me the cave before whose entrance Caliban suns himself, the thicket of high fantastic trees round whose crowns Ariel glides like a miraculous bird: within me also is the air of this island, a southern evening breeze of gold and blue wherein Miranda's beauty swims like a wonder of the sea in its element. Today or never am I all these things at once: I am Prospero's magnificence and Ferdinand's youth, Ariel's elflike devotion and Caliban's hate; I am Antonio the evil, Gonzalo the honest, Stephano the drunken villain. And why, pray, should I not be all these beings? In me there are so many. In me so many meet one another." — True, in each of us there live more beings than we care to admit to ourselves. Somewhere lying dormant within us are the shadows and fears of boyhood's twilight hours forming a cave for Caliban. There is so much space within us. And over many things drifting about in us we have no more power than a shipowner over his vessels tossing about at sea.

So the reader walks off with *The Tempest* in his pocket. The meadow is too near to the highway, the forest already too dark. For a while he strolls to and fro unable to decide, until he settles down on a tree trunk between gossamer threads and mossy branches, and projects his magic theater. It requires a supreme effort of imagination; he has to efface himself, become completely empty, become the scene of action, that island, become completely a stage. Then Prospero emerges from the cave, a shadow of tiredness on his noble face, and Miranda's flowerlike hands reach for the clasp to loosen the dark magic cloak from his shoulders. And now he, the reader, is nothing but an instrument: now the book plays on him.

You will tell me that my reader's name is Charles Lamb or Théophile Gautier, that he is a poet in whom the poems of others come once again to life. But that should make no difference. What matters is Shakespeare's music, and that again and again there must be someone to whom it is granted to hear the whole music of these poems. But it must be as a Whole. — Take *Measure for Measure*, a play full of harshness, with somber passages, with a strange, tart blending of the high and the low; more difficult in language, its motives moving us less quickly than the others—a play that begins to live only after we have heard its whole music. It resembles the faces of certain rare women whose beauty is known only to him who has been happy with them. How frightful is this action in itself, this story of the disloyal judge, disloyal to his profession, disloyal to the wretched convicted, disloyal to the good sister—how harsh and sinister, how heart-constricting, how outrageous, repulsive, and revolting all this is! How harsh and sinister, how painful is Claudio's fate, his fear of death, his clinging to the straw that can save him! And all this only because of a senseless law, because of something no better than a trivial coincidence, a "blank in the lottery!" And grafted on to this misfortune which so outrages us, more misfortune. What a wonderful composition it is! what lights thrown on darkness! what life these lights give the shadows! In the mouth of the one who has to die and is afraid of dying, what a voice, what eloquence, what language, wiser than himself, more profound than his shallow virtue—how death squeezes out of him the best sap! And in the mouth of the girl who is helpless, who is betrayed, what strength, what a sword of God suddenly in her hand! And the others! See how their lives intertwine, how their very presence changes the air: the presence of the old murderer Barnardine, who has been condemned to death for seven years, next to the boy Claudio, who was condemned twenty-four hours ago. Friar Thomas and Friar Peter in the quiet monastery with its peace and seclusion, next to the prison, next to the palace wherein the evil Angelo lurks like a poisonous spider in the masonry. Then all of a sudden we are out of town and there sits Mariana before the "moated grange" and a boy's voice singing that sweet song "Take, O take those lips away" . . . And between this world and that, combining everything like a chorus, the disguised Duke, who now sees at close range those whom he has formerly seen only from above, from afar, he whose presence calms our heart as during a nightmare does the deep knowledge "It is only a dream!" and from whose lips fall those incomparable words about life and death. Between these figures, so that life and light shall play everywhere over living flesh, the shadows emphasizing life, there is still this company of commoner, lower beings, even the least among them not completely denuded of some goodness or wit, some grace or courtesy, not quite incapable of showing goodwill, of saying something kind or uttering an apt analogy. And between all these human beings, what an atmosphere, what a co-existence on this earth, what little yet immeasurably deep and tender gestures towards one another, what looks of pity or mockery exchanged between them! What a Whole, not of calculation, not of reason, not even of emotion, a Whole not so much from the point of view of colors alone or from that of morality, not from the contrast between heaviness and lightness, sadness and gaiety—but from a combination of all this, what a Whole "before God"! What music!

In the performance of *Twelfth Night* by Beerbohm Tree and his troupe, the play ends—and it is said that this was not the director's brilliant idea, but an old English tradition—with each gentleman offering a hand to his lady, and thus, in couples, the Duke and Viola, Olivia and Sebastian, and behind them their retinue dance across and off the stage. Hand in hand they dance, those who had inflamed and tortured one another, sought and deceived and enchanted one another. Thus these figures become figures of a dance, pursuing and not finding, chasing the Wrong and fleeing the Right. This is now the final figure, and for an instant something wafts past it like a shadow, a fleeting memory of the Dance of Death which also makes everything equal, as everything here is equal and together, hands in hands, is creating a double chain, a "figure" wherein the single destiny has as much value as a single spot of color on an ornament, as a single theme in a symphony. Even if this idea were re-created out of an old tradition, it was nevertheless once, the first time, a stroke of genius on the part of one director who invented this perfect symbol of binding together the human bodies (in whose gestures he has expressed for five acts the experiences of each single character), of binding them together at the last moment by a rhythm and expressing in them the wholeness of the Whole. You will say that this director was also a poet. But every creative stage director is a poet. Again and again throughout history Fate chooses one man from among those who "carry within them a stage" and who, in luxurious solitude, play Shakespeare for themselves—chooses the man and gives him a real stage.

And thus, among the hundreds of stages on which Shakespeare is played for show—where he is played, I mean, for tradition's sake, because he constitutes part of the repertory or because his plays contain fine roles—there shines out one stage where he is performed out of sheer passion. Just as Macbeth and Shylock, Othello and Juliet, continue to overpower the body and soul of an actor of genius, so the music of the dramas continues to overpower the soul of a creative director and his whole stage, and lives anew. For everything alive lives only from the living, and the flame only from that which wants to burn.

On announcing that I was going to talk to you about Shakespeare's kings and noblemen, it was agreed that I would not speak of anything but the Whole in Shakespeare's work. It's as though I had said I wished to talk about the solemn and sublime sounds in Beethoven's symphonies, or of light and color in Rubens. When I say "kings and noblemen" your memory is inundated with a flood of figures and gestures incomparable to any vision unless it be that which was granted to the old men on the walls of Troy when before their eyes the dust clouds parted, and the sun was seen gleaming on the armor and faces of the countless heroes so akin to the gods. More figures, images, feelings, surge up in you than you can grasp. You are reminded at once of Lear, who is a king, every inch a king; of Hamlet, who is a prince, a prince to his fingertips; of Richard II, that elder "brother" of Hamlet who talks so much about his royal blood, round whose shoulders hangs the royal cloak as agonizing to wear as that garment immersed in the blood of Nessus and which, when finally torn off, spells certain death. And the face of Henry VI, pale as though his head had been cut off and stuck on a pike, rests for an instant in you, and the face of gentle Duncan, too. In a flash you see the royal, commanding gestures of Antony and feel a breath of the spirit-kingdom on Prospero's island, of the fairy realm of those idyllic kings in long red cloaks and scepters in their hands—Leontes of Sicily, Polixenes of Bohemia, Cymbeline, and Theseus. But this flood of visions continues to rise, and you look into an imbroglio of noble gestures until your head begins to swim. The gestures of command and contempt, of haughty defiance and magnanimity, glitter before your eyes like a thousand flashes of lightning. The words "kings and noblemen" have the power to make continuously fresh floods rise from the well of a memory steeped in Shakespeare. Swamped by a vision and figures almost impossible to grasp, you will search within yourselves for a word that can compress in one idea this whole imaginary world of spirits. You sense that these words conjure up not only three-quarters of all figures created by Shakespeare, but also what happens between these figures as well as what happens between them and those of less importance who stand beside them; you sense that these words apply not only to these figures but also to the empty space around them and to what fills this empty space—what the Italians call *l'ambiente*. You slowly realize that in this world of Shakespeare there really exists a line leading from one point to another, some true relation between the scene in which Kent, the unrecognized, offers his services to Lear because he had something in his countenance which "he would fain call master," and the sylvan idyll of King Cymbeline's sons who grow up in a cave, unfettered, like beautiful young animals although of royal blood; between the sullen feuds of the English barons in the dramas of the kings and the benevolent master's tone in which noble Brutus speaks to Lucius, his page; between the tone of proud Othello, yes, and Cleopatra, a queen, and Falstaff, who is—after all—a nobleman. You feel, as I do, this imponderable, this intangible element, this Nothing which is nevertheless everything, and from my lips you take the words wherewith I wish to name it—the Atmosphere of Shakespeare's work. This word could not be more vague, yet it belongs to those of which we may have to make a very definite, very productive use.

At no other time of the year, however, would I have dared to speak of something so vague and in it to seek something so great than now, that spring has come.

"Now with the drops of this most balmy time / My love looks fresh" . . . and now greater than ever is the courage to see all beautiful things afresh, to dismiss all those clearly defined subjects which are usually discussed—characters, actions, ideas— and to follow this fleeting, barely palpable truth which pervades all of Shakespeare's work.

The moment itself has so much atmosphere. I mean this very moment in the life of Nature, this moment of the not yet fully awakened, not yet luxuriating, still-yearning spring in which the death-anniversary of a human being unites us here, a human being who has become almost a myth to us and of whom we can scarce believe that he ever was a presence among mortal men. It does not appear to me as something essentially different whether we sense the atmosphere of spring, the atmosphere of a Shakespearean drama, or that of a picture by Rembrandt. Here as there I feel a gigantic *ensemble*. (Let me take this sober word from the technique of painting rather than any other.

There are many at my disposal: I could speak of the music of the Whole, of a harmony, of a spiritualization, but all these words strike me as somewhat wilted, slightly soiled by the touch of human hands.) An *ensemble* wherein the difference between great and small has been canceled insofar as one lives for the sake of the other, the great for the small, the dark for the light, where one seeks the other, emphasizes and restrains the other, colors and discolors, and where finally for the soul there exists nothing but the Whole—the indivisible, intangible, imponderable Whole. To dissect the atmosphere of spring was always the passion of the lyric poet. But its essence is nevertheless the *ensemble*. Everywhere the world is burgeoning. The far and the near whisper to one another; the tepid breeze gliding over the still-naked earth breathes an air of oppressive sultriness. Light, like water, is melting everywhere, but no moment is more pregnant with the abundance of spring than that of noon, when darkness falls and heavy, sinister clouds brood over the earth-brown hills and the clamor of delirious bird voices rises from the bare branches into the gloom. And as in a phantasmagoria, everything has changed. The naked landscape, hitherto so sad and deserted, is full of voluptuousness. The darkness doesn't oppress, it exalts. The near is as mysterious as the far. And the voice of a single bird contributes no less to the Whole than the dark forest which lends to the wind the scent of moist earth and budding green.

I could continue to offer you this notion of Atmosphere were I not sure that you have understood me immediately and completely, and were I not afraid to tire you. The death of a human being has its Atmosphere, like spring. The faces of those in whose arms a man has died speak a language that defies words. And in their presence inanimate objects join in this language. A chair that has always stood elsewhere, an open cupboard that has never remained open for long, and a thousand trivial signs appearing at such a moment like traces of ghosts' hands: this is the world which ends at the windowpanes. But the outside world, too, in a mysterious way, shows this fateful, deeply knowing face: the street lamps are burning as on any other day; the passing of the unsuspecting strangers, turning a corner, passing the house, turning another corner—all this condenses itself into something that drags along like an ominous iron chain. These are the moments when the long-forgotten friends return: the emergence of those whose behavior has become queer, who are embittered or utterly estranged, and out of whom now break forth words and looks never heard or seen at any other time. The sudden astonishment: how did we part? how did all this happen? The quick realization: how futile everything is! How alike we all are, how similar to one another! — This, too, is Atmosphere. Here, too, something indefinable connects the near with the far, the great with the small, one moving the other into its proper light, intensifying and subduing, coloring and discoloring one by the other, annihilating all borderlines between the seemingly important and seemingly unimportant, the common and the exceptional—and creates the *ensemble* out of the whole existing material, considering no elements to be incompatible.

The Atmosphere in Shakespeare's work is nobility: the king is merely the greatest nobleman among great noblemen, and each of them has in him something of a king—nobility in the sense of the Cinquecento—that is, infinitely freer, infinitely more human, more colorful than anything which we are accustomed to associate with this notion. It is not only the characters and their feelings born out of Shakespeare's soul which are imbued with this nobility, but precisely and above all the Atmosphere, the air of life, *ce grand air* pervading everything. All these characters (the duller few who do not belong to them exist only to create contrast) are steeped in the element of nobility as the figures in the paintings of Titian and Giorgione are steeped in the golden, luminous element of color. It's in this element that such groups as Romeo, Mercutio, Benvolio, Tybalt, as well as Antonio the noble merchant and his friends, move. The banished Duke in the Ardennes and all those who belong to him, above all Brutus and his household, are surrounded by this aura. This light, this air, is around them in such abundance and with such intensity that it cannot be ignored. A noble consciousness—nay, deeper than that—an existence of almost conscious nobility, a noble breathing, and closely connected with it a remarkable tender and strong feeling for the other person, a mutual almost impersonal affection, a tenderness, reverence for the human. Have I not recalled to you with these words—too weak to express what is ineffably alive—what all these different young people have in common: the melancholic Jaques with the lighthearted Bassanio, the passionate Romeo with the shrewd, shy Mercutio? The element in which these beings are bred is delicately suspended between arrogance and courtesy. It is the youthful attitude of defiance which is nevertheless shocked at the thought of having offended—a readiness to open up and form attachments, yet at the same time remaining detached and complete. Their equilibrium is one of the most beautiful things I know. Like graceful, well-built ships they lie rocking to and fro above their own shadows on the flood of life. Round them there is something exultant, something expansive overflowing into the air, an abundance of life, a glorification of life itself, something definitely welcoming life, something that evokes the Pythian and Nemean odes of Pindar, those radiant salutations of victors. Not only is Prince Henry ultimately their brother, but so, to a certain degree, is Falstaff. They are youths, but Brutus is a man. They are without any other destiny but the destiny of love; they seem to be placed in this picture only as a glorification of life, like glowing reds and resplendent yellows in a painting. Brutus, however, has a lofty destiny of his own. He is modeled of the same clay as they, but he is a more mature person. It is not the manner in which his soul interprets life, but his attitude in life, this nobility without harshness, full of generosity, of goodness and gentleness, this tone whose harmony could shine forth only from a soul in whose depths the profoundest self-respect is rooted. Apart from his destiny which fulfills itself in him—"the genius and the mortal instruments are then in council"—and drives him to the great deed of his life which is then followed by everything else, even by death, as water follows water when a dam is opened; apart from his inner destiny this tragedy (whose hero is Brutus) is illuminated almost exclusively by the light of this noble being in whose ray all other characters mold themselves by coming closer to him. What occurs between Brutus and Cassius is nothing but the reaction of Cassius (who is less noble and knows himself to be less noble) to the atmosphere around Brutus. In Cassius there is a vain, mute, inner wooing of Brutus, a wooing with every torment of jealousy which Cassius does not admit to himself, which Brutus, too, perhaps, if aware of it, does not admit, doesn't want to know, certainly doesn't want to analyze. And in Brutus an amazing forbearance for Cassius; up to the moment of his single outburst he places himself tactfully on the same level; and even then it is his nerves, not his will, which give way. (An hour ago he has received the news of Portia's death, yet he refrains from mentioning it.) And then, on parting, once again: "noble, noble Cassius." Imagine him being capable of saying this, the noble one to the less noble! Of feeling driven to say it twice! This is the attitude of Brutus towards Cassius. And Portia! She has but this one unforgettable scene. Enveloped in the atmosphere of Brutus, her noble face is molded from the light emanating from him. Or does this light emanate from elsewhere? Are both Brutus and Portia molded out of this light and its shadows? Who, before a Rembrandt, can say whether the atmosphere is there for the sake of the figures or the figures for the sake of the atmosphere? But certain places exist simply to catch the whole light, which is the soul of the atmosphere. I have in mind the scenes with the boy Lucius and the other servants. The considerate tone of his voice when he apologizes to Lucius for shortening his sleep to which his youth has so much claim. And this: "Look, Lucius, here's the book I sought for so; I put it in the pocket of my gown. . . . Bear with me, good boy." And then, as Lucius falls asleep while tuning his lute, Brutus steps forward to remove the lute on which his arm has sunk in slumber: "If thou dost nod, thou break'st thy instrument." I don't know what can bring tears to a reader's eye if not such a detail. This is the man who was Caesar's murderer. He is the general in his tent. He is the last Roman; tomorrow at Philippi he will die. And here he is, bending down, and from under the sleeping boy removing a lute so that it shall not be broken. And at the moment of making this small gesture, this plain, homely, almost feminine little gesture—more natural to a woman, a housewife, a mother—at this moment, so near his death (Caesar's ghost is already standing there in the dark), I see his face: it's a face he has never had before, a second face as though taking form from within—a face in which male and female features mingle, as in the death masks of Beethoven and Napoleon. It is here that we are moved to tears, rather than at Lear's curses, rather than when Macbeth, strangled in his own iron torments as in a hundredweight of armor, turns his eye on us and constricts our heart. From such minor details our admiration for Shakespeare is intensified to the pitch of worship. Indeed, in a work of art there is no difference between great and small. Here, when Brutus, Caesar's murderer, picks up the lute so that it shall not be broken, here as nowhere else do we face the tornado of existence that sucks us down. These are the flashes of lightning wherein a heart reveals itself completely. We are reminded of Ottilie in the *Elective Affinities*, who could never forget the anecdote about how Charles I of England, already dethroned and surrounded by enemies, drops the knob of his stick. He looks round and, dumbfounded to see that no one picks it up, stoops himself for the first time in his life. This incident so engraves itself on her heart that from then on she stoops whenever anyone, even a man, drops something. Again, we think of the howl suddenly uttered by Natasha during the hare hunt in *War and Peace*, that wild, triumphant howl of a hound from the throat of an elegant young lady. These are the flashes of lightning I have in mind. And in Shakespeare they are legion. They are the cataclysms of his atmosphere.

I know nothing that so grips the heart as the tone of Lear's voice when he speaks to Edgar. To his daughters he talks like a furious prophet or a patriarch drunk with pain. To his Fool he speaks harshly. But to Edgar, that naked madman whom he has found in a cave, he speaks in a tone (wherein, to be sure, there is something of madness) whose keynote is an extraordinary politeness of the heart, an indescribable courtesy, which makes us realize how this king could sometimes make his people happy when in a gracious mood. It is that same politeness whose glow hovers over gentle Duncan when he comes in and suggests that the air round Macbeth's castle ought to be good since swifts nest there. The same light, too, shines over that brief scene between Richard II and the groom (shortly before his death); and the same but stronger, more exotic, more resplendent light in each scene between Antony and Cleopatra, between Antony and his friends, Cleopatra and her attendants. What reverence for themselves and the grandeur of their existence! What "Olympian air," what magnificent style, when the affairs of the world have to wait in the anteroom while they embrace: "The nobleness of life is to do thus . . ." The same light again, as if penetrating dense storm clouds with furious flashes of lightning, falls on the hundred figures of the proud peers of England whose self-esteem (one of them calls it "our stately presence") shrouds them in wide folds grander, wilder, more real than any ermine-trimmed cloak. But I could continue endlessly saying "It is here! It is there!" for I see it everywhere. I could spend another hour describing how I see in this aura the figures of all these regal, noble women, from Cleopatra to Imogen. I see it everywhere so much, in fact, that I am deeply perplexed when perceiving a figure like Macbeth with almost nothing of this atmosphere around him. This suggests to me that Shakespeare meant to endow him with a peculiar frightfulness, meant to let him be shrouded by an icy air of death. It seems as if the ghastly breath of Hecate had eaten away from the world around Macbeth everything alive, everything that ordinarily unites mankind, leaving nothing of that which surrounds Hamlet as a breath of life. Take the scene with the actors, where Hamlet's whole being expands in a princely, gracious self-indulgence and joy, even delighting others with his self-indulgence. Or the scenes with Polonius, Rosencrantz, and Guildenstern as a conscious use of his princely eminence, an ironic and grievous demonstration of his superiority—implying that even this prerogative is worth nothing, even this privilege is of no avail save as an instrument of self-torture.

Gentlemen! The ideas I have been expounding here seem to me to bind together the whole of Shakespeare's work. They are a mystery and the word "Atmosphere" describes them in as unsatisfactory and almost as superficial a manner as the word "Chiaroscuro" describes a similar mystery in the work of Rembrandt. Were I thinking of the figures alone—and it is the isolated figures, as though standing in a vacuum, that are usually made the subject of observation—then I would have tried to talk of the Shakespearean "attitude." For the important point is to see or to sense the common ground whereon, in life, all these figures stand. Dante's figures are placed in a gigantic architectonic system and the place on which each stands is *its* place according to mystical designs. Shakespeare's figures, on the other hand, are determined not by the stars but by themselves; they carry within themselves hell, purgatory, and heaven, and instead of their place in life they have their attitude. I, however, see these figures not each by itself but each in relation to all the others, and between them not a vacuum but a space mystically alive. I don't see them next to one another separately, like the figures of saints on a painting by an early primitive, but standing out from a common element like the men, animals, and angels in the paintings of Rembrandt.

The drama (I don't mean only Shakespeare's drama) is just as much a picture of the absolute solitude of the individual as a picture of the co-existence of mankind. In the dramas cast out of the volcano of Kleist's fiery soul, this atmosphere, this co-existence of characters, is perhaps the most beautiful part of the whole. His creatures, you will remember, are continually lusting after one another; suddenly, when addressing one an-

other, they change from the distant you to the naked thou, ca-
ress one another with amorous glances, seize one another with
violence, the one yearning to merge into the other but
promptly turning cold, flying asunder in estrangement, then to
go all over again in ardent search of one another. All this fills
Kleist's space with passionate life and movement and creates
something living out of the void.

To sum up: Whatever occurs between these figures seems to
me filled with a life flowing from the same mysterious sources
as the figures themselves. This mirroring of one another, this
humiliating and exalting, restraining and fortifying of one an-
other—all this, for me, is as much the work of a hand of a gigan-
tic genius as the figures themselves. And it is because I cannot,
in Shakespeare's work any more than in Rembrandt's, draw or
admit a dividing line between the figures themselves and that
part of the picture without them that I have seized upon the
word "Atmosphere." The lack of time and the urgency of imme-
diate understanding between us has prevented me from em-
ploying a word even more appropriate and more mysterious—
the word "Myth."

Had I been able with greater intensity than today to evoke
in your minds the power of Rembrandt and with comparable
intensity the power of Homer, then these three primeval
forces—Shakespeare's Atmosphere, Rembrandt's Chiaroscuro,
Homer's Myth—would for a moment have merged into one.
Grasping this glowing key, we would have descended to the
Mothers, and there, where "neither Space, still less Time" exists,
have visualized the deepest creating and longing of distant spir-
its in mystical union with the deepest creating and longing of
our own epoch—to generate atmosphere for its existence, to let
its figures move in the lightness and darkness of life, to imbue its
breath with myth.

BALZAC

THOSE WHO KNOW only this or that book by Balzac do not know this great author. No single volume contains the essence of his poetic genius as *Faust* or the *Poems* contain the essence of Goethe's. Balzac has to be read extensively, and to read him does not require any art. He provides the most natural reading matter for men of the world—and I employ that phrase in its broadest sense—from the solicitor's clerk or merchant's apprentice to the *grand seigneur.* The reading of Goethe, on the other hand, requires from men of the world (I am talking here of men of all ranks, of politicians and soldiers, of traveling salesmen, of distinguished and simple women, of clerics, of all people who are neither professionals nor amateurs of letters, of all those who read not from desire for self-improvement but for entertainment or in order to stimulate their imagination) an occasional minor effort, a certain transition. While it is more than possible that Goethe would deny himself to them in the troubled and confused moments of their existence, Balzac will always be ready to open his door to them. I do not mean this in the literary sense, for the first verse of Goethe's they set eyes on will always be something marvelous, as from another world, an incantation; whereas with Balzac they may easily fall upon three or four boring, tiresome pages, not only at the beginning of a story but possibly wherever they may happen to open the book. Nevertheless, while automatically glancing at these indifferent and rather laborious pages, something will begin to take hold of them, something from which the real reader, the alive reader, can never escape—a vast, indescribably substantial imagination, the greatest, most substantially creative imagination since Shakespeare. Wherever they open the book—be it at a digression on the law of exchange or the practices of usurers, on legitimist or liberal society, the description of a kitchen interior, of a marital scene, of a face or a den, they will feel the *world*, substance, the same substance from which the vicissitudes of their own lives are shaped. They will be able to move over directly from their own lives—from their worries and vexations, from their favorite anecdotes and financial affairs, their trivial troubles and ambitions—without intermediary stages, into these books. I have met the banker who, after his meetings and conferences, picked up without transition his Balzac, in which he kept as bookmarker his last quotation from the Stock Exchange; I have met the *dame du monde* who considered *Les Illusions perdues* or *La Vieille fille* to be the only possible literature to find the way back to herself.

In the evenings, after we have been among people or have entertained guests, Balzac seems the only reading matter strong and pure enough to cure the imagination of its sudden and destructive fever of vanity and to reduce all social matters to their human value. This function of delving straight into the lives of human beings, of curing the ill with the ill, of conquering reality with intensified daemonic reality—I ask myself who among the great authors, on whom our intellectual life counts, can in this respect rival Balzac, unless it be Shakespeare? But to read Shakespeare as former generations read the classics—I mean to read them so that we absorb from him the whole of life, to read him from the point of view of living, and to satisfy through him our profoundest desire for knowledge—this not all of us can do. Not everyone can strain his imagination and make it soar across the distance of three centuries, make it penetrate all the guises of a magnificent but utterly strange epoch, and recognize behind them only the eternally true ups and downs of human actions and sufferings. It is not easy for everyone without the help of the actors, without a very specific talent for re-creative imagination, to unravel the most brilliant telescoping and condensation ever realized, to spread it out into such a broad picture of the world that in it he can rediscover himself and the manifold entangled threads of existence whose interwoven pattern represents his reality.

In a certain sense Goethe is easier to read, and who does not read him? Although he expressed one of his profound and subtle insights when he said that his writings were not qualified to become popular and that their true content would always reveal itself only to the individual who has gone through similar experiences, there seem to be so many of these individuals nowadays that the truth of his words has almost lost its meaning. He, however, who wants to reabsorb one of Goethe's works, who wants to enjoy *Hermann and Dorothea, Wilhelm Meister,* or the *Elective Affinities,* must approach the book with senses already purified. He must leave much of himself, of the atmosphere of his life, behind. He must forget the big city. He must cut through ten thousand threads of the feeling, thinking, and wishing of the moment. He must try to recall his "spiritual body"—I mean his immortal, his absolute, his purely human essence; he must keep in mind the eternal stars and through them purify himself. Once he has achieved this, however, it is of little importance which of Goethe's works he opens. Everywhere he is enveloped by the same enhanced and transfigured reality; he is truly surrounded by a world, a spirit in itself a world. The interpretations and the characters, an idea or the description of a phenomenon of nature, a verse, a figure like Mignon or Ottilie—all these are of the same divine radiant substance. Behind each line he senses the reference to a Whole, to a sublime order. The immense calm of an immense wealth descends almost oppressively on his soul in order to raise this soul again into a state of bliss. But this arm which can raise to the stars does not embrace everyone. The living Goethe, too, gave himself only to a few and to these not at any hour. To him who reaches out for it with a nervous hand, a creation such as the *Elective Affinities* snaps shut like the shell of an oyster. To such people Goethe appears cool, distant, strange. He impresses more than he captivates. They postpone the reading of his work—for calmer days or for a journey. Or he creates in them a nostalgia for their youth, for a higher receptiveness. To them he appears artificial, he who was himself Nature, and cold, he whose loving eye penetrated even the impenetrable primitive rock with warmth. They gaze about in search of something that will help them enjoy him. They reach out for an interpreter or for the wonderful letters and conversations in which he comments on himself, and only in this roundabout way do they return again to his books.

Nothing is more unthinkable than a reader who would come to Balzac's works by an indirect route. The fewest of his innumerable readers know anything about his life. The *littérateurs* know a few minor anecdotes which would be of interest to no one were they not concerned with the author of the *Comédie humaine.* And they know the correspondence with one person containing almost nothing but bulletins about the incessant, gigantic job of writing—an achievement that cannot be compared with any other in the world of literature. It is the strongest proof of the immense power of his work that we are able to read these endless bulletins with a thrill similar to that with which we read Napoleon's reports on his campaigns, on Austerlitz, Jena, and Wagram. His readers know his books, but not him. They say *La Peau de chagrin* and recall a waking dream, an adventurous experience, not the achievement of a poet; they think of old Goriot and his daughters but do not remember the name of the author. Once they have entered this world, ninety out of a hundred readers will always return to it again, after five, after ten, after twenty years. Walter Scott, who once was read with rapture by mature people, has become the reading matter for boys. Balzac will always (or for a long time, for who can speak of always?) remain the reading matter for all stages of life, for men as well as women. The war stories and adventures, *Les Chouans, L'Auberge rouge, El Verdugo,* are for the imagination of a sixteen-year-old boy the next stage after the tales of Red Indians and Captain Cook; the experiences of Rubempré and Rastignac compose the reading of the young man; *Le Lys dans la vallée, Savarus, Modeste Mignon,* that of the young woman. Men and women around forty, the mature but not effete ones, will keep to the most mature—to *La Cousine Bette,* that magnificent book which, although containing only ugly, sad, and terrible facts, I cannot call sinister because it glows with fire, life, and wisdom; to *La Vieille fille,* which combines a plasticity of characterization surpassing all praise with the most profound philosophy of life, and at the same time is intimate, cosy, gay—in every respect an incomparable book that alone would have the power to carry the fame of the author through the generations. I have heard an old gentleman praise the *Contes drolatiques,* and I have heard another old gentleman speak with emotion about the story of César Birotteau, that steady rise of a good man from year to year, from profit to profit, from honor to honor. And if there have been people who cut out of *Wilhelm Meister* the "Confessions of a Beautiful Soul" and burned the rest, then there has surely also been the man who cut Séraphitus-Séraphita out of the *Comédie humaine* and made of it a devotional book. And just such a person, perhaps, was that unknown man who, in a Viennese concert hall, forced his way to Balzac to kiss the hand that had written *Séraphita.*

In Balzac's work everyone finds as much of the great complexity of life as he carries in himself. The more richly a man's experience has been nourished, the stronger the imagination he possesses, the more deeply will he enter into these books. Here no one need leave anything of himself outside. All his emotions, uncleansed as they are, will be brought into play. Here he finds his own inner and outer world, only stranger, more condensed, more illuminated from within. Here are the powers that determine him, here the inhibitions that paralyze him. Here are the diseases of the soul, the greeds, the almost pointless aspirations, the consuming vanities; here are all the demons that burrow within us. Here above all is the great city with which we are familiar, or the province in its peculiar relation to the big city. Here is the money, the colossal power of money, the philosophy of money, transformed into characters, the myth of money. Here are the social stratifications, the political groupings that are more or less still ours; here is the fever of rising in the world, the fever of moneymaking, the fascination of work, the lonely mysteries of the artists, the inventors—everything down to the misery of the petit bourgeois life, to the small money misery, to the laboriously and constantly mended glove, to the gossip of the servant.

The exterior truth of these things is so great that it has been able to continue its existence separate, so to speak, from its object, and to pass on like an atmosphere; the Paris of Louis Philippe has disappeared, but certain constellations, the salon in the province in which Rubempré takes his first step into the world, or Madame de Bargeton's salon in Angoulême have today an astonishing significance for Austria whose social and political condition bears, in a sense, a resemblance to the July Monarchy; and certain features from the life of Rastignac and de Marsay are possibly more significant today for England than for France. But the varnish of this palpable and exciting "truth," the first great glory of the "modern" surrounding his work, will pass. Nevertheless, the inner truth of this world hurled forth by the imagination (which coincides only for moments in a thousand insignificant points with the ephemeral reality) is today stronger and more alive than ever. This world, the most complete and multi-articulated hallucination that ever existed, seems to be charged with truth. Under our reflective gaze its corporeity dissolves into a co-existence of innumerable power stations, of monads whose essence is the most intense substantial truth. In the ups and downs of these careers, these love affairs, money and power intrigues, rural and small town events, anecdotes, monographs of a passion, of a soul sickness, of a social institution, in the maze of close on two thousand human existences, almost everything is touched which, in our cultural life, complicated as it is to the point of confusion, ever plays a role. And almost everything that is said about these myriads of things, relations, phenomena, bristles with truth. I don't know if an attempt has already been made—it could be done at any time—to compile a dictionary whose content would be drawn exclusively from Balzac. It would contain nearly all material, all spiritual and intellectual realities, of our existence. It would include cooking recipes as well as chemical theories; details about money and commercial affairs, precise and useful details which would fill columns; about trade and commerce we would learn many facts that are out of date, but we would also learn other facts that are eternally true and valid. And next to these, under arbitrary slogans, we would have to include the most daring prophecies and anticipations of biological facts of later decades; the articles under the headings "Marriage," "Society," or "Politics" would each comprise a book in itself, and each a book which, among the publications on worldly wisdom of the nineteenth century, would know no equal. The book containing the treatise on "Love" would reach in a boldly designed arc from the most sinister, inscrutable mysteries (*Une Passion dans le désert*) through a chaos bristling with all human possibilities to the most spiritualized, angelic love. By the greatness of its conception and the magnitude of its panorama, this volume would put the one famous book we have on the same subject (and one written by a master's hand) into the shade. This dictionary, however, does exist. It is spun into a world of characters, into a labyrinth of events, and we leaf through it while following the thread of a superbly invented story. The man of the world will find in these volumes the whole range of human situations, so specious yet so true, that constitute social life. The thousand nuances wherewith men and women treat one another well or ill; the imperceptible transitions, the unrelenting gradations, the whole gamut from the truly distinguished to the semi-distinguished, to the vulgar—all this modified and perforated in the most splendid manner by the Human, by the Passionate, and for moments reduced to its nothingness. Man in his struggle for existence (and who does not struggle to make a living, to maintain what he has or to suffer privation?) has his whole world here. The great financier, the struggling physician, the starving and the triumphant inventor, the great and small promoter, the rising businessman, the army contractor, the notary as mediator, the usurer, the stand-in, the pawnbroker—and of each not one but five or ten types. And what types! With all the tricks of their trade, their secrets, their last truths. Painters among themselves maintain the legend that Delacroix must have been the source of the last intimate details of modeling by light and shade described in *Le Chef-d'oeuvre inconnu*; this truth appeared to them too substantial to be discovered by someone not a painter, and a great painter at that. A thinker who has been handed *Louis Lambert* as the monograph on a thinker may find the biographical part weak and may doubt the validity of the character; but as soon as he reaches the thought material transmitted in letters and notes, he will find the consistency of these thoughts, the substantial power of this thinker, so convincing that any doubt about the character will be dispelled. These are thoughts of a real being, this brain has indeed functioned—no matter to what extent we may reject these thoughts, this philosophy of a spiritualistic dreamer. And the married man who, in a pensive hour, comes across the *Physiologie du mariage* will find in this strange book (which, perhaps, owing to a certain semi-frivolous tone, has lost some favor) several pages whose truths are as delicate as they are deep, and worthy of being taken to heart—truths which, when absorbed, expand themselves and continue to live in us with a gentle, radiant power. There is nothing esoteric clinging to these truths. They are presented in a worldly, sometimes in an almost frivolous tone. Interspersed among events and descriptions, they form the most spiritual element in the body of a story, a novel. They are offered to us as life itself offers us its content—in encounters, catastrophes, in the unfolding of passions, in sudden perspectives and insights, in unexpected vistas opening up the dense forest of human existence. Here we find the most passionate and most comprehensive painting of life, and simultaneously an extraordinarily perceptive philosophy ready to take whatever seemingly obscure phenomenon of life for its point of departure. Thus the whole great work, whose world-image is certainly as somber as that of Shakespeare's and at the same time so much more bulky, cloudier, heavier through its own volume, is nevertheless pervaded by a spiritual aliveness—yes, a spiritual gaiety, a deep sense of gratification. What else could we call that which—whenever we come across one of these books—makes us turn the pages back and forth, not read but leaf through them, an act wherein lies a far more subtle, nostalgic love? What else could we call that which can turn for us the mere enumeration of the titles of these hundred books or the record of the characters appearing in them into a kind of summary perusal whose enjoyment is complex and violent, like that of a favorite poem?

The amassing of such an enormous bulk of substantial truths is not possible without organization. The talent to organize is as much a creative gift as the merely productive one. Or rather, they are only different aspects of one and the same power. From the truth of the countless isolated phenomena follows the truth of the relationship between them: thus a world is created. As with Goethe, I feel myself here in a definite relationship to the Whole. I find an invisible coordinating system by which I can orientate myself. Whatever I read, be it one of the great novels, one of the stories, one of the fantastic philosophic rhapsodies; whenever I become engrossed in the secrets of a soul, in a political digression, in a description of a lawyer's office or a small grocery—never do I lose the sensation of being related to the Whole. I feel around me an organized world. The great secret is that this world surrounding me without any gaps, this other, more condensed, more intense reality, does not affect me as an oppressive burden, as a nightmare taking my breath away. It does not make us stop short, does not petrify us; rather, the sight of it pours fire into our veins. For this world itself does not stand still but is constantly in motion. It is in flux, *infinitis modis*, to use a technical term of medieval thinkers. In this most complete vision to have sprung from a human brain since Dante, the world is conceived not as static but dynamic—observed, moreover, so minutely that it forms a gapless scale, presenting the whole texture of life, from thread to thread. Yet everything is seen in motion. Never was the ancient wisdom of *Panta rei* more magnificently conceived and transformed into characters. Everything is transition. Behind these books whose totality represents, after *Don Quixote*, the greatest epic conception of the modern world, the idea of epic art form seems to come to life. To describe human beings, how they flourish and perish like the flowers on the earth—Homer did nothing else. Dante's world is static. It does not move; rather, he himself moves, and walks past it. Balzac himself we do not see, but we see with his eyes how everything changes. The rich turn poor, and the poor rich. César Birotteau rises and Baron Hulot goes down in the world. Rubempré's soul appeared like an untouched fruit, and before our eyes we see it transformed; we see him seize the rope to put an end to his tarnished life. Séraphita extricates herself and soars off to heaven. Each one is no longer what he was— each becomes what he is not. Here we are as deep in the core of the epic *Weltanschauung* as with Shakespeare we are in the core of the dramatic. Everything is flowing, everything on the way. Money is merely the brilliantly conceived symbol of this constant motion, and at the same time its vehicle. Through money everyone gets everywhere. And it is the nature of the world, conceived in this magnificent and epic fashion, that everyone gets everywhere. We find transitions everywhere, nothing but transitions, in the moral as well as in the social world. The transitions between vice and virtue—two mythical concepts which no one knows quite how to grasp—are as finely graded and as continuous as those between rich and poor. Hidden in the most far removed and most contradictory things lie certain secret relationships through which everything is connected with everything. Between a concierge in his basement and Napoleon in Saint-Cloud, there can flash up for a moment a secret affinity meaning far more than a mere witticism. Since in the world everything affects everything, why should this not be conditioned by the most secret analogies? Everything is in flux; no rigid block remains, either in the spiritual world or in everyday existence. "Love" and "Hatred" appear sufficiently separate and clearly enough defined. And there are in Balzac's work characters in whose heart one of these feelings merges as imperceptibly into the other as the colors of glowing iron. Does Rosalie hate Albert Savarus or does she love him? In the beginning she loves him, in the end she seems to hate him. She acts under an obsession that is perhaps both love and hatred at once. And were we able to ask her, she could not inform us by which of the two emotions she feels tortured. Here we are separated by an abyss from the world of the eighteenth century with its notions (such as "virtue") which are clear, well-defined, and dogmatic, well-suited to replace clear and theological concepts. Here any mythology, even that of words, is dissolved. And nowhere are we closer to Goethe. Here quite close—yes, in the same bed—rushes the deep stream of his ideas. But it was the innate gesture of his spiritual being to turn at this moment to the opposite side. The driving forces of his nature were so powerful that they threatened to overwhelm him. He had to oppose them with the Permanent, with Nature, Laws, Ideas. The eye of his soul was fastened on the changeless amidst the changes. This is how we see his face; this is how the mask of the contemplative magician was formed. Balzac's face we don't see as an Olympic mask enthroned above his work. Only in his books do we occasionally think we see it appearing, like that of a seer, cast up by chaotic obscurities, by whirling lava, but it is not in our power to retain it. Each generation will see it differently; each as a titanic face, and after its fashion will make out of it a symbol of inexpressible inner experiences. We are surprised that we do not possess a likeness of this face by that hand which created the *Massacre of Chios* and *Dante's Barque*. He would have painted the thirty-year-old Balzac as the titan he was, as a demon of life, or he would have treated his face as a battlefield. It is a surprising hiatus that later the mask of the fifty-year-old man was not bequeathed to us by Daumier. His miraculous crayon and his equally miraculous brush would have made the faunlike quality of the man spring forth from the dark and would have ennobled it with the wild solitude of genius. But perhaps these generations were too close to him, and it required perspective for something like Rodin's creation to emerge—this completely symbolic, superhuman face wherein a terrible weight of matter is coupled with the dark, sultry quality of the demoniac, a face in which the synthesis of utterly opposite worlds has taken place, a face that reminds us of a fallen angel and simultaneously of the dim and boundless sadness emanating from primeval Greek demons of the earth and sea.

Each generation which, steeped in Balzac's work, conjures up this vision will create within this face a similar synthesis between the whole burden of life and the most secret urge towards the conquering of this burden, towards redemption, towards a transcendence of it. This Belonging to the dark, bulky burden of life (forever renewing itself) and at the same time the desire to transcend it, this deepest urge of the spirit for the spiritual: that is the signature of this great tragic face which, unlike Goethe's mask gazing up over our heads into eternity, looks through us, right through the burden of life. This enormous world constructed from our life—the life of lust, of selfishness, of errors, of the grotesque, sublime and ridiculous passions—this world in whose medley the concepts Comedy and Tragedy are as dissolved as are Vice and Virtue, this world is fundamentally all movement, all urge, all love, all mystery. This apparent materialist is actually a passionate, ecstatic seer. The essence of his characters is aspiration. All forces of suffering, forces of love, all artistic exertion, all monomanias, these titanic powers, the great motors of his world, are aspirations: they all aim towards some highest ideal, towards something indefinable. Vautrin, the genius as criminal, and Steinbock the genius as artist, Goriot the father, Eugénie Grandet the virgin, Frenhofer the creator—they are all focused towards an Absolute which will reveal itself, as ships tossed about at night in a storm are focused on the existence of a polar star, even though darkness conceals it. In the depths of their cynicism, in the turmoil of their tortures, in the abyss of renunciation, they seek and find God, whether or no they call Him by name.

All these characters endowed with such physical presence are really nothing but the transitory embodiments of one nameless power. Through these infinite relativities breaks an Absolute; angels and demons look at us from the eyes of these people. All mythology, even the last, the most tenacious, that of words, is here dissolved. But a new, mysterious, most personalized mythology supplants all the others. Its conception is magnificent, so definite and yet vague that hundreds of thousands of people can adopt it and make out of it something like a myth of modern life. All these characters that force themselves on our imagination as "real" appear to us, in an almost supernatural light which descends from the summit of this work, as good and bad genii, beings in whom the earthly instincts are temporarily incarnate. But nothing in this conception is schematic. Here no dogmas are established, rather visions. Taine in his great essay on Balzac measures these intuitions, these floating truths—all of which are true only for the one moment and in the one place where they happen to be—by a yardstick which they do not allow. From a poet's work one cannot isolate details. Everything which within a world is truth—yes, more than truth, boundless premonition—becomes a miscarried phantasmagoria when taken out of context. We are concerned here with forms of vision. The thinker sees principles, abstractions, formulas, where the poet sees character, the human being, the demon.

Nevertheless, even when observed with the cold eye, the most grandiose synthesis has been accomplished. Here Novalis the magician encounters the titanic beginnings of true naturalism; here is the link between Swedenborg and Goethe or Lamarck. Here we find, to a certain degree, the last word of Catholicism, and at the same time an anticipation of Robert Mayer's discoveries breaks through the clouds like a star. The power of his work which is to subjugate more than one generation lies in his spirit's miraculous penetration of the reality of life, the *vraie vérité,* down to the most trivial human miseries. The spirituality of the nineteenth century, that whole enormous synthetic spirituality, is here compressed into the substance of life like a luminous vapor penetrating all fibers. When the precipitations of this vapor are strong and clearly crystallized as in *Louis Lambert,* in *La Recherche de l'absolu,* in *Le Chef-d'oeuvre inconnu,* there emerge concatenations of thoughts, forebodings, aphorisms, comparable only to the *Fragments* of Novalis. But whereas with Novalis these crystallizations are almost all that has reached us, in Balzac they are but a by-product of these psychophysical processes. Much more remarkable still is the phenomenon that develops when the compressed power of this spirituality drives the living substance forward, when characters result who thus driven make us feel the sway of spiritual forces in the very core of life. Hence Claës, the tireless searcher after the Absolute; hence Louis Lambert and Séraphita. And hence, above all, Balzac's conception of love. It is the most incomparable, most individual creation. All aspiration, it is at the same time the medium of the most mysterious synthesis between the spiritual and the sensual. It, this love, is a mysterious phenomenon which I have no desire to dilute with words. It does not occupy great space in this bulky work. And yet what warms and illuminates this work is just this love, and without it I could not imagine this immense weight, this dark world of human beings, as anything but terrible.

IN BALZAC we find a world teeming with characters. None among them is so powerfully conceived, so complete in himself, as to exist alone, divorced from his background in the immortal completeness of his gesture, like Don Quixote, King Lear, or Odysseus. The material is more brittle, the vision not of that radiant clarity that produces characters molded in the purest, strongest light, like Homer's Achilles or Nausicaa, or in delicate twilight, like Mignon or Ottilie. In Balzac everything is interwoven, one thing conditions the other. It would be as impossible to isolate the single detail from his work as it would from a picture by Rembrandt or Delacroix. Here as there the grandiose consists of a stupendous wealth of color value which up and down, *infinitis modis*, like Nature herself, produces an unbroken scale. Those figures appear as freely moving deities: how they may have come into existence is an inscrutable secret. Balzac's, on the other hand, are single notes in a titanic symphony. Their springing into existence seems to us more comprehensible; we believe we carry in our blood the elements out of which their sinister hearts are formed, and we believe we inhale them with the air of the great cities. Yet here also a last, higher truth pervades everything. Just as the scale from darkness to brightness in a painting by Rembrandt resembles the earthly light and earthly darkness only by being unbroken, convincing, and absolutely right, so there vibrates here, in the myriads of small features wherewith a teeming world is described, a barely definable ultimate truth. The plasticity of this world borders on the too weighty, its gloom on nihilism, the worldliness of its treatment on the cynical. But the colors with which they are painted are pure. A choir of angels by Fra Angelico is not painted with a cleaner brush than the characters in *La Cousine Bette*. To these colors, the truly fundamental elements of the soul, clings nothing dull, nothing sickly, nothing blasphemous, nothing base. They are imperishable; they cannot be harmed by any evil breath. Through them vibrates an absolute joyfulness that is untouched by the gloom of its theme, as the divine joyousness of the sounds in a symphony by Beethoven can at no moment be perturbed by the fearful nature of its musical expression.

SEBASTIAN MELMOTH

THIS NAME was the mask behind which Oscar Wilde concealed his face, ravaged by gaol and the signs of approaching death, so as to live out a few more years of his life in the dark. It was the fate of this man to bear three successive names: Oscar Wilde, C_{33}, Sebastian Melmoth. The sound of the first suggests only splendor, pride, seduction. The second sounds terrifying, one of these marks which society brands with a fiery iron into the naked human shoulder. The third is the name of a ghost, a half-forgotten Balzacian character. Three masks, one after the other: the first with a fine brow, sensual lips, moist, magnificent, impudent eyes—a mask of Bacchus; the second a mask of iron with eyeholes through which gazes despair; the third a wretched costumier's domino hired to conceal a slow death from the eyes of mankind. Oscar Wilde glittered, enchanted, offended, seduced, betrayed and was betrayed, stabbed others' hearts and was himself stabbed in the heart. Oscar Wilde wrote his reflections upon *The Decay of Lying*, wrote *Lady Windermere's Fan* and *Salomé*. C_{33} suffered. C_{33} wrote *The Ballad of Reading Gaol* and that letter from Reading Gaol entitled *De Profundis*. Sebastian Melmoth wrote no more, dragged himself through the streets of Paris, died, and was buried.

And today Sebastian Melmoth, behind whose coffin five people walked, is exceedingly famous. Today all that he experienced, perpetrated, and endured is on everyone's lips. Today everyone knows that he sat in a kind of rabbit hutch and with his fine fingers bleeding had to produce oakum by picking old ropes to pieces. Everyone knows the story of the foul bath he had to climb into, the dirty water into which the convicts had to climb one after the other, Oscar Wilde the last of all since he was the last in line. "Oscar Wilde," a man muttered behind him as they were being led round the prison yard, "I realize that you must suffer more than any of us." Even these words, muttered through the motionless lips of some convict, are very famous today. They form a detail of a legend that is full of wonder, as something wonderful invariably appears when life takes the trouble to treat fate poetically.

But people say, "What a transformation!" They say, "Oscar Wilde of the earlier phase, and Oscar Wilde of the later." They talk of an aesthete transformed into a new man, a believer, almost a saint. They have developed the habit of saying certain things about certain romanticists, and such things are too easily repeated. They should not be repeated. Firstly, because they were very likely incorrect in the first place; and secondly, because times change and it is senseless to pretend that things repeat themselves while in reality new, infinitely differentiated, infinitely surprising things are constantly rising to the surface. There's no point in trying to make out that Oscar Wilde's fate and Oscar Wilde's character were two different entities and that Fate had attacked him as a snarling mongrel attacks a harmless peasant child carrying a basket of eggs on its head. We should not always talk and think in clichés.

Oscar Wilde's character and Oscar Wilde's fate are one and the same. He walked towards his catastrophe with the same steps as Oedipus, the seeing-blind one. The aesthete was tragic. The dandy was tragic. He raised his hands in the air and drew the lightning towards him. People say, "He was an aesthete, and suddenly unfortunate entanglements overwhelmed him, a snare of unfortunate entanglements." We should not blanket everything with words. An aesthete! This signifies nothing. Walter Pater was an aesthete, a man who lived by the enjoyment and the re-creation of beauty, and towards life his attitude was one of reserve and reverence, full of propriety. An aesthete is, by nature, steeped in propriety. Oscar Wilde, however, was a figure of impropriety, tragic impropriety. His aestheticism had a convulsive quality. The jewels among which he professed voluptuously to delve were like death-dimmed eyes, petrified because they could not bear the sight of life. Incessantly he felt the threat of life directed towards him. He was forever surrounded by a tragic air of horror. He kept challenging life unceasingly. He insulted reality. And he sensed life lying in wait in order to spring upon him out of the darkness.

People say, "Wilde spoke in witty paradoxes while duchesses hung on his lips, while his fingers plucked an orchid to pieces and his feet lay among cushions of ancient Chinese silk; but then misfortune descended upon him and he was pushed into the bath ten convicts had used before him." Yet it is false to talk of life in such trite terms, wrong to drag everything down to the level of a case of disaster. The marvelously polished words, the sentences—their cynicism near to torture, their worldliness to vertigo—which fell from these beautifully curved, seductive, impudent lips were actually not meant for the ear of the lovely duchesses, but for the ear of an Invisible Listener who lured him with horror, like the Sphinx of whom he thought endlessly while all the time denying her, and whose name "Reality" passed his lips merely in order that he might jeer at and humiliate it. And his limbs which toyed with orchids and lounged among cushions of ancient silks were in reality filled with an awful longing for the ghastly bath from which, however, at its first touch, they shrank in nauseated repugnance.

This is why it must have been deeply moving to have seen Oscar Wilde at one moment of his life. I mean the moment when he (over whom no one but his fate had any power)—against the pleading of his friends and almost to the horror of his enemies—turned and denounced Queensberry. For then the mask of Bacchus with its full, beautifully curved lips must have been transformed in an unforgettable manner into the mask of the seeing-blind Oedipus or the raging Ajax. At that moment he must have worn round his magnificent brow the band of tragic fate, so rarely visible.

We must not make life more banal than it is, nor turn our eyes away so as not to behold this band when for once it can be seen on a brow.

We must not degrade life by tearing character and fate asunder and separating his misfortune from his fortune. We must not pigeonhole everything. Everything is everywhere. There are tragic elements in superficial things and trivial in the tragic. There is something suffocatingly sinister in what we call pleasure. There is something lyrical about the dress of a whore and something commonplace about the emotions of a lyric poet. Everything dwells simultaneously in man. He is full of poisons that rage against one another. There are certain islands whose savage inhabitants pierce the bodies of their dead relatives with poisoned arrows, to make sure that they are dead. This is an ingenious way of expressing metaphorically a profound thought and of paying homage to the profundity of Nature without much ado. For in truth the slowly killing poisons and the elixir of gently smoldering bliss all lie side by side in our living body. No one thing can be excluded, none considered too insignificant to become a very great power. Seen from the viewpoint of life, there is not one thing extraneous to the Whole. Everything is everywhere. Everything partakes of the dance of life.

In the words of Jalal-ud-din Rumi, "He who knows the power of the dance of life fears not death. For he knows that love kills."

FROM THE *BOOK OF FRIENDS*

Man perceives in the world only what already lies within him; but to perceive what lies within him man needs the world; for this, however, activity and suffering are indispensable.

The young suffer their powerful impressions, the mature produce them.

To approve is more difficult than to admire.

While growing older we recognize that throughout all the vicissitudes of life we are not free of guilt; but in each of us there dwells our own form of innocence, which is what sustains us without our knowing how.

Egotism offends not so much by deeds as by lack of understanding.

Apropos the notion "Experience," there exist two irritating kinds of people: those who lack experience and those who pride themselves too much on their experience.

Allegory is a great medium which should not be despised. What friends really mean to one another can be demonstrated better by the exchange of a magic ring or a horn than by psychology.

Who observes manners in social intercourse lives off his interest; who disregards them breaks into his capital.

There are no two people on this earth who could not be turned into deadly enemies by a devilishly contrived indiscretion.

Children are entertaining because they are easily entertained.

Under certain circumstances a woman will tolerate a man's conversation about his love for another woman, but the whole emphasis must lie on love, not on the object of that love.

Manners rest on a twofold assumption: to show the other every attention yet not to intrude upon him.

Where is your Self to be found? Always in the deepest enchantment that you have experienced.

Those who feel little coherence in themselves talk about the adherence to ideas, but ideas are nothing to which one can adhere; they are something transcendent which reveals itself to us in sublime moments and then vanishes again.

In the present which surrounds us there are no fewer fictitious elements than in the past, whose reflection we call history. Only by interpreting one fictitious element through the other does something worthwhile develop.

When I think of myself and anything else at the same time—be it only the map of Greece—then I look into myself as through a window.

Powerful imaginations are conservative.

To grow more mature is to separate more distinctly, to connect more closely.

The past has been incorporated into our memory so that we shall overestimate it.

The most dangerous form of stupidity is a sharp intellect.

Depth must be hidden. Where? On the surface.

Fiery air amidst burning logs looks like crystal-clear moving water.

There is more freedom within the narrowest limits, within the most specialized task, than in the limitless vacuum which the modern mind imagines to be the playground for it.

At every moment of the present there is always a hidden element whose emergence could alter everything: this is a dizzy-making thought, but one which gives us comfort.

Nations speak such different languages that they can neither offend nor do justice to one another.

Minor intellects—the so-called brilliant ones—stir up, but do not dominate, the ideas of their time.

An author, whether he wishes it or not, is always at war with the age he lives in. He experiences every resistance of the epoch, but during his lifetime he will never learn whether the weights that threatened to smother him were made of iron or paper.

The famous author lives merely in a different form of obscurity from the author of whom no one speaks.

What the inferior writer knows least how to appreciate in the superior—because he is not aware of it, indeed, cannot even divine it—is perseverance: the real tenacious drive.

Every spoken word presupposes a listener, every written word a reader; to create its audience is the hidden but more important aspect of literary achievement.

The average raconteur relates how something might occur. The good raconteur makes something occur before our eyes as though it were occurring. The master raconteur relates his story as though something which occurred long ago were occurring again.

Good taste is the ability continuously to counteract exaggeration.

The worst style develops when a man imitates something while pretending to feel superior to the object of his imitation.

To youth the so-called Interesting is remarkable, to a more mature age the Good.

The purest poesy is a state of being completely out of one's own Self, the most perfect prose a complete returning to one's own Self. The latter is perhaps even rarer than the former.

In a work of art of a higher order, as much as in an organic formation, it is not the isolated form which is so magical, but the emergence of one form from another.

LIBRETTI

THE CAVALIER OF THE ROSE

A Comedy for Music in Three Acts

CHARACTERS

Maria Theresa, *the Princess of Werdenberg, known as the*
   Marschallin after her husband's military title of Field Marshal
Octavian, *nicknamed Quinquin, a young gentleman of noble family*
Baron Ochs of Lerchanau, *her distant cousin*
Valzacchi, *an Italian intriguer*
Annina, *his companion*
Major-Domo of the Princess
A Noble Widow
Her Three Noble Daughters
A Singer
A Flautist
A Notary
His Clerk
A Hairdresser
His Apprentice
A Milliner
An Animal Seller
A Scholar
A Little Blackamoor
Footmen and servants

The place: Vienna.
The time: The first decade in the reign of Maria Theresa.

Act I

The Princess's bedroom. Left, in the alcove, the great tent-shaped four-poster. Near the bed a three-leaved Chinese folding screen, with clothes lying about behind it. Further away from it, an occasional table and a few chairs. On a chaise longue left lies a sword in its scabbard. Right, big double doors into the antechamber. Center, barely visible, is a small door let into the wall. Otherwise no doors. Between the alcove and the small door stand a dressing table and a few chairs against the wall. The bed curtains are drawn back.

Octavian is kneeling on a footstool before the bed, left, with his arm half round the Princess, who is lying in bed. Her face cannot be seen, only her very beautiful hand and her arm with the lace sleeve falling from it.

OCTAVIAN

What you were! What you are!
No one can know, no one can guess!

PRINCESS

sitting up among the cushions

Is that a complaint? Would my Quinquin
prefer that many knew it?

OCTAVIAN

Sweetheart, no, blessed am I
to be the only one that knows what you are.
No one can guess! No one can know!
You, you—what does the "you" mean, what "you and I"?
Has it a meaning?
Words, just words, isn't that all it is? Tell me!
And yet, and yet—there's something in them,
a swaying, a tugging, a squeezing, a yearning,
as my hand now moves to yours,
the will to be near you, to enfold you,

this is what "I" am and it wants you near,
but the "I" dissolves in the "you,"
I am your boy—but when my senses are reeling,
then where is your boy?

PRINCESS *softly*

You are my boy, you are my treasure!

OCTAVIAN

Why is it day? I don't want the day!
What is day for? Then you belong to everyone.

The Princess laughs softly.

OCTAVIAN

Are you laughing at me?

PRINCESS *affectionately*

Am I laughing at you?

OCTAVIAN

Sweetheart.

PRINCESS

Treasure, you, my treasure child.

A soft tinkle of bells

Listen.

OCTAVIAN

I don't want to.

PRINCESS

Quiet, pay attention.

OCTAVIAN

I don't want to hear *anything*! What could it be?

The tinkling comes nearer.

Footmen perhaps, with letters and cards
from Saurau, or Hartig, or the Portuguese envoy.
But I'll let nobody in here. Here I am master.

*The small door in the center opens and a tiny Blackamoor in
yellow, hung with silver bells, carrying a tray with the chocolate,
trips over the threshold.*

PRINCESS

Quick, there—hide there. It's the breakfast.

*Octavian slips behind the nearer leaf of the screen. The door is
shut behind the Blackamoor by invisible hands.*

PRINCESS

For heaven's sake, throw your sword behind the bed!

*Octavian dashes for his sword and hides it. The Princess lies back
after pulling the bed curtains to. The little Blackamoor puts the tray
on the small table, pushes this forward, moves the left-hand sofa
nearer it, bows deeply to the bed, his little arms crossed over his breast.
Then he dances daintily backwards, his face turned always towards
the bed. At the door he bows once more and vanishes.*

*The Princess comes out between the bed curtains.
She has put on a light, fur-bordered wrap.*

Octavian comes out from between the wall and the screen.

PRINCESS

Madcap, careless boy!
Leaves his sword lying about in a lady's bedroom?
Don't you know any better manners?

OCTAVIAN

If my behavior is beginning to offend you,
if it irks you to find me so unpracticed in such matters,
then I really don't know what you see in me at all.

PRINCESS *affectionately, on the sofa*

Let my lord and treasure stop philosophizing and come here.
There's a time for everything, and now it's breakfast.

OCTAVIAN

sits down next to her. They breakfast very affectionately.
Octavian lays his face on her knee. She strokes his hair.
He looks up into her face. Softly

Marie Thérèse.

PRINCESS

Octavian.

OCTAVIAN

Bichette.

PRINCESS

Quinquin.

OCTAVIAN

Treasure!

PRINCESS

Darling boy!

They continue breakfast.

OCTAVIAN *gaily*

The Field Marshal's stuck in the Croatian forest hunting bear
and lynx.
And I, a mere youngster, I stick here, and what do I hunt?
Oh, I can't believe my luck, my luck!

PRINCESS

as a shadow crosses her face

Leave the Field Marshal in peace.

I dreamt of him last night.

OCTAVIAN
Last night you dreamt of him? Last night?

PRINCESS
I'm not responsible for my dreams.

OCTAVIAN
Last night you dreamt about your husband?

PRINCESS
Don't make such big eyes at me, I can't help it. All at once there
  he was, at home again.

OCTAVIAN
The Field Marshal?

PRINCESS
There was a clatter down in the yard, horses and people, and
  there he was.
Suddenly I woke up in a fright—why, just look at me,
look how silly I am—I can still hear the bustle in the yard,
I can't get it out of my ears. Don't you hear something too?

OCTAVIAN
Yes, of course I hear something, but why must it be your
  husband?
Think where he now is—in the Raitzenland, beyond Esseg.

PRINCESS
That's really a long way, is it?
Good, then it must be something else. All is well.

OCTAVIAN
You're looking so worried, Thérèse.

PRINCESS

Well, you know, Quinquin—even if it is a long way—
the Field Marshal's so quick. Once—

OCTAVIAN *jealously*

What happened once?

The Princess listens distractedly.

OCTAVIAN *jealously*

What happened once? Bichette?
Bichette! What happened once?

PRINCESS

Oh, be a dear boy now, you don't have to know everything.

OCTAVIAN

throws himself onto the sofa

Look how she treats me! Oh I'm a miserable creature!

PRINCESS *listening*

Don't be difficult now. Now it's serious—it *is* the Field Marshal.
If it were a stranger, the noise would be over there, in my
    antechamber.
It must be my husband, trying to come in through the dressing
    room
and arguing with the footmen.
Quinquin, it's my husband!

Octavian makes a dash for his sword and runs right.

PRINCESS

Not there, that's the antechamber.
That's where the tradespeople are waiting and half a dozen
    footmen.
There, that way!

Octavian runs across to the small door.

PRINCESS

Too late. They're in the dressing room already.
There's only one thing for it. Hide! There!

OCTAVIAN

I'll bar his way! I'm staying with you!

PRINCESS

There behind the bed! There among the curtains! And don't
  stir!

OCTAVIAN *hesitating*

If he catches me there, what'll become of you, Thérèse?

PRINCESS *pleading*

Hide, hide, treasure.

OCTAVIAN *by the screen*

Thérèse!

PRINCESS *stamping impatiently*

Quiet, I said!

With flashing eyes

                          I should like to see them try!
Let anyone just try to get through with me standing here.
I'm not a Neapolitan general—where I stand, I stand.

Goes resolutely up to the small door and listens.

Splendid fellows, my footmen, won't let him in,
telling him I'm asleep. Splendid fellows!
That voice?
Why, that isn't the Field Marshal's voice!
They're calling him "Your Lordship." It's a stranger.
Quinquin, it's a caller.

She laughs.

Quick, get into your clothes,
but keep hidden,
don't let the footmen see you.
That loud, stupid voice—I ought to know that.
Who can it be? Oh heavens, it's Ochs.
It's my cousin, Lerchenau, Ochs of Lerchenau.
What can he want? Oh my goodness!

She cannot help laughing.

Quinquin, do you hear, Quinquin, don't you remember?

She goes a few steps over to the left.

Five or six days ago—the letter—
we were sitting in the carriage
and they brought me a letter to the carriage door.
That was the letter from Ochs.
And I have no notion what was in it.

Laughs.

You know who's to blame for that, Quinquin.

VOICE OF MAJOR-DOMO *outside*
May it please your Lordship to wait in the gallery!

VOICE OF THE BARON *outside*
Where did the fellow learn his manners?
Baron Lerchenau don't kick his heels in an anteroom.

PRINCESS
Quinquin, what are you up to? Where've you got to?

*Octavian, in a woman's skirt and bodice, his hair done up
in a handkerchief and ribbon like a mobcap, comes forward
and curtsies, speaking like a country girl.*

OCTAVIAN

Please your Highness, not been long in your Highness's service.

PRINCESS

You darling boy.
And I can't give you more than just a peck.

Kisses him quickly.

He's breaking my door down, my lord cousin.
But you, go on, be off with you!
Slip boldly out through the footmen.
You're a clever rascal. And mind you come back, treasure,
but in man's clothes and through the front door, if you please.

Sits down, her back to the little door, and begins to sip her chocolate.

Octavian goes quickly towards the little door and tries to get out. At the same moment the door is wrenched open and Baron Ochs forces his way past the footmen who are trying to hold him back. Octavian, as he is trying to make his escape with lowered head, collides with him. Octavian presses himself back coyly against the wall to the left of the door. Three footmen who have been swept in with the Baron stand uncertain what to do.

BARON

with hauteur to the footmen

No question that her Highness'll receive me.

He comes forward, while the footmen on his left try to bar his way. To Octavian, with interest.

Your pardon, my pretty child!

Octavian turns coyly against the wall.

BARON

with graciousness and condescension

I said, "Your pardon, my pretty child!"

The Princess looks over her shoulder, then stands up,
and comes to meet the Baron.

BARON

with gallantry to Octavian

Haven't really hurt you, my dear, have I?

THE FOOTMEN *pulling at his clothing*
Her serene Highness!

The Baron makes a French bow with two repeats.

PRINCESS

How well your Lordship looks.

BARON

bows again, then to the footmen

Now d'you see how charmed her Highness is to see me?

Advances towards the Princess with cavalier nonchalance,
offers her his hand, and leads her forward.

And why shouldn't your Highness be charmed?
What's an early call among people of rank?
Why, I remember Princess Brioche now,
called on her day after day to pay my compliments
while she was in her bath,
with nothin' but a little screen between her and me.
I must say I'm astonished

Looking round angrily.

that your Highness's fellows—

PRINCESS

Forgive us,

they did but do as they were told,
I had a bad headache this morning.

> *At the Princess's nod the footmen have brought forward*
> *a small sofa and an armchair, and gone off.*

> *The Baron keeps looking over his shoulder.*

> *Octavian, having sidled along the wall towards the alcove, tries*
> *to busy himself as inconspicuously as possible about the bed.*

> *The Princess sits down on the sofa, after offering the Baron the armchair.*

BARON

> *tries to sit down, his attention wholly taken up with*
> *the pretty chambermaid. To himself.*

A pretty child! A precious little morsel!

PRINCESS

> *standing up and once more, with ceremony, offering him a seat*

I pray your Lordship.

> *The Baron sits down reluctantly and tries not to turn*
> *his back completely on the pretty maid.*

PRINCESS

I'm still not quite recovered.
So my cousin will perhaps have the indulgence to—

BARON

Of course.

> *He turns round to look at Octavian.*

PRINCESS

My chambermaid, a young thing from the country,
I'm afraid your Lordship finds her a nuisance.

BARON

Quite delightful! What? Oh, not the least little bit. Me? On
the contrary!

He beckons to Octavian with his hand, then turns to the Princess.

Your Highness will be surprised perhaps
that a betrothed man

Looking around.

should nonetheless—in the meantime—

PRINCESS

A betrothed man?

BARON

As to which your Highness, of course, will be sufficiently
informed from my letter—
Delicious little creature! Can't be fifteen!

PRINCESS

The letter, of course, yes, the letter, now who is it then,
who's the lucky girl?
I have the name on the tip of my tongue.

BARON

What?

Over his shoulder.

Fresh as a kitten! Washed and bloomin'! Delightful!

PRINCESS

Who is she, just remind me, your lady bride?

BARON

The young Miss Faninal. I made no secret of the name to
your Highness.

PRINCESS

Of course. Where's my memory? Only, the family—not local
  people, are they?

*Octavian busies himself with the tray, thus getting still
more behind the Baron's back.*

BARON

Yes, local people indeed, your Highness.
One ennobled by her Majesty's gracious favor.
He has the contract for supplyin' the army in the Netherlands.

*The Princess impatiently signals with her eyes to
Octavian to remove himself.*

BARON

completely misunderstanding her look

I see your Highness knittin' her lovely brows at the misalliance.
But let me say, the girl's as pretty as an angel.
Fresh from the convent. She's an only child.
The father owns twelve houses in the Wieden,
as well as his town house on the Platz am Hof,
and his health is said to be not all that good.

PRINCESS

My dear cousin, I understand very well what quarter the
  wind is in.

Nods to Octavian to remove himself.

BARON

And if your Highness will graciously permit the expression, of
  good noble blood I have enough, I think, for two in my veins.
A man is what he's born, *corpo di Bacco!*
My lady wife shall have the precedence where her rank entitles
  her,
we'll see to that, and as for the children,

if there's any reluctance to allow them
the golden key—*va bene!*
They'll content themselves with the twelve iron keys
to the twelve houses in the Wieden.

PRINCESS

Indeed, yes, my cousin's children, I feel sure,
will not go tilting at windmills.

Octavian tries to back across towards the door with the tray.

BARON

Why such a hurry with the chocolate?
There now, easy does it!

Octavian stands uncertainly, turning away his face.

PRINCESS

Go on, be off with you!

BARON

If I confess to your Highness
that I've hardly tasted a morsel of breakfast.

PRINCESS *resigned*

Here then, Mariandel. Serve his lordship.

Octavian comes and offers the tray.

BARON

taking a cup and helping himself to chocolate

Hardly a morsel, your Highness. Sittin' up in the coach since
   five o'clock this mornin'.

Softly

Really delicious creature. Stay here, my love. I've got somethin'
   to tell you.

My whole domestic staff, grooms, attendants, the whole lot—

He eats noisily.

all down in the courtyard here, complete with my almoner—

PRINCESS *to Octavian*
Go now.

BARON
Just another biscuit? Stay a moment!

Softly

You're a sweet little creature, you're a precious thing!

To the Princess.

—are on the way to the "White Horse," that's where we're
puttin' up, till the day after tomorrow, that is.

Half-aloud

I'd give a lot just for a little tête-à-tête—

To the Princess, very loud

—the day after tomorrow—

Quickly to Octavian

—somewhere with you, just the two of us.

Princess cannot help laughing at Octavian's impudent impersonation.

BARON
Then we move to Faninal's.
Of course I must first send my best man—

Angrily over his shoulder

can't you just wait?—
to announce me to the lady bride

and present her with the silver rose
as is customary among the high nobility.

PRINCESS

And which of our relations has your Lordship chosen
to perform this office?

BARON

The desire to seek your Highness's advice
has emboldened me to present myself thus attired at your
   Highness's levee.

PRINCESS

My advice?

BARON

As solicited, with all respect, in my humble missive.
I have surely not had the infelicity with my poor supplication
to arouse your Highness's displeasure?

Leaning back.

You could turn me round your little finger,
and well you know it!

PRINCESS

Why, of course, a best man
for your Lordship's first visit to the bride,
one of our relations—now whom could we—I'll—
Cousin Jörger? Or let me see—Cousin Lamberg?

BARON

I leave it in your Highness's most lovely hands.

PRINCESS

Very well. Will you dine with me, cousin?
Tomorrow, shall we say? By then I shall have a name to suggest.

BARON

Your Highness is condescension itself.

PRINCESS *trying to get up*

Meanwhile—

BARON *half-aloud, to Octavian*

Mind you come back to me! I shan't go until you do.

PRINCESS *to herself*

Oho!

Aloud, to Octavian

Stay a moment!

To the Baron

Can I now be of any further service
to my cousin?

BARON

I am almost ashamed to trouble your Highness—
a recommendation to your Highness's notary—
it's a matter of the marriage contract.

PRINCESS

My notary often comes in the mornings. Go and see, Mariandel,
if he's not waiting in the antechamber.

BARON

Why send the girl?
Your Highness deprives herself of service
for my sake.

Holds Octavian back.

PRINCESS

Let her be, cousin, she can perfectly well go.

BARON

That I cannot allow. Stay here at her Highness's nod.
There'll soon be one of the footmen comin' in—
'pon my word, I'll not let this little pearl
be cast among the swinish herd of flunkies.

Strokes her.

PRINCESS

Your Lordship shows too much concern.

The Major-Domo enters.

BARON

There, didn't I say so?
He's come to report to your Highness.

PRINCESS *to the Major-Domo*

Struhan, is my notary waiting in the antechamber?

MAJOR-DOMO

Your Highness's notary awaits your Highness,
the steward too, then your Highness's chef,
then too, sent by his Excellency Count Silva,
a singer with a flautist.
Otherwise the usual riffraff.

BARON

*has pushed his chair behind the Major-Domo's broad back and
is tenderly pressing the supposed maid's hand*

Ever had dinner alone
with a man of the world
in a private room?

Octavian pretends to be very embarrassed.

BARON

No? You'd be surprised! Like to try?

OCTAVIAN *softly, shamefacedly*

Oh I'm sure I don't know if I ought.

The Princess, inattentively listening to the Major-Domo, notices the two and cannot help laughing softly.

The Major-Domo bows and steps back, giving the Princess an unobstructed view of the tableau.

PRINCESS *to the Major-Domo*

Ask them to wait.

The Major-Domo goes off.

The Baron sits back in his seat as unconcernedly as he can manage and assumes a ponderous expression.

PRINCESS *laughing*

I see my cousin doesn't waste his chances.

BARON *relieved*

With your Highness I see one can be quite open.
No shifts and evasions, no false proprieties,
no standing on ceremony.

He kisses the Princess's hand.

PRINCESS *amused*

But, as an engaged man?

BARON

half standing up, coming close to her

Does that make a lame duck out of me?
Should I not rather be like a good hound on a trail,
double keen to sniff out every bit of game?

PRINCESS

I see your Lordship makes a profession of it.

BARON *standing up*

I should think I do.
Like to see anythin' which'd suit me better.
Must say I'm sorry for your Highness
that your Highness—how shall I say?—
has experience only in defense.
Parole d'honneur! There's nothin' like the attackin' side.

PRINCESS *laughing*

I can well believe it has many attractions.

BARON

There's not a season of the year, not an hour of the day—

PRINCESS

Not one?

BARON

Which isn't—

PRINCESS

Which isn't?

BARON

Right for coaxing some small favor
out of the boy Cupid.
A man's not a stag or a capercaillie
held at the mercy of the seasons
but a lord of creation free of the calendar.
May, for instance, is a good month for the love game
as every child knows,
but I say:
June, July, August are better still.
Those are the nights!
Up in our country then there's an influx
of young girls over from Bohemia—
they come for the harvest and are otherwise good and biddable.

I often keep two or three of them for myself
in the house till November.
Then, and not before, I send them home.
And what a mixture they make,
the round young Bohemian maids,
sweet and heavy on the palate,
with those of our own sort, the German strain,
dry and sharp-tastin' as a mountain wine.
And what a mixture they make all together!
And everywhere there's watchin' and lyin' in wait
and slippin' through the palin's,
creepin' to one another and lyin' around together,
and everywhere there's singin'
and swayin' of hips
and milkin'
and mowin'
and dabblin' and splashin' in brook and horse pond.

PRINCESS

And my cousin lets nothing escape him?

BARON

Could I but be as blessèd Jupiter
in a thousand shapes,
I'd have a use for every one.

PRINCESS

What, even the bull? Would you be as rough as that?

BARON

All accordin'! Accordin' to the case.
There are as many ways to a woman's favor
as there are women.
I know how to take them each one as she wants.
There's the little waif
stands there as if she couldn't count up to five

and yet when it comes to the point, upon my word
she's all there, I can tell you.
And then there's the one that loses her head
with giggles and sobs—she's a particular favorite.
Or at the other extreme the one
in whose eye sits a cold, hard devil,
but even for her there comes the moment when that eye melts.
And when that same devil inside her lets it be known
that the hour of reckonin' has struck,
like a fish gaffed and landed,
if I may so put it, that's a game worth the candle—
can't have too much of that.

PRINCESS

A devil, my word, that's yourself!

BARON

And is there some poor Cinderella, savin' your presence,
for whom no one has a glance,
sloppin' about in a dirty smock, savin' your presence,
squattin' in the ashes behind the kitchen range,
even she, even she taken at the right moment,
even she has everythin' that's needed.
That look of astonishment! Can't understand what's
    happenin'!
And terror! And last of all such overpowerin' bliss
that the master himself
should graciously stoop to her lowliness.

PRINCESS

My cousin knows his business, that I can see.

BARON

Then there are those who want you to creep up on them
soft as the wind caressin' the fresh-mown hay.
Others again you have to stalk from behind like a lynx,

catch hold of the milkin' stool and tip them over
headlong—first makin' sure there's some hay nearby.

PRINCESS

No! You're altogether too expert.
Be my good cousin and leave this child alone.

BARON *back on his dignity*

Let your Highness but give me the little creature
to wait upon my future wife.

PRINCESS

What, my little girl here? What should she do?
The lady bride must be well provided already
and not dependent on your Lordship's selection.

BARON

That's a fine piece of goods, Goddamn it!
There's a drop of the best blood there all right.

PRINCESS

Your Lordship has a keen eye.

BARON

It's only fittin'.

Confidentially

See nothin' wrong in people of quality being thus waited on
    by noble blood,
I've a child of my own pleasure here with me.

PRINCESS

What? Not a girl? I sincerely hope not!

BARON

No, a son: has the lineaments of a Lerchenau in his face.

Keep him as a valet.
When your Highness shall please to order me
to place the silver rose in your hands,
he it will be who brings it.

PRINCESS

It will be a pleasure. But wait a moment. Mariandel!

BARON

Let your Highness give me the maid. I won't let go.

PRINCESS

Oh dear. Mariandel, go and get that miniature.

OCTAVIAN *softly*

Thérèse, Thérèse, take care.

PRINCESS *softly*

Go on, bring it. I know what I'm doing.

BARON

gazing after Octavian

Could be a young princess.
It's my intention to present my bride
with a true copy of my family tree
together with a lock of the first Lerchenau's hair—
he was a great founder of monasteries
and chief steward of the imperial domains in Carinthia
and the Wendish March.

Octavian brings the miniature.

PRINCESS

Will your Lordship have the young gentleman there as
best man?

BARON

At your Highness's recommendation, unseen—no need
to look.

PRINCESS

My young cousin, Count Octavian.

BARON

Octavian—

PRINCESS

Rofrano, second brother of the Marquess.

BARON

Could wish for no one of better quality.
Should be exceedingly obliged to his young Lordship.

PRINCESS

Look at him.

Holds out the miniature to him.

BARON

looking alternately at the miniature and the maid

The likeness!

PRINCESS

Is it not?

BARON

Feature for feature.

PRINCESS

I have often had my thoughts about it.

BARON

Rofrano! One is somebody, comin' from such a house, even if only by the servants' entrance.

PRINCESS

That's why I keep her as something extra special.

BARON

It's only fittin'.

PRINCESS

Always about my person.

BARON

Quite right.

PRINCESS

But now go, Mariandel, be off with you.

BARON

How so? She'll be comin' back?

PRINCESS *ignoring his remark*

And let the people in from the antechamber.

Octavian goes towards the double doors, right.

BARON *after him*

My lovely child!

OCTAVIAN *at the door, right*

You may go in.

Runs to the other door.

BARON *after him*

Your humble servant! Grant me a moment's audience.

OCTAVIAN

shutting the small door in his face

Be back soon.

At the same instant an elderly chambermaid comes in through the same door. The Baron retires disappointed. Two Footmen come in from the right and bring a screen out from the alcove. The Princess goes behind the screen, accompanied by the chambermaid. The dressing table is pushed forward into the center. Footmen open the double doors right. There enter: the Notary, the Chef, followed by a scullion carrying the menu book; then the Modiste, a Scholar with a folio, and the Animal Dealer with several minute dogs and a little monkey. Valzacchi and Annina, gliding swiftly behind these, take up the front place left. The Noble Mother with her Three Daughters, all in mourning, take up their position on the right. The Major-Domo leads the Tenor and the Flautist to the front. The Baron, towards the back, beckons a Footman to him and gives him an order, signaling: "Here, through the back door."

THE THREE NOBLE DAUGHTERS

kneeling down

Three poor but noble orphans
implore your Highness's aid.

MODISTE

Le chapeau Paméla. La poudre à la reine de Golconde.

ANIMAL DEALER

Monkeys, your Highness, all mischief and slyness!
Birds of Africa too, in every hue.

THE THREE ORPHANS

Our father on the field of honor
gave his young life, his daughters three
have but one wish, to do the same.

MODISTE

Le chapeau Paméla! C'est la merveille du monde!

ANIMAL DEALER

Parrots gay in every hue
from Africa and India too.
Lapdogs so small,
housebroken one and all.

> *The Princess steps forward and everyone bows or curtsies deeply.*

> *The Baron has come forward left.*

PRINCESS

May I present the Notary to your Lordship?

> *With a bow to the dressing table, where the Princess has seated
> herself, the Notary approaches the Baron, left. The Princess beckons
> the youngest of the Three Orphans to herself, takes a purse handed her
> by the Major-Domo, and gives it to the girl with a kiss on the fore-
> head. The Scholar is about to step forward and present his folio when
> Valzacchi bounds forward and pushes him to one side.*

VALZACCHI

> *producing a black-bordered newspaper*

The Black Gazette, serene Highness!
All secret news printed here!
Only for high-placed personage!
Corpse found in back room
of noble count's town house.
Citizen's wife and her lover
poison the husband—
last night at three A.M.

PRINCESS

Don't bother me with this tattle!

VALZACCHI

Your pardon!
Tutte quante confidences
from high society!

PRINCESS

I won't hear a word of it!

Valzacchi with a regretful bow jumps back.

*The Three Orphans, with their Mother bringing up the rear, have
kissed the Princess's hand.*

THE THREE ORPHANS

in marching order for departure

May Providence upon your Highness all its wealth and blessings
show'r!
In our hearts your Highness's bounty be remember'd every
hour.

They go off with their Mother.

*The Hairdresser moves up hastily, his Apprentice dashing after him
with flying coattails. The Hairdresser scrutinizes the Princess, then
puts on a gloomy expression as he takes a step backwards to study
her appearance on this particular day. The Apprentice meanwhile
unpacks, laying the things out on the dressing table. The Hairdresser
pushes some of the people back to give himself room for maneuver.
After brief consideration his plan is formed, he throws himself with
determination upon the Princess, and begins to dress her hair. A Foot-
man in pink, black, and silver approaches, bringing a note. The
Major-Domo is quickly on the spot with a silver salver on which he
presents the note to the Princess. The Hairdresser breaks off, to let
her read it. The Apprentice hands him a fresh curling iron. The
Hairdresser brandishes it. It is too hot. The Apprentice, after a
questioning look at the Princess, who nods, hands him the note,*

*which he smilingly uses to cool his iron. At the same time the Singer
has taken up his position, holding a sheet of music before him. The
Flautist reads his accompaniment over his shoulder.*

*Three Footmen have taken up position right front, while others
stand in the background.*

SINGER

Di rigori armato il seno
Contro amor mi ribellai,
Ma fui vinto in un baleno
In mirar due vaghi rai.
Ahi! che resiste puoco
Cor di gelo a stral di fuoco.

*The Hairdresser hands the iron to his Apprentice and applauds
the Singer. Then he continues his arrangement of the curls.*

*A servant has meanwhile admitted through the small door the Baron's
valet, almoner, and body servant. They are three dubious-looking
figures. The valet is a tall young lout, both stupid and impudent. He
carries under his arm a red morocco casket. The almoner is a village
curate run wild, a four-foot-high but strong and insolent-looking
gnome. The body servant, before he was stuck into ill-fitting livery,
no doubt carted dung. The almoner and the valet seem to be
quarreling about the precedence and treading on one another's toes.
They make a course along the left-hand side of the stage towards
their master and take their stand near him.*

BARON

seated, to the Notary, who stands before him taking his instructions

As bride-price—entirely separate, however,
and before the dowry—you take my meanin', Mr. Notary?—
the house and estate of Gaunersdorf returns to me,
free of encumbrances and with undiminished privileges
as they were by my late father possessed.

NOTARY *short of breath*

If your Right Honorable Lordship will permit me most
    humbly to advise,
a bride-price is only to be demanded or stipulated
as given by the husband to the wife,
not by the wife to the husband.

BARON

That may be so.

NOTARY

It is so—

BARON

But in a special case—

NOTARY

The forms and provisions know no special case.

BARON *shouting*

Damn the forms and provisions!

NOTARY *terrified*

Craving your pardon!

BARON

softly again, but insistently and in a tone of lofty self-respect

Where the lusty scion of a great and noble house
condescends to grace with his presence,
before God and the world, and, so to speak,
in view of her Imperial Majesty,
the marriage bed—you take my meanin'?—
of a young Miss Faninal who's as good as a commoner,
corpo di Bacco then if that isn't a case
where a bride-price as a fittin' token of grateful devotion

in return for the conferment of such noble blood
can very well pass from wife to husband.

*The Singer makes as if to start singing again but waits
until the Baron is quiet.*

NOTARY *softly to the Baron*
Perhaps if the affair is separately—

BARON *softly*
You miserable pedant, as bride-price I want the place!

NOTARY *softly*
—treated as a part of the dowry well hedged round with
stipulations—

BARON *half-aloud*
As bride-price! Can't you get it into your thick head?

NOTARY *the same*
—as a presentation *inter vivos* or—

BARON *shouting*
As bride-price!

SINGER

during the conversation between the two

Ma sì caro è'l mio tormento
Dolce è si la piaga mia
Ch' il penare è mio contento
E 'l sanarmi è tirannia.
Ahi! che resiste puoco—

*Here the Baron raises his voice so loudly that the Singer
breaks off abruptly, and the Flautist with him.*

The terrified Notary retires into the corner.

The Princess nods to the Singer to approach her and reaches out her hand for him to kiss. Singer and Flautist withdraw with deep bows.

The Baron acts as though nothing had occurred, nods affably to the Singer, then joins his servants, pushes back the forelock which has been combed in peasant fashion onto his valet's forehead. Then he goes to the small door as if he were looking for somebody, opens it, peeps outside, is angry that the maid does not return, in his anger sniffs around the bed, shakes his head, comes forward again.

PRINCESS

looking at herself in the hand mirror, half-aloud

My dear Hippolyte,
today you have made an old woman of me.

The Hairdresser, much distressed, goes feverishly to work again on the Princess's coiffure and alters it once more.

The Princess's face remains sad.

PRINCESS

over her shoulder to the Major-Domo

Everybody out!

Four Footmen form a chain and push the waiting people out through the doors, which they then fasten shut.

Valzacchi, with Annina behind him, has crept right round the stage behind everybody's backs to where the Baron is standing and they introduce themselves to him with exaggerated servility.
The Baron steps back.

VALZACCHI

Your Lordship looks for something, I can see.
Your Lordship in need of something.
I can find it. I can provide it.

BARON

Who are you, what do you know about me?

VALZACCHI

Your Lordship's face speaks without tongues.
Like antique. *Come statua di Giove.*

BARON

Quite an intelligent fellow, this.

VALZACCHI

Attach us to your Noble Lordship's suite!

Falls to his knees, and Annina likewise.

BARON

You?

VALZACCHI

Uncle and niece.
Two work better than one, at everything.
Per esempio: your Lordship has young wife—

BARON

How do you know that, you devil you?

VALZACCHI *zealously*

Your Lordship has cause for jealousy: *dico per dire!*
Could happen today or tomorrow. *Affare nostro!*
Every step the lady she take,
every carriage the lady she ride,
every letter the lady get—
we're on the spot.
There we are.
At the corner, in the chimney, under the bed—
there we are.

ANNINA

Your Lordship will not regret.

> *They hold their hands out to him, soliciting money;*
> *he acts as if he did not notice.*

BARON *half-aloud*

Hm! The things you can find in Vienna!
Just as a test. D'ye know the girl Mariandel?

ANNINA *half-aloud*

Mariandel?

BARON *the same*

The little maid in the house here with her Highness.

VALZACCHI *softly to Annina*

Sai tu, cosa vuole?

ANNINA *the same*

Niente!

VALZACCHI *to the Baron*

Sure, sure! My niece will provide.
Be sure of it, your Grace.

> *Holding out his hand once more, which the Baron again*
> *affects not to see.*

> *The Princess has got up. The Hairdresser makes a deep bow*
> *and hurries off, the Apprentice after him.*

BARON

leaves the two Italians standing and approaches the Princess

May I present the counterpart to your Highness's dainty
  chambermaid?
The likeness, I am told, is unmistakable.

The Princess nods.

BARON

Leopold, the casket.

The young valet awkwardly presents the casket.

PRINCESS *laughing a little*
My warmest congratulations to your Lordship.

BARON

takes the casket out of the youth's hands and nods to him to withdraw

And now let me show you the silver rose.

Is about to open it.

PRINCESS

Pray do not bother to open it.
Be so good as to put it down there.

BARON

Perhaps the maid might take charge of it?
Shall she be called?

PRINCESS

No, let it be. She's too busy now.
But let your Lordship rest assured: I shall bid Count Octavian
    wait on you
and the Count will do it for my sake
and as your Lordship's cavalier will call
to present your Lordship's rose to his lady bride.
Meanwhile just put it there.
And now I must bid my cousin adieu.
It is time now for the company
to withdraw, and I must to church.

Footmen open the double doors.

BARON

By your inexhaustible favor to me
your Highness this day has put me to shame.

Bows formally and makes a ceremonial departure.

The Notary follows him at his nod. After him the Baron's three servants,
in shambling procession. The two Italians in lithe and obsequious
silence attach themselves to it. The Footmen close the doors and the
Major-Domo withdraws.

PRINCESS *alone*

There he goes, the puffed-up evil wretch,
and gets the young and pretty thing
with a pocketful of money thrown in
as if it were a law of nature.
And prides himself moreover on its being himself
who is giving something away.
Why should I worry myself about it then? It's the way of
    the world.
I, too, can remember a girl who once
was drafted fresh from the convent into the holy estate of
    matrimony.

Takes the hand mirror.

Where is she now? Might as well look for the snows of
    yesteryear!
It's easily said, but can it really be true
that I was that little Resi
and that it's I who will one day be the old woman?
The old woman, the old princess.
"Look, there she goes, the old Princess Resi!"
How can such a thing happen?
Why does the good God arrange it so?
When I am still the same person.
And if He must arrange it so,
why then does He let me look on at myself

with such a clear understanding? Why doesn't He hide it
   from me?
It's all a mystery, so much is mysterious.
And we are here to endure it.
And in the How, there lies the whole difference—

Octavian enters from right, in morning dress with riding boots.

PRINCESS *half-smiling*

Ah, there you are again.

OCTAVIAN

And you are sad.

PRINCESS

It's all over. You know how I am.
Half the time gay, half the time sad.
I cannot choose my thoughts.

OCTAVIAN

I know why you are sad, my treasure.
Because you're upset and have had a fright.
Aren't I right? Confess!
You had a fright,
my darling, my love,
because of me, because of me.

PRINCESS

A little bit perhaps.
But I took hold of myself and told myself:
Nothing will come of it.
And would much have come of it?

OCTAVIAN

And it wasn't the Field Marshal after all.
Only a comic cousin, and you belong to me.
You belong to me.

PRINCESS

Careful, Tavie, not to hug me too often.
Who hugs most, they say, holds least.

OCTAVIAN

Say you belong to me, say you belong to me.

PRINCESS

Oh be gentle now, be gentle and clever and good
No, please do not be as all men are.

OCTAVIAN

As all men?

PRINCESS

As the Field Marshal and Cousin Ochs.
Let my boy not be as all men are.

OCTAVIAN *angrily*

I don't know how all men are.

Gently

I know only that I love you,
Bichette, they've changed my Bichette for another.
Where's my Bichette?

PRINCESS *calmly*

She's here, let my lord and treasure be reassured.

OCTAVIAN

She's here, is she? Then I will hold her
and press her to me so that she doesn't escape me again.

PRINCESS

disentangling herself from his embrace

Oh let my Quinquin be good. I have a feeling

as if the frailty of all temporal things
had seeped into my very heart—
for we can hold nothing,
for we can grasp nothing,
for everything runs through our fingers,
everything, as we reach for it, dissolves,
everything melts away like dream and mist.

OCTAVIAN

When my Bichette has me here,
my finger hooked in hers,
my eyes seeking hers,
is that the moment for such feelings?

PRINCESS *very seriously*

Quinquin, today or tomorrow you will go off
and give me up for the sake of another,

Octavian tries to stop her mouth.

one younger and more lovely than I.

OCTAVIAN

Are you trying to thrust me from you with words,
because your hands will not do it for you?

PRINCESS

The day will come quite of its own accord. For who are you?
A young lord, a younger son.
Your brother the head of your house.
Is he not bound to seek you a bride?
As if everything in the world
hadn't its proper time and its laws.
Today or tomorrow the day will come, Octavian.

OCTAVIAN

Not today, not tomorrow. I love you.
Not today, not tomorrow.

PRINCESS

Today or tomorrow or the day after.
I don't want to torment you, my love.
I'm saying what is true, saying it to myself as much as to you.
Easy for you and me I want to make it.
Easy is what we must be,
with heart and hands at ease,
holding and taking, holding and letting go. . . .
Those who are not so,
are punished by life and get no pity of God.

OCTAVIAN

My God, how she says it—only to show me
she doesn't care for me any more.

He weeps.

PRINCESS

Be a good boy, Quinquin.

He weeps more violently.

Be a good boy.
Now it's I who must console the child
for the prospect that he will sooner or later leave me.

She strokes him.

OCTAVIAN

Sooner or later!
Who's putting the words into your mouth today, Bichette?

He stops his ears.

PRINCESS

Sooner or later.
Do those words offend you so?
Yet time, when you get down to it, Quinquin,

time doesn't alter circumstances.
Time is a strange thing.
While one just lives for the moment, it is nothing.
But then all at once
we feel nothing else but it,
it's all around us, it's right inside us,
it trickles away in our faces, it trickles in the mirror,
in my temples it flows away.
And between me and you there it is flowing too.
Soundless, as an hourglass.
Ah Quinquin!
Often I hear it flowing incessantly.
Often I get up in the middle of the night
and stop all the clocks.

OCTAVIAN

My lovely darling, are you determined to *make* yourself
  miserable?

PRINCESS

Only we must not be afraid of it.
Time too is a creature of the Father
who has created us all.

OCTAVIAN

Today you talk like a parson.

An awkward silence

Does that mean that I shall never again
be allowed to kiss you
till you gasp for air?

PRINCESS *gently*

Quinquin, you must go now, you must leave me.
I am going to church now.
And later I shall drive to see my uncle Greifenklau,

who is old and paralyzed,
and lunch with him—that will cheer the old man.
And this afternoon I will send you a footman,
Quinquin, and let you know
whether I am driving in the Prater.
And if I drive
and you would like,
you shall come to the Prater too
and ride beside my carriage.
Be good now and do as I say.

OCTAVIAN

As you command, Bichette.

He goes. A pause.

PRINCESS *alone*

I didn't even kiss him.

She rings agitatedly. Footmen come in from right.

Run after his Lordship the Count and
ask him back for a word with me.

A pause

I let him go and never even kissed him.

The Footmen come back out of breath.

FIRST FOOTMAN

His Lordship's off and away.

SECOND FOOTMAN

Right at the gate his Lordship mounted.

THIRD FOOTMAN

The groom was waiting.

FOURTH FOOTMAN

Right at the gate they mounted and off like the wind.

FIRST FOOTMAN

Off round the corner, gone like the wind.

SECOND FOOTMAN

Ran after them, we did.

THIRD FOOTMAN

Shouted we did.

FOURTH FOOTMAN

All to no purpose.

FIRST FOOTMAN

Off round the corner, gone like the wind.

PRINCESS

Very good, you may go now.

The Footmen withdraw.

PRINCESS *calling after them*

Send Mohammed.

The little Blackamoor enters with a tinkling of bells and bows.

PRINCESS

There take this casket—

The Blackamoor zealously takes the morocco casket.

PRINCESS

But you don't know where. To Count Octavian.

Hand it over and say:
The silver rose is inside.
His Lordship knows all about it.

The Blackamoor runs off.

The Princess rests her head on her hand.

Curtain

PLAYS

THE DIFFICULT MAN

A Comedy in Three Acts

CHARACTERS

Hans Karl Bühl, *Count*
Crescence, *his sister, Countess Freudenberg*
Stani, *her son, Count Freudenberg*
Helen Altenwyl, *daughter of*
Altenwyl, *Count*
Antoinette Hechingen, *wife of*
Hechingen, *Count*
Neuhoff, *Baron*
Edine ⎫
Nanni ⎬ *Antoinette's bosom friends*
Huberta ⎭
Agathe, *Antoinette's maid*
Neugebauer, *Count Bühl's secretary*
Lukas, *Count Bühl's butler*
Vincent, *a new footman of Bühl's*
A Famous Man
Servants *of Bühl and Altenwyl*

Act I

*A medium large room in a rather old Viennese palace,
fitted up as a study.*

SCENE I

Lukas comes in with Vincent.

LUKAS

This is called the study. Relations and close friends are shown
in here, or else, but only on special instructions, into the green
drawing room.

VINCENT

coming farther in

What does he study? Estate business? Or what? Political affairs?

LUKAS

This door in the wall is for the secretary to come in by.

VINCENT

So he has a private secretary, too? Miserable creatures, they are.
Slinking good-for-nothings. Does this one count for anything
in the house?

LUKAS

This door leads into the dressing room. We'll go in there now
and lay out his dinner jacket and his tails so that he can choose
which he likes, since he hasn't given any special instructions.

VINCENT

nosing round all the furniture

So what? Do you think I need to be taught my duties? There's
time enough till tomorrow morning, and we'd do better to have

a heart-to-heart talk now. It's a good many years since I learned all about gentlemen's service, so just stick to the needful; I mean the special peculiarities. Come on! Put me in the picture.

LUKAS

straightening a picture that is hanging a little askew

He can't bear to see a picture or a looking glass hanging the least bit awry. When he starts pulling out all the desk drawers or hunting for a mislaid key, he's in a very bad mood.

VINCENT

Oh, trifles like these don't matter. But didn't you tell me that the sister and the nephew who live upstairs in the house have to be announced every time they come to see him?

LUKAS

polishing a looking glass with his handkerchief

Exactly like any other visitor. He insists on that.

VINCENT

What's he getting at? He must want to keep them at arm's length. Then why does he let them live here? I suppose he has more than one house? But they're his heirs. They must be wishing him dead.

LUKAS

Her ladyship Countess Crescence and Count Stani? God forbid! I don't know what to make of you.

VINCENT

You can cut out the preaching. What's he after, keeping them in the house? That's what interests me. You see, it throws a light on his future intentions. These I must know before I let myself in for this job.

LUKAS

What future intentions?

VINCENT

Don't throw my words in my teeth! This all means a lot to me. If things suit me here, I might settle down for life. When you've retired, I could take everything in hand. From all I hear, this place would probably suit me very well. But I want to know where I am. Now, since he's bringing his relations into the house, it looks as if he means to begin a new kind of life. At his age and after his years at the front that's quite understandable. When a man won't ever see forty again—

LUKAS

His lordship will be forty next year.

VINCENT

Put it in a nutshell, he wants to be done with love affairs. He's had enough of little bits of fluff.

LUKAS

I don't understand that kind of talk.

VINCENT

But of course you understand me very well, my *dear* sir. — Anyhow, that bears out what the woman at the lodge told me. The main point now is: does he mean to get married? In that case there'll be nothing in it for me, with a lawful mistress in the house. Or might he settle down to a bachelor life with me? Tell me what you think about it. That's the main point for me, that is, you see. (*Lukas clears his throat loudly*) What's the idea, making me jump?

LUKAS

Sometimes he's actually in the room before you hear a footfall.

VINCENT

What's he getting at? Does he try to trap people? Is he as spiteful as that?

LUKAS

When that happens, you have to go away quietly.

VINCENT

What a horrible habit to have. I'll soon break him of that.

SCENE II

HANS KARL

has come in noiselessly

Just wait a moment, Lukas. Is that you, Neugebauer?

Vincent is standing to one side in the dark.

LUKAS

Beg to inform your Lordship this is the new footman, who was four years with his Highness, Prince Palm.

HANS KARL

Just carry on what you were doing with him. Let Mr. Neugebauer bring me the papers about Hohenbühl. And I'm not at home to anyone.

A bell is heard.

LUKAS

That's the bell in the small antechamber.

He goes out.

Vincent stands still.

Hans Karl has moved up to the desk.

SCENE III

LUKAS

comes in and announces

Her ladyship Countess Freudenberg.

Crescence has come in on his heels.

Lukas leaves the room, Vincent likewise.

CRESCENCE

Am I disturbing you, Kari? Do forgive me—

HANS KARL

Not at all, my dear Crescence.

CRESCENCE

I'm on my way up to dress—for the soirée.

HANS KARL

At the Altenwyls'?

CRESCENCE

You're coming too, aren't you? Or not? I should just like to know, my dear.

HANS KARL

If it's all the same to you, I'd rather perhaps make up my mind later, and then perhaps ring up from the Club when I've decided. You know how I dislike being tied down.

CRESCENCE

Oh yes.

HANS KARL

But if you have been counting on me—

CRESCENCE

My dear Kari, I'm old enough to get home by myself—besides, Stani will be there and he'll pick me up. So you're not going?

HANS KARL

I'd rather think it over a while yet.

CRESCENCE

A soirée's none the more attractive for being thought over, my dear. Besides, I fancied that being at the front would have got you out of the way of thinking things over quite so much. (*Sits down beside him as he stands beside the desk.*) Let Kari be a good boy now and give up being so horribly erratic and so unable to make up his mind about anything that I have to carry on a war to the knife with his friends, what with one of them calling him a hypochondriac and another saying he's a wet blanket and a third that he can never be depended on. — You've come back in such excellent shape, too, exactly as you used to be when you were twenty-two and I was infatuated with my brother.

HANS KARL

My dear Crescence, are you paying me compliments?

CRESCENCE

Not at all, I'm just telling you the truth: now Stani is an excellent judge of such things, and he thinks you simply the finest gentleman in society; with him it's Uncle Kari this, and Uncle Kari that, and the greatest compliment one can pay him is to say that he resembles you, which of course he does—in his movements he's just you all over again. He has never known anything more elegant than your way of handling people, the grand air, the distance you set between you and everyone else—and yet the complete composure and bonhomie you show even to the humblest—but, like me, he can't help noticing your weaknesses; he adores decisiveness, strength, positiveness, and he hates shilly-shallying just as much as I do!

HANS KARL

Let me congratulate you on your son, Crescence. I am sure you will always find great happiness in him.

CRESCENCE

Still—*pour revenir à nos moutons*—goodness me, when a man's been through what you've been through and yet has carried on as if it were nothing at all—

HANS KARL *embarrassed*

But everyone did that!

CRESCENCE

Allow me to say: by no means everyone. But I should have thought that it would enable a man to get over his fits of nerves!

HANS KARL

People in a drawing room still make me nervous. An evening party gives me the horrors, I simply can't help it. I can quite well understand people who keep open house, but not those who go there.

CRESCENCE

Then what is it that frightens you? Surely we can talk it over. Are you bored by the old people?

HANS KARL

Oh, I find them charming, they have such good manners.

CRESCENCE

Or is it the young ones who get on your nerves?

HANS KARL

No, I don't mind them at all. It's the occasion itself that is simply a horror, don't you see, the whole thing—the whole thing is such a twisted tangle of misunderstandings. Oh, these chronic misunderstandings!

CRESCENCE

After all you've gone through at the front, I simply don't understand why it hasn't hardened you.

HANS KARL

Crescence, that doesn't make a man less susceptible, but more so. How is it you don't understand that? I find tears starting to my eyes over some little stupidity—or I grow hot with embarrassment about some trifling nuance that nobody else even notices, or it happens that I say out loud what I am thinking—in any such state it's impossible to mix with people. I can't describe it more precisely, but it's too much for me. To be honest with you, two hours ago I gave instructions to make my excuses to the Altenwyls. Perhaps another soirée, sometime soon, but not this one.

CRESCENCE

Not this one. But why not this particular one?

HANS KARL

It's too much for me, just in general.

CRESCENCE

When you say in general you mean something in particular.

HANS KARL

Not at all, Crescence.

CRESCENCE

Of course you do. Aha. Well, on this point I can reassure you.

HANS KARL

On what point?

CRESCENCE

As far as Helen is concerned.

HANS KARL

What has Helen to do with it?

CRESCENCE

My dear, I'm neither deaf nor blind, and that Helen was head over heels in love with you from the time she was fifteen until not so long ago, let us say until the second year of the war, I have plenty of evidence, in the first, second, and third place.

HANS KARL

But, Crescence, you're just imagining things—

CRESCENCE

Do you know, about three or four years ago, when she was quite a young debutante, I used to fancy that she was the one person in the world who could hold you, who could be your wife. But as sure as I live I'm glad that it hasn't turned out like that. Two such complicated people, that would be no good.

HANS KARL

You do me too much honor. I'm the least complicated person in the world. (*He has pulled out a drawer of the desk.*) But I cannot think how you should hit on such an idea—I'm fond of Helen, she's a kind of cousin—after all, I've known her since she was little—she could be my daughter.

Hunts in the drawer for something.

CRESCENCE

More likely mine. But I shouldn't like her to be my daughter. And much less should I want that Baron Neuhoff for a son-in-law.

HANS KARL

Neuhoff? Is that really a serious affair?

CRESCENCE

She's going to marry him.

Hans Karl slams the drawer shut.

CRESCENCE

I regard it as a settled thing, in spite of the fact that he's a wild outsider, blown in from some Baltic province or other where the wolves howl good night in the snow—

HANS KARL

Geography was never your strong point. Crescence, the Neuhoffs are a Holstein family.

CRESCENCE

Well, it's the same thing. Wild outsiders, that's what I said.

HANS KARL

And, besides, one of the first families. As well-connected as anyone could be.

CRESCENCE

But, really, that's only what it says in the *Gotha*. How could one make sure of that from as far away as here?

HANS KARL

You're very set against the man.

CRESCENCE

Why shouldn't I be? When one of the best of our girls such as Helen gets notions about a wild outsider like him, in spite of the fact that he'll never in his life have any position here—

HANS KARL

You think not?

CRESCENCE

Never in his life! — In spite of the fact that she's not taken in by his high-flown talk, flying, in short, in the face of herself and the world— (*A short pause. — Hans Karl with some violence jerks out another drawer.*) Can I help you to look for something? You're upsetting yourself.

HANS KARL

Oh, thanks very much, I'm not really looking for anything, I put the wrong key in the lock.

SECRETARY

appears at the little door

Oh, I beg your pardon, please excuse me.

HANS KARL

I'll be free in a minute or two, my dear Neugebauer.

The Secretary retreats.

CRESCENCE

rises and comes up to the desk

Kari, if it's to do you even a small favor, I'll put an end to that affair.

HANS KARL

What affair?

CRESCENCE

The one we're speaking of: Helen and Neuhoff. I could put an end to it overnight.

HANS KARL

What?

CRESCENCE

As sure as I live, she's as much in love with you now as she was six years ago, and it would need only a word, the merest shadow of a hint—

HANS KARL

Which I beg you for God's sake not to give her—

CRESCENCE

Oh, sorry. Very well.

HANS KARL

My dear, with all due respect to your energetic temperament, people, thank goodness, are not so simple as all that.

CRESCENCE

My dear, people, thank goodness, are very simple if one takes them simply. Well, this bit of news, I see, is no great blow to you. All the better—you've stopped being interested in Helen, I'll keep that in mind.

HANS KARL *standing up*

But I don't know how you ever got the idea that I needed to stop being interested. Do other people have the same fantastic notion?

CRESCENCE

Very likely.

HANS KARL

You know, that's enough to make me want to go to the soirée.

CRESCENCE

To give Theophilus Neuhoff your blessing? He'd be delighted. He'd crawl on hands and knees to be taken into your confidence.

HANS KARL

Don't you find that, considering all this, I should have shown myself at the Altenwyls' long ago? I'm extremely sorry that I made my excuses today.

CRESCENCE

Well, ring them up again: say it was a mistake made by a new footman and that you're coming.

Lukas comes in.

HANS KARL *to Crescence*

You know, I'd still like to think it over.

LUKAS

There's someone waiting to see your Lordship.

CRESCENCE *to Lukas*

I'm just going. Get on the telephone quick to Count Altenwyl, and say that his lordship will be coming to the soirée tonight. It was a mistake.

Lukas looks at Hans Karl.

HANS KARL

not meeting Lukas's eyes

In that case he'd have to ring up the Club first and say that Count Hechingen is not to expect me for dinner, or later on.

CRESCENCE

Of course, he can do that too. But first Count Altenwyl, so that people know where they are. (*Lukas goes out. She rises to her feet.*) And now I'll leave you to your business affairs. (*On the way out*) Which Hechingen were you going to see? Nandi?

HANS KARL

No, Adolf.

CRESCENCE *coming back*

Antoinette's husband? Isn't he an utter fool?

HANS KARL

Do you know, Crescence, I'm no judge of that. Long conversations always make me feel that the clever things people say are foolish and that the foolish things, if anything, are clever.

CRESCENCE

And I'm convinced, anyhow, that there's more to him than to her.

HANS KARL

Well, in the old days I never knew him at all, or, rather— (*He has turned towards the wall and pokes at a picture which is hanging not quite straight.*) —only as the husband of his wife—and then out there at the front we became friends. You know, he's a thoroughly decent fellow. We were together in the winter of '15, twenty weeks in our station in the Carpathian forest, I with my gunners and he with his sappers, and we shared our last crusts together. I developed a great respect for him. There were plenty of brave men out there, but I never met one who faced death with such complete equanimity, almost a kind of comfortable ease.

CRESCENCE

If his relations could hear you they'd fling their arms round your neck. You'd better speak to his fool of a wife, then, and bring about a reconciliation between them, you'd make two families happy. This idea that she keeps dangling over them of a divorce or a separation, it's all the same, is getting on everyone's nerves. Besides, it would be to your own advantage to have the situation made regular.

HANS KARL

How so?

CRESCENCE

You may as well know it: there are people spreading the absurd rumor that if she got an annulment you'd marry her. (*Hans Karl is silent.*) I don't say that it's people of any standing who are making up such unlikely nonsense. (*Hans Karl is silent.*) Have you been to see her at all since you came back from the front?

HANS KARL

No. I ought to go, of course.

CRESCENCE

looking at him sideways

Well, go to see her tomorrow and stir up her conscience.

HANS KARL

bends down as if to pick up something

I don't really know if I'm exactly the right man to do that.

CRESCENCE

It would be an act of simple kindness. It would let her under-
stand that she was on the wrong track when she tried her hard-
est two years ago to get you involved with her.

HANS KARL

not meeting her eyes

That's only a notion of yours.

CRESCENCE

Exactly as she's trying to do with Stani today.

HANS KARL *in astonishment*

Your Stani?

CRESCENCE

Ever since springtime. (*She had got as far as the door, but turns round again and comes back to the desk.*) There's a great, great favor my Kari could do me—

CRESCENCE

HANS KARL

But for goodness' sake, you've only to tell me what it is!

He offers her a chair, she remains standing.

CRESCENCE

Let me send Stani downstairs for a moment or two, and Kari can make the situation clear. Tell Stani that Antoinette is—well, the kind of woman who's not worth compromising oneself for. In a word, put Stani off her.

HANS KARL

And how do you think that's to be done? If he's in love with her?

CRESCENCE

But men are never so much in love as all that, and you're an oracle for Stani. If you would just bring the conversation round to that point—will you promise?

HANS KARL

Yes, well—if it can be done naturally—

CRESCENCE

again at the door, speaks from there

You'll find the right approach. You have no idea what an authority you are for him. (*On the point of going out, she turns once more and comes forward to the desk.*) Tell him that you find her anything but elegant—and that you would never have had anything to do with her. Then he'll drop her overnight. (*She makes for the door again, and again turns round.*) You know, don't be too severe about it, but not too casual either. Don't be too subtle about it.

And he mustn't have the slightest suspicion that I'm behind it—he has the fixed idea that I'm trying to marry him off—of course I am, but all the same—he mustn't suspect it; he's exactly like you in that: the mere idea that anyone might try to influence him—! (*Once more she makes the same maneuver.*) Do you know, I'd very much like to get it all settled at once, why waste an evening? And that provides you with a line of action too: you make it clear to Antoinette how much you disapprove her go-ings-on—you lead her round to the subject of her marriage—you sing Adolf's praises—and that gives you something to do and keeps the whole evening from being aimless.

> *She goes out.*

SCENE IV

VINCENT

> *has come in from right, looks round first to see if Crescence has gone, then*

I don't know if the butler has mentioned it, there's a young woman out there, a lady's maid or something like that.

HANS KARL
What does she want?

VINCENT
From Countess Hechingen, to be precise. Seems to be a kind of confidential messenger. (*Coming still nearer.*) Not a poor creature with nothing to say for herself.

HANS KARL
That I shall judge for myself, show her in.

> *Vincent goes out right.*

SCENE V

LUKAS

comes in quickly through the middle doors

Has it been announced to your Lordship? Countess Hechingen's maid, Agathe, is here. I told her I absolutely could not say whether your Lordship was at home.

HANS KARL

Good. I have sent to say I am at home. Did you ring up Count Altenwyl?

LUKAS

I beg your Lordship's pardon. I noticed that your Lordship didn't want the call to be made, but didn't want to contradict her ladyship—so for the time being I have not telephoned.

HANS KARL *smiling*

Well done, Lukas. (*Lukas goes as far as the door.*) Lukas, what do you think of the new footman?

LUKAS *hesitating*

Perhaps we should wait to see how he turns out.

HANS KARL

An impossible man. Pay him off. Send him packing!

LUKAS

Very good, your Lordship. I thought as much.

HANS KARL

But say nothing about it for tonight.

SCENE VI

Vincent shows in Agathe. Both servants go out.

HANS KARL

Good evening, Agathe.

AGATHE

To think of seeing you again, your Lordship! I'm all of a flutter.

HANS KARL

Won't you sit down?

AGATHE *standing*

Oh, your Lordship, only don't be angry because I've come in-stead of that Brandstätter.

HANS KARL

But, my dear Agathe, we're old acquaintances. What has brought you to see me?

AGATHE

Oh dear, your Lordship knows quite well. I've come about the letters. (*Hans Karl is taken aback.*) Oh, my goodness, oh, excuse me, I can't bear to think of how my lady impressed on me not to spoil things by putting my foot in it.

HANS KARL *hesitatingly*

The Countess did write to tell me that certain letters belonging to her which are in my possession would be called for by a Herr Brandstätter on the fifteenth. Today is the twelfth, but of course I can hand over the letters to you instead. Immediately, if that is what the Countess wishes. I know that you are very devoted to the Countess.

AGATHE

Certain letters—what a way to speak, your Lordship. I know quite well what letters these are.

HANS KARL *coldly*

I shall have them brought in at once.

AGATHE

If she could only see us together like this, my poor lady. It would
be a comfort to her, it would do her a little good. (*Hans Karl
begins to hunt about in a desk drawer.*) After these dreadful seven
weeks, since ever we knew that our Count had come back from
the war and yet we hadn't a single sign of life from him—

HANS KARL *looking up*

You hadn't a sign of life from Count Hechingen?

AGATHE

From him! When I say "our Count" that's what we call *you* be-
tween ourselves, your Lordship. We don't call Count Hech-
ingen "our Count"!

HANS KARL *very embarrassed*

Ah, excuse me, I couldn't be expected to know that.

AGATHE *tentatively*

Until this very afternoon we believed that you were to be at
Count Altenwyl's soirée. And then Countess Altenwyl's maid
told me on the telephone: he's made his excuses. (*Hans Karl
stands up straight.*) He's made his excuses, Agathe, cried my poor
lady, he's not going because he's heard that I'm to be there!
That means it's all over—and she gave me a look that would
have melted a stone.

HANS KARL

very politely, but with the intention of putting an end to this

I fear that the letters in question are not here in my desk. I'll
send for my secretary at once.

AGATHE

Oh, goodness, does the secretary have these letters? My lady must never find that out!

HANS KARL

The letters, needless to say, are in a sealed package.

AGATHE

A sealed package! Have things gone as far as that?

HANS KARL

speaks into the house telephone

My dear Neugebauer, could you come over here for a moment? Yes, I am free now. — But never mind those papers—something else has cropped up. At once? No, just finish adding up your figures. In three minutes' time, that will do.

AGATHE

He'd better not catch sight of me, he'll remember who I am.

HANS KARL

You can slip into the library, I'll put on the light for you.

AGATHE

How could we imagine that all of a sudden everything would be over.

HANS KARL

escorting her to the library door, stops, wrinkles his forehead

My dear Agathe, since you are so well-informed—I don't understand it, for I wrote to the Countess from the field hospital, a long letter, this last spring.

AGATHE

Yes, that abominable letter.

HANS KARL

I don't understand you. It was a very friendly letter.

AGATHE

It was a treacherous letter. How it made us tremble when we read it, that letter! Upset we were, and humiliated.

HANS KARL

But why on earth, I should like to know!

AGATHE *looking at him*

Why? Because you praised Count Hechingen in it up to the skies—and said that in the end one man is the same as another and any man will do instead of any other.

HANS KARL

I certainly never used such expressions. Thoughts of that kind never entered my head!

AGATHE

But that was what it all amounted to. Oh, we've read the letter often enough. And this, cried my lady, this is the result of nights spent under the stars in solitary meditation, this letter, in which he says plainly: one man is the same as another, our love was only moonshine, forget me and turn to Hechingen again—

HANS KARL

Not one single word of all that was in the letter.

AGATHE

The words don't matter. We understood the sense of it well enough. The humiliation of it, the mortifying conclusions to be drawn. Oh, we know well enough what was meant. This self-deprecation is just a deceitful trick. When a man starts accusing himself in a love affair, he's accusing the affair itself. And in no time it's us who are standing in the dock. (*Hans Karl is silent.*

Agathe comes a step nearer.) I put up a good fight for our Count, when my lady said: Agathe, you'll see, he wants to marry the Altenwyl girl, and it's only because of that he's trying to patch up my marriage again.

HANS KARL

Did the Countess actually think that of me?

AGATHE

In her worst hours, when she'd been brooding over it. Then she would have a flash of hopefulness again. No, she would cry then, no, I'm not afraid of Helen—for she runs after him; and anyone who runs after Kari is done for as far as he's concerned, and she doesn't deserve him, either, for she's quite heartless.

HANS KARL

setting something straight

If I could only convince you—

AGATHE

But then she would suddenly despair again—

HANS KARL

How far I am from—

AGATHE

O God, she would cry, he hasn't been seen anywhere yet! Could that mean—?

HANS KARL

How far I am from—

AGATHE

Suppose he were to get engaged to her before my very eyes—

HANS KARL

How *can* the Countess—

AGATHE

Oh, men do that kind of thing, but not you, surely, your Lordship?

HANS KARL

Nothing in the world is farther from my thoughts, my dear Agathe.

AGATHE

Oh, I kiss your hand, your Lordship!

Quickly kisses his hand.

HANS KARL

withdrawing the hand

I hear my secretary coming.

AGATHE

For we know, we women, that something so blissful can't last forever. And yet that it should suddenly stop all at once, that's what we can't get used to!

HANS KARL

You'll see me in a minute. I'll give you the letters myself and— Come in! Just come in, Neugebauer.

Agathe goes off right.

SCENE VII

NEUGEBAUER

comes in by the wall door

Your Lordship summoned me.

HANS KARL

If you would be so good as to come to the help of my bad memory. I'm looking for a packet of letters—private letters, sealed up—about two fingers thick.

NEUGEBAUER

Inscribed by your Lordship with a date? June 15 to October 22, 1916?

HANS KARL

That's right. Then you know—

NEUGEBAUER

I've had those documents in my hand, but I can't think where, for the moment. In the pressure of work among so many different memoranda that are piling up daily—

HANS KARL

without the slightest reproach

I can't understand how these very private letters should come to be mixed up with business documents—

NEUGEBAUER

If there is occasion to fear that your Lordship has the faintest doubt of my discretion—

HANS KARL

But that has never entered my mind—

NEUGEBAUER

Be so good as to let me look for them at once; I'll do my utmost to clear up this very regrettable mishap.

HANS KARL

My dear Neugebauer, you're making far too much of a trifling occurrence.

NEUGEBAUER

For some time now I have been aware that something in me has begun to irritate your Lordship. It is true that my education has been confined to inward accomplishments, and if it has perhaps failed to equip me with an unimpeachable social manner, this defect might perhaps be balanced in the eyes of a benevolent judge by other qualities, which it would certainly be difficult for a man of my character to remind you of, if I had to do so in person.

HANS KARL

I have no doubt of it, my dear Neugebauer. You give me the impression of being overworked. I wish you would stop work rather earlier of an evening. Why not go for a stroll in the evenings with your fiancée? (*Neugebauer is silent.*) If it is private affairs that are worrying you, perhaps I could come to your assistance in some way and lighten your burden.

NEUGEBAUER

Your Lordship takes it for granted that it's only financial worries a man of my kind can have.

HANS KARL

That's not at all what I meant. I know you are engaged to be married, and so of course a happy man—

NEUGEBAUER

I don't know if your Lordship is referring to the housekeeper of Castle Hohenbühl?

HANS KARL

Yes, haven't you been engaged to her for five years?

NEUGEBAUER

The lady I'm at present engaged to is the daughter of a senior civil servant. She was engaged to my best friend, who lost his life in the war six months ago. Even while he was alive she was fond of me—and I have regarded it as a sacred trust from the deceased to offer this young girl a support for her lifetime.

HANS KARL *hesitatingly*

And your former long-standing engagement?

NEUGEBAUER

I brought it to an end, of course. Naturally, in the most correct and conscientious manner.

HANS KARL

Ah!

NEUGEBAUER

Naturally I shall honor all the commitments I had entered into, and take that extra burden with me into my new marriage. No small burden, I admit. (*Hans Karl is silent.*) Perhaps your Lordship does not sufficiently appreciate the severe moral seriousness that presses down on life in our lowly circles, so that the only course open to us is to exchange hard duties for others still harder.

HANS KARL

I always supposed that when a man thought of getting married he felt happy about it.

NEUGEBAUER

Personal inclinations cannot take first place in our humble world.

HANS KARL

To be sure, to be sure. Well, you'll find me the letters if you can.

NEUGEBAUER

I'll hunt for them until midnight if necessary.

Goes out.

HANS KARL *to himself*

I wonder what it is about me that makes everyone so much in-
clined to read me a lesson, and that always makes me wonder
ever so faintly whether I don't deserve it?

SCENE VIII

STANI

appears in the middle door, in full evening dress

Excuse me, I only want to say good evening, Uncle Kari, if I'm
not disturbing you.

HANS KARL

on his way to the library door right, stops and stands still

Not at all.

Offers him a chair and a cigarette.

STANI

taking the cigarette

But of course it puts you out when people come in without
being announced. You're very like me in that. I can't stand it
either when somebody gate-crashes me. I need time to put my
thoughts a bit in order first.

HANS KARL

Please don't apologize, this is your home.

STANI

I beg your pardon, it's yours—

HANS KARL

Go on, sit down.

STANI

No, truly, I shouldn't have had the face to come in if I hadn't heard Neugebauer squawking away—

HANS KARL

He's just this moment gone.

STANI

Or else I should never have— You see, the new footman ran after me in the corridor about five minutes ago and told me— without being asked, mind you—that you were talking to Antoinette Hechingen's maid and shouldn't be disturbed.

HANS KARL *half to himself*

He did, did he? — Delightful fellow!

STANI

So of course I wouldn't have on any account—

HANS KARL

She was only bringing me back some books.

STANI

Does Toinette Hechingen read books?

HANS KARL

Apparently. One or two old French things.

STANI

Eighteenth century, I suppose. To match her furniture. (*Hans Karl is silent.*) Her boudoir is charming. That small chaise longue of hers! It's a signed piece.

HANS KARL

Yes, the small chaise longue. Riesener.

STANI

Yes, Riesener it is. What a good memory for names you have!
The signature's underneath.

HANS KARL

Underneath at the foot.

STANI

She's always dropping little combs out of her hair, and when
one bends to pick them up one can see the inscription. (*Hans
Karl crosses right and shuts the library door.*) Do you feel a draught?
Are you susceptible?

HANS KARL

Yes, at the front my gunners and I got as full of rheumatism as
old hounds.

STANI

Do you know, she thinks the world of you, does Antoinette.

HANS KARL

lights up and smokes

Ah!

STANI

But truly, beyond compare. It was only because she thinks me
wonderfully like you that I had any chance with her in the be-
ginning. For instance, our hands. She goes into ecstasies about
your hands. (*He spreads out his own hand and gazes at it.*) But not
a word of all this to Mamma, please. It's just a thoroughgoing
flirtation, not by any means a *liaison*. But Mamma exaggerates
everything to herself.

HANS KARL

My dear Stani, is it likely that I should ever mention such a thing?

STANI

Bit by bit, of course, she's been finding out the differences between us. *Ça va sans dire.*

HANS KARL

Antoinette?

STANI

She told me all about the beginning of her friendship with you.

HANS KARL

But I've known her for ages.

STANI

No, I mean what happened two years ago. In the second year of the war. When you were on leave after your first wound, and spent some days at Grünleiten.

HANS KARL

Does she date our friendship from then?

STANI

Of course. Since then you've been her greatest friend. As counselor, as confidant, as anything you please, simply *hors ligne.* You've been an angel to her, she says.

HANS KARL

She's inclined to exaggerate, our Antoinette.

STANI

But she gave me all the particulars, about how she was terrified to be left alone at Grünleiten with her husband, who happened to be on leave too, and how she had sent a message to Feri Uhlfeldt, who was chasing after her at that time like the devil, asking him to come next day, and how she caught sight of you in the theater that very evening and it came over her like an inspiration so that she begged you to drive back with her and spend the evening with her *à trois* with Adolf.

HANS KARL

I hardly knew him in those days.

STANI

Yes, by the way, that's something she can't understand. How you could have become so friendly with him later on. Such a dull pedantic fool, such a blockhead.

HANS KARL

There she's unfair to her husband, very!

STANI

Well, I'm not going to take sides. But she has a delightful way of telling it all.

HANS KARL

That's her strong point, these little confidences.

STANI

Yes, that's how she leads one on. The whole of that evening, I can see it all before me, how she showed you the garden after supper, the charming terraces beside the river, how the moon rose—

HANS KARL

She went into so much detail, did she?

STANI

And how in that one evening's conversation with her you were able to talk her out of having anything to do with Feri Uhlfeldt. (*Hans Karl smokes and says nothing.*) That's what I admire so much in you; you have little to say, you are so absentminded, yet you have such a strong influence. That's why I find it quite natural, though so many people never stop talking about it, that you've been a year and a half in the Upper House without ever rising to speak. Absolutely right for someone like you! A great gentleman like you makes himself felt by his mere presence! Oh, I'm taking you as a model to study. Give me a year or two and I'll get there. At the moment I'm still too full of passion. You never go out for anything and never try to talk people into anything, that's just what's so elegant in you. Any other man in your shoes that evening would have become her lover.

HANS KARL

with a twinkle in his eye

Do you think so?

STANI

Positively. But of course I understand well enough that at your time of life you're too serious for that. It's no longer a temptation to you: that's how I explain it to myself. You know, that's me all over: I do like to account for everything. If I'd had time to stay at the University—science, that would have been my subject. I should have hit on themes, on problems, on questions that simply don't occur to other people. A life without reflection is no life for me. For instance, now: when a man realizes that he's no longer young, does it come over him all of a sudden? — That must be a most unpleasant moment.

HANS KARL

Well, you know, I think it comes on quite gradually. When someone lets you precede him one day through a doorway and you say to yourself: of course, he's much younger than I am, although he's a full-grown man.

STANI

Very interesting. How closely you observe things. You're altogether like me in that. And then do you just get used to being old?

HANS KARL

Well, there are still moments that give you a shock. For instance, when you suddenly realize you have stopped believing that there are people who can explain everything to you.

STANI

But there's one thing I don't understand, Uncle Kari, that, as experienced and well-preserved as you are, you don't get married.

HANS KARL

Now!

STANI

Yes, now. For you're past the stage of looking for little adventures. You know, I could quite well understand that any woman would still be inclined to take an interest in you. But Toinette has made it clear to me why no woman's interest in you ever becomes serious.

HANS KARL

Ah!

STANI

Yes, she's given a lot of thought to it. She says you don't hold a woman because you haven't enough heart.

HANS KARL

Ah!

STANI

Yes, you lack the essential quality. That, she says, is the enormous difference between you and me. She says your hand is always loose on its wrist, ready to let go, and a woman feels that, and even if she were on the point of falling in love with you it would prevent the crystallization.

HANS KARL

Is that how she puts it?

STANI

Indeed, that's her great charm, she makes good conversation. You know, I demand that absolutely: any woman who is to hold me must be able to make conversation as well as being absolutely devoted.

HANS KARL

She does it enchantingly.

STANI

Absolutely. She has charm and spirit and temperament, but there's one thing she doesn't have: breeding.

HANS KARL

Do you think so?

STANI

You know, Uncle Kari, I'm a very fair-minded man; a woman can have given me, a hundred times over, the utmost proofs of her goodwill towards me—I'll grant her good points yet remain firmly aware of her bad ones. You understand, I think everything out and always make a division into two categories. So I put women into two main categories: those made for love affairs and those for marriage. Antoinette belongs to the first category. Let her be Adolf Hechingen's wife a hundred times over, for me she's not a wife but—the other kind.

HANS KARL

That's where she belongs, of course. If one likes to divide people into such categories.

STANI

Absolutely. That's why, by the way, it's utterly stupid to try reconciling her to her husband.

HANS KARL

But if he is her husband after all? Forgive me, perhaps that's a very bourgeois notion.

STANI

You know, if I may go on, I make my categories and stick to them absolutely, affairs of gallantry on one side, marriage on the other. Marriage is not an experiment. It's the result of coming to a right decision.

HANS KARL

From which you are of course far removed.

STANI

Not at all. Ready to take the decision at any moment.

HANS KARL

At this very moment?

STANI

I find myself extraordinarily well qualified to make a woman happy, but please don't tell Mamma that, I want to keep complete freedom of action. I'm exactly like you in that. I can't bear being driven into a corner. (*Hans Karl smokes.*) The decision must be instantaneous. At once or not at all, that's my motto!

HANS KARL

Nothing in the world interests me so much as how a man can move from one situation into another. So you would never postpone a decision?

STANI

Never, that's absolute weakness.

HANS KARL

But there's such a thing as complications?

STANI

I refuse to admit them.

HANS KARL

Suppose there were contradictory obligations interfering with each other?

STANI

In that case one chooses which are the ones to honor.

HANS KARL

But in making this choice one can be sometimes rather at a loss.

STANI

How so?

HANS KARL

Well, let us say hampered by self-reproach.

STANI

That's for hypochondriacs. I'm a very sound specimen. At the front I hadn't a single day's illness.

HANS KARL

Ah, you're always absolutely satisfied that you've done the right thing?

STANI

Yes, if it weren't the right thing I should have behaved differently.

HANS KARL

I don't just mean correct behavior—but, to put it briefly, you let blind chance, or shall we say destiny, guide you?

STANI

How so? I always keep things well in hand.

HANS KARL

Yet sometimes in such decisive moments one is tempted to let a fantastic notion intervene: the notion of a Higher Necessity.

STANI

What I do is simply necessary, or I shouldn't do it.

HANS KARL *showing interest*

Forgive me if I take an example from actual life—that's not really the thing to do—

STANI

But please do—

HANS KARL

Let us suppose that a certain situation brought you close to the decision to get married.

STANI

Today or tomorrow.

HANS KARL

But then you're already more or less tied up with Antoinette.

STANI

I should break with her at once!

HANS KARL

Ah! Without any occasion for it?

STANI

But the occasion for it is at hand all the time. Look, our affair has been going on since the spring. Yet for the last six or seven weeks there's been something about Antoinette, I don't know what—to say I suspect her would be to say too much—but the mere idea that she might be preoccupied with someone else besides me, you know, I'm absolutely against that.

HANS KARL

I see.

STANI

You know, I can't help it. I shouldn't like to call it jealousy, it's rather a not being able to understand how a woman attached to me could be interested in someone else at the same time— do you follow me?

HANS KARL

But Antoinette's so innocent whenever she's up to mischief. It makes her almost more endearing than ever.

STANI

There I simply don't understand you.

SCENE IX

NEUGEBAUER

has come in quietly

Here are the letters, your Lordship. I found them in the first place I looked—

HANS KARL

Thank you. Please give me them. (*Neugebauer hands over the letters.*) Thank you.

Neugebauer goes out.

SCENE X

HANS KARL

after a short pause

Do you know whom I think of as a born husband?

STANI

Well?

HANS KARL

Adolf Hechingen.

STANI

Antoinette's husband? Ha ha ha!—

HANS KARL

I say it in all seriousness.

STANI

But Uncle Kari!

HANS KARL

In his attachment to his wife there is a Higher Necessity.

STANI

He's a born—I won't say what!

HANS KARL

What happens to him matters to me.

STANI

For me he comes into the category of men lacking instincts. Do you know whom he hangs on to when you're not in the Club? Me. Me, of all people! He has a flair!

HANS KARL

I'm fond of him.

STANI

But he's inelegant from top to toe.

HANS KARL

But he has a kind of inward grace.

STANI

An inelegant, long-winded bore.

HANS KARL

He needs a bottle of champagne to quicken his blood.

STANI

Don't let him hear that, he'll take it literally. I can't stand a man of no elegance when he's been drinking.

HANS KARL

I'm fond of him.

STANI

He takes everything literally, including your friendship for him.

HANS KARL

He's entitled to take that literally.

STANI

Forgive me, Uncle Kari, you're not a man to be taken literally; anyone who does that falls into the category of men lacking instincts.

HANS KARL

But he's such a good, decent fellow.

STANI

He may be, if you say so, but that's no reason for his continually harping on your kindness. That gets on my nerves. An elegant man can show bonhomie, but he can't be a kind man. Excuse me, I say to him, Uncle Kari is a great gentleman and therefore of course a great egotist. You forgive me?

HANS KARL

It's no use, I'm fond of him.

STANI

That's so eccentric of you! But you have no need to be eccentric. You have the wonderful quality of presenting yourself as you are, without the slightest effort—as a great gentleman. Without any effort! That's the great thing. Second-rate men are always making efforts. Take that Theophilus Neuhoff who's been cropping up everywhere this last year. What kind of existence has such a creature except a continuous wretched effort to copy a way of life that simply isn't his?

SCENE XI

LUKAS

comes in hastily

May I ask—has your Lordship given instructions that visitors from outside are to be shown in?

HANS KARL

Absolutely not. What's all this?

LUKAS

Then the new footman must have mixed things up. The porter's lodge has just telephoned to say that Herr Baron Neuhoff is on his way up. Please tell me what to do with him.

STANI

You see, just when we were speaking about him. That's no accident. Uncle Kari, that man is my *guignon,* and I conjure him up. A week ago at Helen's, just when I was going to tell her what I thought of Herr von Neuhoff, in that very moment he appeared in the doorway. Three days ago I was just leaving Antoinette—who should be in the anteroom but Herr von Neuhoff? Yesterday morning at my mother's I had something urgent to discuss with her, and as soon as I reached the anteroom what I found was Herr von Neuhoff.

VINCENT

comes in, announces

Herr Baron Neuhoff is in the anteroom.

HANS KARL

Now of course I'll have to receive him.

Lukas makes a gesture that the visitor is to be admitted.

Vincent opens the folding doors and shows him in.

Vincent and Lukas go out.

SCENE XII

NEUHOFF

comes in

Good evening, Count Bühl. I made so bold as to enquire if you were at home.

HANS KARL

Do you know my nephew Freudenberg?

STANI

We have met before.

They sit down.

NEUHOFF

I was to have had the pleasure of meeting you tonight at the Altenwyls'. Countess Helen had promised herself some small satisfaction in bringing us together. My disappointment was all the more grievous when I learned from Countess Helen this afternoon that you had begged to be excused.

HANS KARL

You have known my cousin, have you, since last winter?

NEUHOFF

Known, yes—if one dare use such a word in reference to her. There are moments when one suddenly realizes how ambiguous the word is; it describes the most superficial relationship in the world and at the same time the deepest mystery of communion between person and person. (*Hans Karl and Stani exchange a look.*) I have the good fortune to see Countess Helen frequently and to be bound to her by ties of devotion. (*A short, somewhat embarrassed pause*) This afternoon—we were both in Bohuslawsky's studio—Bohuslawsky is painting my portrait, that's to say, he's tormenting himself unreasonably about catching the expression of my eyes; he says there's a certain something in them that can be seen only at rare moments—it was he who begged Countess Helen to come and see the portrait and give him her opinion about the eyes—well, she said to me: Count Bühl isn't coming, you should go to see him. Just pay him a visit, quite simply. He is a man with whom natural lack of affectation achieves everything and calculated behavior nothing at all. A wonderful man in our calculating world, was my answer—but that's what I thought he was like, that's what I guessed him to be, at our very first meeting.

STANI

Did you meet my uncle at the front?

NEUHOFF

On the Staff.

HANS KARL

Not the most congenial company to be found in.

NEUHOFF

One could tell how you felt about it, for you said extremely little.

HANS KARL *smiling*

I'm no great conversationalist, am I, Stani?

STANI

Among close friends you are!

NEUHOFF

You've put your finger on it, Count Freudenberg, your uncle likes to make his payments in gold; he can't demean himself to accept the paper currency of ordinary intercourse. His words can give away nothing less than intimate friendship, and that is beyond price.

HANS KARL

You are extremely kind, Baron Neuhoff.

NEUHOFF

You should have your portrait painted by Bohuslawsky, Count Bühl. He would catch your essence in three sittings. You know that he's renowned for his portraits of children. Your smile has just a suggestion in it of a child's laughter. Don't misunderstand me. What is it makes real dignity so inimitable? Because there is a residue of the childlike in it. By way of this childlike quality Bohuslawsky would get round to imbuing your portrait with something which is extremely rare in our world and distinguishes you in the highest degree: dignity. For we live in a world that lacks dignity.

HANS KARL

I hardly know what world you're referring to: at the front we met with human dignity in plenty, all of us—

NEUHOFF

That's why a man like you was in his element at the front. How great were your achievements, Count Bühl! I have in mind the noncommissioned officer in hospital who was buried in the same trench with you and thirty of your riflemen.

HANS KARL

My brave sergeant, Franz Hütter! Did my cousin tell you about him?

NEUHOFF

She permitted me to accompany her when she visited the hospital. I shall never forget the dying man's expression and what he said. (*Hans Karl is silent.*) He spoke only about you. And in what a tone! He knew that the lady he was speaking to was a relative of his captain's.

HANS KARL

Poor Franz Hütter!

NEUHOFF

Perhaps Countess Helen wished to let me have an impression of you such as a thousand social encounters could not have provided.

STANI *a little sharply*

Perhaps she wished above all to see the man himself and to hear about Uncle Kari.

NEUHOFF

For a being like Helen Altenwyl it takes a situation of that kind to bring out her true self. Beneath her perfect simplicity, her pride of race, there lies hidden a stream of loving feeling, a sympathy that radiates through every pore: to anyone whom she loves and respects she is bound by inexpressible ties that nothing can disrupt and nothing disconcert. Woe to the husband who fails to respect this unutterable sense of affinities in her, who would be narrow-hearted enough to wish to monopolize for himself all these radiations of sympathy. (*A short pause. Hans Karl smokes.*) She is like you, one of these people whom one cannot win, who must bestow themselves upon one. (*Again a short pause. Continues with great, perhaps not wholly genuine, assurance.*) I am a wanderer, my curiosity has driven me half round the world. I am fascinated by what is difficult to know; I am drawn to whatever hides itself. A proud and precious creature like Countess Helen I should like to see in your company,

Count Bühl. She would become a different being, she would blossom out; for I don't know anyone who is so responsive to human quality.

HANS KARL

We're all a little that way inclined here. Perhaps my cousin is not so unusual in that respect.

NEUHOFF

The social circle which ought to surround a creature like Helen Altenwyl should consist, I think, of men like you. Every culture puts out its own flowers: substance without pretension, nobility mellowed by infinite grace, is what the culture of this ancient society produces, which has succeeded in doing what the ruins of Luxor and the forests of the Caucasus could not do, to hold an inconstant creature like myself spellbound in its magic circle. But do explain one thing to me, Count Bühl. It is precisely the men of your stamp—to whom society owes its true character—that one meets all too seldom in it. You seem to avoid society.

STANI

Oh, not at all. You will meet Uncle Kari this very evening at the Altenwyls', and I'm even afraid that, pleasant as this little talk has been, we must soon give him the opportunity of dressing.

He has risen from his chair.

NEUHOFF *rising*

If we must, then I shall say adieu for the present, Count Bühl. If ever, in any circumstances whatsoever, you need a knight-errant (*already making for the door*), who is willing to enter, unconditionally and reverently, into the service of the noble and the good wherever he finds it, please call upon me. (*Hans Karl and Stani behind him escort him. As they reach the door the telephone rings.*) Do stay where you are, you are wanted on the telephone.

STANI

May I escort you to the stairway?

HANS KARL *at the door*

I thank you very much for your friendly visit, Baron Neuhoff. (*Neuhoff and Stani go out. Hans Karl left alone with the loudly ringing telephone goes to the wall and presses the button of the house telephone, calling.*) Lukas, switch off the telephone! I can't stand that indiscreet machine! Lukas!

The telephone stops ringing.

SCENE XIII

STANI

comes back

Only for a moment, Uncle Kari. I must hear what you think of this gentleman!

HANS KARL

What you think of him seems to be already cut-and-dried.

STANI

Oh, I find him simply impossible. I simply don't understand a type like that. And yet he comes of quite a good family!

HANS KARL

So you think he's utterly unacceptable?

STANI

But, I ask you: every word he speaks is a gaffe.

HANS KARL

He wants to be very amiable, he wants to win people over.

STANI

But a gentleman keeps his countenance, he doesn't crawl into the bosom of an utter stranger.

HANS KARL

And, besides, he believes that a man can make something of himself—now, I should regard that as naïve or the result of a faulty upbringing.

STANI

walking to and fro in agitation

All these tirades about Helen!

HANS KARL

That a girl like Helen should discuss one of us with him doesn't particularly amuse me either.

STANI

I'm sure there's not a word of truth in it. A fellow who blows hot and cold at the same time.

HANS KARL

Something like it must have happened as he said. But there are people who can't help distorting every nuance.

STANI

You're so tolerant!

HANS KARL

I'm simply growing old, Stani.

STANI

It infuriates me, anyhow; his whole tone is an affront, the false assurance, the oily glibness, that twiddling with his odious little pointed beard.

HANS KARL

He has intelligence, but it's of a kind to make one feel queasy.

STANI

These unspeakable indiscretions. I ask you, what business of his is the expression on your face?

HANS KARL

Au fond, perhaps one should be sorry for a man like that.

STANI

I call him an odious creature. But I must go up to Mamma now. I'll be seeing you anyhow in the Club tonight, Uncle Kari. (*Agathe peeps through the door right, thinking Hans Karl is alone. Stani turns and comes forward again. Hans Karl waves Agathe back.*) You know, I just can't simmer down. First, the vulgarity of flattering a man like you to your face.

HANS KARL

No, that wasn't very elegant.

STANI

Secondly, the parading of God knows how thick a friendship with Helen. Thirdly, the probing to see if you were interested in her.

HANS KARL *smiling*

Do you think he wanted to spy out the ground?

STANI

Fourthly, his unbounded indiscretion in hinting at his future situation. He practically announced himself as her husband-to-be. Fifthly, his odious perorations, which make any retort quite impossible. Sixthly, his impossible exit lines. He delivered himself of a regular birthday oration, a whole leading article. But I'm keeping you, Uncle Kari. (*Agathe has peeped again through the door; the same business as before. Stani is already nearly through the door but comes forward again.*) Just a word more, if I may? There's one thing I can't understand, that this affair with Helen doesn't affect you more.

HANS KARL

Why me?

STANI

Well, Helen's too close to me for these impossible phrases about "devotion" and "being bound to her" not to stick in my throat. I've known Helen all her life, like a sister!

HANS KARL

The moment comes when sisters leave their brothers.

STANI

But not for a Neuhoff! No, no!

HANS KARL

A small modicum of insincerity goes down well with women.

STANI

A fellow like that shouldn't be allowed anywhere near Helen.

HANS KARL

We shan't be able to prevent it.

STANI

We'll see about that! Not anywhere near her!

HANS KARL

He has announced our coming relationship.

STANI

What state of mind must Helen be in to get involved with this creature!

HANS KARL

You know, I've learned not to draw conclusions about a woman's state of mind from anything she does.

STANI

Not that I'm jealous; but to think of a person like Helen as the wife of this Neuhoff—it's so sheerly incredible—the idea is simply beyond my grasp—I must talk it over with Mamma at once.

HANS KARL *smiling*

Yes, do that, Stani.

Stani goes out.

SCENE XIV

LUKAS *comes in*

I'm afraid the telephone was switched on here.

HANS KARL

I don't want it to be.

LUKAS

Very well, your Lordship. The new footman must have turned the switch without my noticing him. He has his fingers and his ears everywhere he has no business to have them.

HANS KARL

Pack him off tomorrow morning at seven o'clock.

LUKAS

Very good. It was Count Hechingen's man who was ringing up. The Count would like to speak to you himself about whether your Lordship is going to Count Altenwyl's soirée or not this evening. Because Countess Hechingen will be there.

HANS KARL

Ring up Count Altenwyl's now and say I have had a previous engagement canceled and beg to be allowed to come to the soirée after all. And then put me on to Count Hechingen; I'll speak to him myself. And meanwhile ask the lady's maid to come in.

LUKAS

Very good.

Goes out. Agathe comes in.

SCENE XV

HANS KARL

takes the packet of letters

Here are the letters. Tell the Countess that I can part with these letters because of the beautiful memories I have that nothing can destroy; I shall have them always with me not in a letter, but everywhere.

AGATHE

Oh, I kiss your hand! You make me so happy. For now I know that my lady will soon meet our Count again.

HANS KARL

She will meet me tonight. I'm going to the party.

AGATHE

And dare we hope that she—that the man who meets her will be the same as ever?

HANS KARL

She has no better friend.

AGATHE

Oh, I kiss your hand.

HANS KARL

She has only two sincere friends in the world, myself and her husband.

AGATHE

Oh, goodness, I don't want to hear that. Oh my goodness, what bad luck that our Count has grown so friendly with Count Hechingen. My poor lady has indeed been spared nothing.

HANS KARL

nervously moving away a step or two

Do women really have so little intuition of what a man is like? And of who is really fond of them?

AGATHE

Oh, anything but that. We'll believe anything your Lordship tells us, but not that—that's too much!

HANS KARL

pacing up and down

So not that. Not to be able to help! Not even so little!

Pause

AGATHE

shyly, coming nearer to him

Or you might try, all the same. But not through me: I'm not clever enough to be a go-between. I shouldn't find the right words. And not in writing, either. That only causes misunderstandings. But face to face: yes, surely! Then you might persuade her. What couldn't you persuade my lady to! Not perhaps at the first try. But time and again—if you make an appeal to her better feelings—how could she resist you?

The telephone rings again.

HANS KARL

goes to the telephone and speaks into it

Yes, speaking. Here. Yes, I'm listening. I'll wait. Count Bühl. Yes, in person.

AGATHE

I kiss your hand.

She goes out quickly through the middle doors.

HANS KARL *at the telephone*

Hechingen, good evening to you. Yes, I've thought better of it. I've agreed to go. I'll find an opportunity. Certainly. Yes, that was partly why I made up my mind to go. A soirée's the very thing, since I don't play bridge and I don't think your wife does either. There's no need. No need for that either. For your pessimism! Pessimism, I said! There's no need for you to be cast down. Throw it off absolutely! All alone? Then try the old bottle of champagne. I'll certainly report the result to you before midnight. Don't be too hopeful either, of course. You know that I'll do my utmost. It suits with my own feeling, too. Suits with my own feeling! What? The connection bad? I said: it suits with my own feeling. Feeling! A word that doesn't matter. No, not absurd, a word. I said: a word that doesn't matter. What word? Feeling! No, I only said it didn't matter because you didn't catch it for so long. Yes. Yes. Yes! Adieu. Over! (*He rings off.*) There are people who make everything complicated, and yet he's such a decent fellow!

SCENE XVI

STANI

once more in the middle doors

Am I presuming too much, Uncle Kari?

HANS KARL

Not at all, I'm at your disposal.

STANI

coming forward beside him

I must tell you, Uncle Kari, that meanwhile I've had a talk with Mamma and come to a decision. (*Hans Karl looks at him.*) I'm going to get engaged to Helen Altenwyl.

HANS KARL

You're going to—

STANI

Yes, I've made up my mind to marry Helen. Not today and not tomorrow, but fairly soon. I've thought it all out. On the stairs, as I was going up to the second landing. By the time I reached Mamma on the second floor I had it all cut-and-dried. The idea struck me in a flash, you know, when I saw that you weren't really interested in Helen.

HANS KARL

Aha.

STANI

Do you understand? That was just one of Mamma's notions. She always says that one never knows where one is with you— possibly, she says, you did, after all, toy with the idea of marrying Helen—and you're still the head of the family for Mamma, she's altogether a Bühl at heart.

HANS KARL

half turned away

Dear Crescence!

STANI

But I contradicted everything she said. After all, I know you through and through. I've always felt that there wasn't anything in the idea of your being interested in Helen.

HANS KARL

suddenly turning round

And your mother?

STANI

Mamma?

HANS KARL

Yes, how did she take it?

STANI

All for it, of course, delighted. She went quite red in the face with joy. Does that surprise you, Uncle Kari?

HANS KARL

Just a little, just a shade—I've always had the impression that your mother always thought of Helen in a particular way.

STANI

An aversion?

HANS KARL

Not at all. Just an intention. A supposition.

STANI

An earlier one? Some time ago?

HANS KARL

No, half an hour ago.

STANI

Pointing in what direction? But Mamma is such a weathercock! She forgets such things in no time. Any decision that I come to brings her to her knees at once. She yields to the man in me. She adores the fait accompli.

HANS KARL

So you have decided?

STANI

Yes, I have decided.

HANS KARL

In a twinkling, like that!

STANI

That's the whole point. That's what impresses women so much in me. And that's just how I always keep the initiative. (*Hans Karl smokes.*) You see, perhaps you did once think of marrying Helen—

HANS KARL

Goodness, years ago maybe. In an idle moment, as one thinks of so many things.

STANI

Do you see? I never thought of it at all! And yet, in the very moment when I do think of it, I put it into execution. — Is something disturbing you?

HANS KARL

I couldn't help thinking about Antoinette for a moment.

STANI

But everything in the world has to come to an end sometime.

HANS KARL

Of course. And you're not bothering at all about whether Helen's free or not? She seems, for instance, to have given this Neuhoff grounds for hope.

STANI

That's exactly what I'm depending on. The hopes of a Herr von Neuhoff I can merely ignore. But that Helen should consider for a moment a Theophilus Neuhoff proves only that she has no serious preoccupation at all. Complications of that nature aren't worth thinking about. They're freaks of caprice, or shall we say, aberrations.

HANS KARL

She's not easy to fathom.

STANI

But I know her genre. When it comes to the point, she couldn't take an interest in any type of man except our own kind: anything else is an aberration. You're so quiet, do you have one of your headaches?

HANS KARL

Not at all. I'm admiring your courage.

STANI

You, admiring courage!

HANS KARL

This is a different courage from the kind in the trenches.

STANI

I do understand you so well, Uncle Kari. You're thinking of the other chances I may be missing. You feel that perhaps I'm disposing of myself too easily. But, you see, there again I have quite a different outlook: I'm all for common sense and definite conclusions. Forgive me for saying so, Uncle Kari, but *au fond* you're an idealist: your thoughts fly off to the absolute, to some ideal of perfection. That's a very elegant way of thinking, but it can't be realized. *Au fond* you're like Mamma; you think nothing's good enough for me. Now I've thought this matter out as it is. Helen is a year younger than I am.

HANS KARL

A year?

STANI

She's of an excellent family.

HANS KARL

One could not be better born.

STANI

She's elegant.

HANS KARL

Very elegant.

STANI

She's rich.

HANS KARL

And above all, so lovely.

STANI

She's well-bred.

HANS KARL

Incomparably so.

STANI

And in my opinion, above all she has the two qualities most essential in marriage. First: she cannot tell a lie; second: she has the best manners in the world:

HANS KARL

She is charmingly considerate, as only old women usually are.

STANI

Her mind lights up everything.

HANS KARL

You needn't tell me that. I love talking to her.

STANI

And in time she'll adore me.

HANS KARL

to himself, involuntarily

That's possible, too.

STANI

Not only possible. Quite certain. Marriage does that for women of her genre. In a liaison everything depends on chance and circumstance, so that fantastic things may happen, deceptions and God knows what. In marriage all is based on a permanent relationship; in the long run each partner absorbs the quality of the other to such an extent that no real difference can arise: always provided that the marriage is based on a right decision. That's the meaning of marriage.

SCENE XVII

LUKAS *entering*

Her ladyship Countess Freudenberg.

CRESCENCE

comes past Lukas, moving rapidly

Well, what does my Kari say to the boy now? I'm more than delighted. Let us have congratulations!

HANS KARL

a little absently

My dear Crescence, I wish him the greatest success.

Stani silently takes leave.

CRESCENCE

Send the car back for me.

STANI

It's at your disposal. I'm going on foot.

Exit.

SCENE XVIII

CRESCENCE

His success will depend very much on you.

HANS KARL

On me? But it's written on his forehead that he'll always get what he wants.

CRESCENCE

Helen will go by your judgment.

HANS KARL

How so, Crescence, in what way?

CRESCENCE

And her father Altenwyl of course even more. Stani's an eligible young man but not a brilliant match. I'm under no illusions about that. But if my Kari backs him up, a word from him has tremendous weight with the older people. I'm sure I don't know why.

HANS KARL

Simply because I'm almost one of them myself.

CRESCENCE

None of this airiness about old age! You and I are neither old nor young. I do hate half-and-between situations. I'd rather be quite on the shelf with gray hair and horn-rimmed spectacles.

HANS KARL

That's why my sister has begun matchmaking so early.

CRESCENCE

I've always wanted to do it for my Kari, as long as twelve years ago. But he always put up a dumb, obstinate resistance.

HANS KARL

My dear Crescence!

CRESCENCE

Haven't I said a hundred times: let my Kari tell me what he wants and I'll take it in hand.

HANS KARL

Often enough, God knows, Crescence.

CRESCENCE

But one never knew where one stood with Kari. (*Hans Karl nods.*) And now Stani's simply going to do what Kari never would. I can hardly wait to see little children running about again in Hohenbühl and Göllersdorf.

HANS KARL

And falling into the lake! Do you remember how they fished me out half-drowned? Do you know—I sometimes have the idea that nothing new happens in the world.

CRESCENCE

What's in the back of your mind?

HANS KARL

That whatever happens has been long ready, waiting some-
where, and only comes to light suddenly. You know, like the lake
at Hohenbühl, when the water's been drawn off in autumn and
suddenly the carp and the tails of the stone Tritons are all there
which one could hardly see before. A grotesque idea, what!

CRESCENCE

Has something suddenly upset you, Kari?

HANS KARL

pulls himself together

On the contrary, Crescence. I thank you as warmly as I can, you
and Stani, for the way you have quickened my life with your
vitality and your decisiveness.

He kisses her hand.

CRESCENCE

Does my Kari find that it does him good to have us beside him?

HANS KARL

Haven't I a very fine evening ahead of me? First, a serious talk
with Toinette—

CRESCENCE

But there's surely no need for that now!

HANS KARL

Oh, I might as well talk to her, I had my mind made up to it in
any case, and then as Stani's uncle I have those various im-
portant conversations to take in hand.

CRESCENCE

The most important thing is to present Stani to Helen in a
good light.

HANS KARL

So I have a regular program. Does Crescence see how she is reforming me? But do you know—I have an idea—first I'll go for an hour to the circus, they have a clown there—a kind of Simple Simon.

CRESCENCE

Furlani, it is. Nanni's quite crazy about him. It's not the kind of thing that amuses me.

HANS KARL

I find him enchanting. He delights me much more than the wittiest talk of anybody on earth. I shall enjoy myself enormously. I'll go to the circus, then have something to eat in a restaurant, and then turn up in a very good mood at the soirée and carry out my program.

CRESCENCE

Yes, my Kari will come and prepare Helen to hear what Stani has to say, you can do that kind of thing so well. You would have made such a wonderful ambassador if you had stuck to your career.

HANS KARL

It's rather late now for that too.

CRESCENCE

Well, have a good time and don't be too long in following us.

Hans Karl escorts her to the door. Crescence goes out.

SCENE XIX

Hans Karl comes forward again. Lukas has come in with him.

HANS KARL

I'm going to wear my tails. I'll ring in a minute.

LUKAS

Very good, your lordship.

Hans Karl goes out left.

SCENE XX

VINCENT

comes in right

What are you doing now?

LUKAS

I'm waiting for the dressing-room bell to ring, then I'm going in to help.

VINCENT

I'll come with you. It's quite good for me to get in the way of it.

LUKAS

You haven't been asked for, so you will keep out.

VINCENT

helping himself to a cigar

Well, he's an easygoing, amenable kind of creature, his relations do what they like with him. In a month's time I'll be winding him round my little finger. (*Lukas locks the cigar cabinet. A bell is heard. Lukas hurries.*) Don't go yet. Let him ring twice. (*He sinks into an armchair. Lukas goes out behind him. Vincent to himself.*) He's sending his love letters back, he's marrying off his nephew, and he himself has made up his mind to an old bachelor's life with me. That's just what I thought would happen. (*Over his shoulder, without turning round*) Well, my *dear* sir, I'm very pleased with everything, I'm going to stay!

Curtain

Act II

At the Altenwyls'. A small drawing room in eighteenth-century style. Doors left, right, and in the middle. Altenwyl with Hans Karl entering from the right. Crescence with Helen and Neuhoff standing in conversation left.

SCENE I

ALTENWYL

My dear Kari, I am doubly obliged to you for coming, since you don't play bridge and are therefore willing to put up with the modest odds and ends of entertainment one can still provide in a drawing room. You know already that you will find here only the same familiar faces, no artists or other celebrities—indeed, Edine Merenberg is extremely scornful of such old-fashioned hospitality, but neither Helen nor I relish the kind of social intercourse Edine rates so highly, where with the first mouthful of soup she asks her neighbor whether he believes in the transmigration of souls or has ever sworn brotherhood with a fakir.

CRESCENCE

I must give you the lie there, Count Altenwyl, for I met an entirely new face at my bridge table, and Mariette Stradonitz whispered to me that he's a world-famous scholar we've never heard of simply because we're all illiterate.

ALTENWYL

Professor Brücke is a great celebrity in his subject and a welcome political colleague of mine. He enjoys enormously being in a drawing room where he meets with no colleagues from the academic world, so that he is, as it were, the sole representative of learning in a purely social circle, and since my house can offer him this modest indulgence—

CRESCENCE

Is he married?

ALTENWYL

At any rate I have never had the honor of meeting Madame Brücke.

CRESCENCE

I find famous men odious, but their wives are still worse. Kari agrees with me there. We're all for trivial people and trivial conversations, aren't we, Kari?

ALTENWYL

I have my own old-fashioned predilections, Helen knows what they are.

CRESCENCE

You should back me up, Kari. I find that nine-tenths of what passes for intellectual conversation is just twaddle.

NEUHOFF *to Helen*

Are you equally severe, Countess Helen?

HELEN

We have every reason, we of the younger generation, to feel that if anything in the world makes our flesh creep it's the art of conversation: words that flatten everything real under a dead layer of soothing syrup.

CRESCENCE

Do back me up, Kari!

HANS KARL

Let me off this time. Furlani doesn't put one in the frame of mind to be brilliant.

ALTENWYL

In my opinion, the art of conversation is a lost art nowadays: it consists not in pouring out words oneself like a waterfall but in stimulating others. In my time one used to say: with my guest I must manage the conversation so that when his hand is on the door latch he'll feel that he has been brilliant, then on the way downstairs he'll think me brilliant. Nowadays, if you'll excuse my rudeness, no one understands how to make conversation or how to keep silent—oh, allow me to present Baron Neuhoff to you, my cousin Count Bühl.

NEUHOFF

I already have the honor of Count Bühl's acquaintance.

CRESCENCE *to Altenwyl*

It's to Edine you should be saying all these clever things—she drives her cult of important people and printed books to ridiculous lengths. I begin to hate the very words: important people—they sound so domineering!

ALTENWYL

Edine is a very clever woman but she's always trying to kill two birds with one stone: to improve her education and also make something on the side for her charities.

HELEN

Forgive me, Papa, she's not really a clever woman, rather a silly one, for she would give her eyes to have clever people round her but always picks the wrong ones.

CRESCENCE

It surprises me that her wild woolgathering doesn't cause more confusion.

ALTENWYL

People like her have guardian angels.

EDINE

arriving through the middle door

I see that you're speaking about me, please go on doing it, don't
be embarrassed.

CRESCENCE

Well, Edine, have you met the famous man yet?

EDINE

I'm furious, Count Altenwyl, that you gave him to her as a partner
and not to me. (*Sits down near Crescence.*) You have no idea how
much I'm interested in him. After all, I read these people's books.
Only a week or two ago I read a thick book by this Brückner.

NEUHOFF

He's called Brücke. He's the second President of the Academy
of Sciences.

EDINE

In Paris?

NEUHOFF

No, here in Vienna.

EDINE

But on the book it said: Brückner.

CRESCENCE

Perhaps a printer's mistake.

EDINE

The book was called *On the Origin of All Religions*. What learning
was in it, what depth! And such a fine style!

HELEN

I'll bring him to you, Aunt Edine.

NEUHOFF

If you allow me, I'll find him and bring him here as soon as he's disengaged.

EDINE

Please do, Baron Neuhoff. Tell him I've been longing to meet him for years.

Neuhoff goes out left.

CRESCENCE

He'll ask for nothing better, I should think, he's a fairly thorough—

EDINE

Don't be in such a hurry to call people snobs; didn't Goethe too think every duchess and countess a—dear me, I'd better be careful what I say.

CRESCENCE

She's got on to Goethe again, our Edine.

Looks round for Hans Karl, who has moved right with Helen.

HELEN *to Hans Karl*

You like Furlani so much, do you?

HANS KARL

A man like him is a real recreation to me.

HELEN

Does he have such clever tricks?

She sits down right, Hans Karl beside her.

Crescence goes out through the middle door.

Altenwyl and Edine have sat down left.

HANS KARL

He has no tricks at all. He's just the zany, the simple Simon.

HELEN

A kind of buffoon, then?

HANS KARL

No, that would be overdoing it. He never does that, nor does he do caricatures either. He plays his role: the man who wants to understand everybody and help everybody and yet brings everything into the utmost confusion. He makes the silliest blunders, the gallery rocks with laughter, and yet he does it with such elegance, such discretion, that one realizes how much he respects himself and everything in the world. He makes a hash of everything; wherever he intervenes there's a complete mess, and yet one wants to cry out: "He's right, all the same!"

EDINE *to Altenwyl*

But a cultivated mind gives us women much more to hold on to! Antoinette, for instance, lacks that completely. I keep telling her she should cultivate her mind, it gives one other things to think of.

ALTENWYL

In my time conversation had quite a different set of values. We thought highly of a witty repartee: we used to lay ourselves out to be brilliant.

EDINE

What I say is: when I make conversation I want to be taken out of myself. I want to get away from the everyday round. I want to find myself in a different world!

HANS KARL *to Helen, continuing his conversation*

You see, Helen, all these feats are difficult enough—these balancing tricks and juggling and the rest of it—they all need a fabulous concentration of willpower and even intelligence. More intelligence, I fancy, than most conversations—

HELEN

I'm sure of that.

HANS KARL

Absolutely. But what Furlani does is on a much higher level than what all the others do. All the others are following a purposeful line and look neither right nor left, they hardly even breathe till they have achieved their purpose: that's the whole content of their trick. But he apparently has no purpose of his own at all—he only enters into the purposes of others. He wants to join in everything the others are doing, he's so full of goodwill, he's so fascinated by every single bit of their performance: when he balances a flowerpot on his nose he's balancing it only out of politeness, so to speak.

HELEN

But doesn't he let it drop?

HANS KARL

Yes, but the point lies in the way he lets it drop. He lets it drop out of sheer ecstasy and bliss, because he's managed to balance it so well! He believes that once you are doing a thing well it should go on happily of itself.

HELEN *to herself*

And that's usually more than the flowerpot can bear and so it falls down.

ALTENWYL *to Edine*

This businesslike tone that's so prevalent today! And, I ask you, even between men and women: a kind of open pursuit of conscious purpose in social intercourse!

EDINE

Yes, I detest that too. One needs a little artistic maneuvering, a touch of hide-and-seek—

ALTENWYL

Young people today have forgotten that to travel hopefully is better than to arrive—they're so headlong, so direct!

EDINE

Because they haven't read enough! Because they don't cultivate their minds enough!

During this exchange they have risen and go off together left.

HANS KARL *to Helen*

When one is watching Furlani, the cleverest clowns strike one as vulgar. He's wonderful to watch in his lovely nonchalance— but his very nonchalance of course needs twice as much skill as the tension of the others.

HELEN

I can understand why you find him sympathetic. Anything that betrays a purpose lurking behind it seems a little vulgar to me too.

HANS KARL

Oho, tonight I myself am laden with purposes, and these purposes concern you, Countess Helen.

HELEN

drawing her brows together

Countess Helen! Do you say "Countess Helen" to me?

Huberta appears in the middle door and darts a swift but knowing glance at Hans Karl and Helen.

HANS KARL

without noticing Huberta

No, but seriously, I must beg you to have five minutes' talk with me—later on, sometime or other—we neither of us play bridge.

HELEN

a little uneasy but very self-controlled

You make me feel apprehensive. What can you have to say to me? It sounds unpromising.

HANS KARL

If it's going to bother you, then for goodness' sake we'll call it off.

Huberta has vanished.

HELEN *after a short pause*

Very well, then, if you like, but later on. I see Huberta, she seems to be bored. I must look after her.

She rises.

HANS KARL

You're so delightfully considerate.

Has also risen.

HELEN

Now you must say good evening to Antoinette and the other ladies. (*She leaves him but pauses in the middle door.*) I'm not considerate: I'm only aware of what's going on inside people and get worried about it—and then I react by showing people the regard I have for them. My good manners are just a kind of nervous defense, to keep people at arm's length.

She goes out. Hans Karl follows her slowly.

SCENE II

*Neuhoff and the Famous Man appear together
in the doorway left.*

THE FAMOUS MAN

now in the middle of the room, looks through the doorway right

Over there, in the group beside the fireplace, is the lady whose
name I wanted to ask you.

NEUHOFF

The one in gray? That's the Duchess of Pergen.

THE FAMOUS MAN

No, I've known her a long time. The lady in black.

NEUHOFF

The Spanish Ambassadress. Have you been introduced to her?
Or may I—

THE FAMOUS MAN

I should very much like an introduction. But perhaps we'd bet-
ter arrange it in this way—

NEUHOFF

with barely perceptible irony

I am entirely at your service.

THE FAMOUS MAN

If you would perhaps be so good as to mention me first to the
lady, explaining my reputation to her, since she's a foreigner,
and my standing in the world of science and in society—then I
could follow it up at once by getting Count Altenwyl to intro-
duce me.

NEUHOFF

But with the greatest pleasure.

THE FAMOUS MAN

A scholar of my standing is not concerned merely to increase his acquaintance, but to be known and recognized for what he is.

NEUHOFF

No doubt about it. Here comes Countess Merenberg, who is particularly looking forward to meeting you. May I—

EDINE *coming forward*

This is a great pleasure. With such an eminent man, Baron Neuhoff, I beg you not to introduce him to me but to present me to him.

THE FAMOUS MAN *bowing*

I am very happy, Countess.

EDINE

I don't need to tell you, do I, that I am one of the most enthusiastic readers of your famous books. I'm always transported by your deep philosophy, your immense learning, and your beautiful prose style.

THE FAMOUS MAN

You astound me, Countess. My books are hardly light reading. True, they are not intended exclusively for professional scholars but the public they envisage must have a rather unusual depth of understanding.

EDINE

No, no, not at all! Any woman could benefit from reading such fine, profound books which lift her into a higher sphere: that's what I never tire of telling Toinette Hechingen.

THE FAMOUS MAN

May I ask which of my works has had the privilege of attracting your attention?

EDINE

But of course that wonderful book *On the Origin of All Religions*! That has such depth, and such uplift, it's an education in itself—

THE FAMOUS MAN *icily*

Hm. It is certainly a book much talked about.

EDINE

But not nearly enough. I've just been saying to Toinette that we ought all of us to have it for bedside reading.

THE FAMOUS MAN

The press in especial has gone beyond all bounds in staging publicity for this opus.

EDINE

How can you say such a thing! Such a book is surely one of the greatest—

THE FAMOUS MAN

It has interested me considerably, Countess, to find you one of the enthusiasts for this production. I myself am quite unacquainted with the book and could only with difficulty bring myself to add one to the circle of those who read such compilations.

EDINE

What? Are you not the author?

THE FAMOUS MAN

The author of this journalistic potpourri is my colleague Brückner. There is certainly a fatal similarity in our names, but the likeness ends there.

EDINE

It shouldn't be allowed for two famous philosophers to have names so like each other.

THE FAMOUS MAN

It is certainly regrettable, especially for me. In any case, Herr Brückner is far from being a philosopher. He's a philologist, or rather a drawing room philologist, or, better still, a philological journalist.

EDINE

I'm terribly sorry to have got so mixed up. But I'm sure I must have some of your famous works in my house, Professor. I read everything that helps one along a bit. I've just got a very interesting book about Semi-Pelagianism lying on my table, and another called *The Soul of Radium*. If you would come to see me sometime in the Heugasse—

THE FAMOUS MAN *coldly*

I should be honored, Countess. But I am already overwhelmed with engagements.

EDINE

is on the point of going but stands still again

But I'm terribly sorry that you're not the author! For now I can't ask you the question I wanted to ask. And I would have wagered anything that you were the one man who could answer it so that my mind is set at rest.

NEUHOFF

Won't you put your question to the Professor, all the same?

EDINE

You're certainly a man of even more profound learning than the other one. (*To Neuhoff*) Should I really? It's something that matters a great deal to me. I would give my eyes to have my mind set at rest.

THE FAMOUS MAN

Won't you sit down, Countess?

EDINE

looking anxiously around in case someone should come in, says quickly

What do you imagine Nirvana would be like?

THE FAMOUS MAN

Hm. For an extempore answer to that question you had much better apply to Herr Brückner.

A short pause

EDINE

And now I must go back to my bridge table. Good evening for the present, Professor.

She goes out.

THE FAMOUS MAN

obviously upset

Hm.—

NEUHOFF

Poor, dear Countess Edine. You shouldn't take her too seriously.

THE FAMOUS MAN *coldly*

This is not the first time a member of the lay public has mistaken me for that other—I almost begin to believe that the charlatan Brückner is deliberately working to that end. You can hardly conceive how painful is the inward impression left by a grotesque and false misunderstanding such as we have just experienced. To see a trumpery pretense of sham knowledge, heralded by the fanfares of a rascally press, in full sail on the broad stream of popularity—to see oneself mistaken for that, against which one believed oneself inviolably shielded behind the icy silence of indifference—

NEUHOFF

But you don't need to tell me all that, my dear Professor! I can feel for you and with you down to the smallest detail. To see oneself misunderstood in one's best qualities, all one's life— that is the destiny—

THE FAMOUS MAN

In one's best qualities.

NEUHOFF

To see precisely that side of oneself misjudged which is what chiefly matters—

THE FAMOUS MAN

One's whole lifework confounded with a piece of journalistic—

NEUHOFF

That is the destiny—

THE FAMOUS MAN

Which in a rascally press—

NEUHOFF

—of the unusual man, as soon as he lets himself down to the level of trivial people, of women who cannot tell the fundamental difference between an empty mask and a man of weight and standing!

THE FAMOUS MAN

To find even in a drawing room the hateful signs of mob rule—

NEUHOFF

Don't be so upset. How can a man of your eminence—nothing that an Edine Merenberg and all the nobodies may say can come anywhere near you.

THE FAMOUS MAN

It's the fault of the press, that witches' brew of this, that and everything. But here I should have thought I might be safe from it. I see that I have overestimated the exclusiveness of this circle, at least where the intellectual life is concerned.

NEUHOFF

Intellect and these people! Life—and these people! All the people you see here ceased to exist long ago. They're nothing but shadows now. Nobody who circulates in these rooms belongs to the real world in which the intellectual crises of this century are resolved. Just look around you: consider that figure in the next room, from the part in his hair to the soles of his feet balancing himself in the complete assurance of unlimited triviality—besieged by women and girls—Kari Bühl.

THE FAMOUS MAN

Is that Count Bühl?

NEUHOFF

In person, the renowned Kari.

THE FAMOUS MAN

I've had no opportunity to make his acquaintance so far. Are you a friend of his?

NEUHOFF

Not particularly, but enough to sum him up for you in a couple of words: absolute, arrogant nonentity.

THE FAMOUS MAN

He has an extraordinary pre-eminence in the highest society.
He's regarded as a personality.

NEUHOFF

There's nothing in him that could stand up to examination. In
a purely social sense I appreciate him half out of habit; but you
lose less than nothing in not knowing him.

THE FAMOUS MAN

keeps on staring in that direction

I should be very interested to make his acquaintance. Do you
think it would compromise me to make the first approach?

NEUHOFF

You would be wasting your time, as with all these people here.

THE FAMOUS MAN

I should be very pleased to be properly introduced to Count
Bühl, by one of his intimate friends, say.

NEUHOFF

I have no wish to pass for one of these, but I'll arrange it for you.

THE FAMOUS MAN

I am much obliged to you. Or do you think it wouldn't be com-
promising for me to accost him of my own accord?

NEUHOFF

In either case you do dear Kari too much honor if you take him
so seriously.

THE FAMOUS MAN

I don't deny that I attach much importance to obtaining the
discriminating and incorruptible approval of high society to

add to the plaudits my learning has already brought me from a wide international public, and which I may regard as the sunset glow of a far-from-commonplace day spent in the service of knowledge.

They go out.

SCENE III

Antoinette with Edine. Nanni and Huberta meanwhile have appeared in the middle door and are coming forward.

ANTOINETTE *to them all*

Do say something, do give me some advice, for you see how upset I am. I'll make a hopeless mess of everything if you don't help me.

EDINE

I'm all for leaving her by herself. She must meet him as if by chance. If we act as a convoy we'll simply frighten him off.

HUBERTA

He's not so shy. If he wanted to speak to her by herself he would just look through us.

ANTOINETTE

So let's sit down here, anyhow. Stay beside me, all of you, but not as if on purpose.

They all sit down.

NANNI

We can just go on talking comfortably: the chief thing is, it mustn't look as if you're running after him.

ANTOINETTE

If only one had Helen's *raffinement,* she runs after him at every step and makes it look as if she were keeping out of his way.

EDINE

I'm all for leaving her alone. She should simply go to meet him as if nothing had happened.

HUBERTA

How can she meet him as if nothing had happened, in the state she's in?

ANTOINETTE *nearly in tears*

Don't tell me that I'm in a state! Try to take my mind off myself! Or else I'll lose all my self-possession. If only I had someone to flirt with!

NANNI *beginning to rise*

I'll bring Stani along.

ANTOINETTE

Stani would be less than no good to me. As soon as I know that Kari's in the same house, the others simply don't exist for me any longer.

HUBERTA

Maybe Feri Uhlfeldt would still exist.

ANTOINETTE

If Helen were in my shoes, she'd know what to do. Without turning a hair she would make a screen out of Theophilus and operate from behind him.

HUBERTA

But she hasn't even looked at Theophilus, she's been shadowing Kari all the evening.

ANTOINETTE

Must you tell me that too, so that I can go as white as a sheet? (*Rises.*) Is he talking to her?

HUBERTA

Of course he's talking to her.

ANTOINETTE

All the time?

HUBERTA

As often as I've peeped in.

ANTOINETTE

Oh my goodness, if you keep on telling me horrid things I won't be fit to look at!

She sits down again.

NANNI *making to rise*

If your three friends are too much for you, we can go away. I'd as soon be playing bridge.

ANTOINETTE

Do stay with me, do give me some advice, do tell me what I'm to do.

HUBERTA

Since she sent her maid to see him only an hour ago, she can hardly meet him now with her nose in the air.

NANNI

I see it the other way about. She must behave as if he didn't matter to her. I know that from playing cards: it's when you play your hand lightly that you have luck. You must always keep inside yourself the feeling of being on top.

ANTOINETTE

Being on top is exactly what I feel like, isn't it!

HUBERTA

But you'll handle him quite wrongly if you give yourself away like that.

EDINE

If she would only let us give her a line to follow! I know what men are like.

HUBERTA

Let me tell you, Edine, men aren't all as like as peas.

ANTOINETTE

The most sensible thing would be for me to go home.

NANNI

Who would throw in a hand so long as there was a chance left?

EDINE

If she would only listen to sensible advice. I have such a good instinct for these psychological situations. There's absolutely no reason why her marriage shouldn't be annulled, it's been like a prison for her all these years, and when it's annulled Kari will marry her if the affair is only half reasonably managed.

HUBERTA *who has glanced right*

Hush!

ANTOINETTE *starts*

Is he coming? Oh God, how my knees are trembling.

HUBERTA

It's Crescence coming. Pull yourself together.

ANTOINETTE *to herself*

My God, I can't stand her, nor she me either, but I'll commit every sort of *bassesse* before her because she's his sister.

SCENE IV

CRESCENCE

comes in from right

Good evening, how are you all? Toinette looks quite out of sorts.

Not a word among you? So many young women! Stani shouldn't have gone off to the Club, should he?

ANTOINETTE *with an effort*
We're getting on very well for the present without gentlemen.

CRESCENCE *still standing*
What do you think of Helen tonight, isn't she looking wonderful? When she's a young married woman she'll be so imposing that nobody will stand a chance against her!

HUBERTA
Is Helen so much in your good graces of a sudden?

CRESCENCE
You're all very charming too. But Antoinette should take more care of herself. She looks as if she hadn't slept for three whole nights. (*Going.*) I must tell Poldo Altenwyl how brilliant I find Helen tonight.

Goes out.

SCENE V

ANTOINETTE
My God, now I have proof positive that Kari's going to marry Helen.

EDINE
How do you make that out?

ANTOINETTE
Didn't you sense that she's beginning to cry up her future sister-in-law?

NANNI
Nonsense, don't be so despairing about nothing and less than nothing. He'll be coming through the door in a minute.

ANTOINETTE

If he comes in when I'm like this I'll be quite— (*Puts her little handkerchief to her eyes.*) —done for.

HUBERTA

We'd better go. She'll calm down meanwhile.

ANTOINETTE

No, you two go and see whether he's still talking to Helen and interrupt him if he is. You've often enough interrupted me when I wanted to be alone with him. And Edine can stay here.

They have all risen. Huberta and Nanni go out.

SCENE VI

Antoinette and Edine sit down again left, at the back.

EDINE

My dear child, you've handled this whole affair with Kari quite wrongly from the first.

ANTOINETTE

How can you tell that?

EDINE

Because Mademoiselle Feydeau gave me all the details, so I know how you bungled the whole situation even at Grünleiten.

ANTOINETTE

That malicious gossip, what does she know about it!

EDINE

It's not her fault if she heard you running barefoot down the stairs and saw you wandering with him in the moonlight with your hair down your back. — You've simply taken the whole affair much too *terre à terre* from the beginning. Of course men are very *terre à terre,* but that's just why on our side we must bring in some higher element. A man like Kari Bühl has never in all his life met anyone who could have instilled a bit of idealism into him. And so he himself is incapable of introducing anything finer into a love affair, and so it goes on, ad infinitum. If you had only asked some advice from me in the beginning, if you had let me prescribe a line for you to follow, and recommend you a book or two—you would have been his wife at this moment!

ANTOINETTE

Please, Edine, don't exasperate me.

SCENE VII

HUBERTA *appears in the doorway*

Well, Kari's coming. He's looking for you.

ANTOINETTE

Holy Mother of God!

They have risen.

NANNI

who has been peeping out right

And Helen's on her way here from the other drawing room.

ANTOINETTE

My God, at the very moment when everything's in the balance she has to come here and ruin it all. Stop her somehow. Go and meet her. Keep her away from here!

HUBERTA

Do put some kind of a good face on it.

NANNI

We can just slip away quietly.

SCENE VIII

HELEN *comes in right*

You look as though you've just been talking about me. Have you? (*Silence*) Are you enjoying yourselves? Shall I collect some gentlemen for you?

ANTOINETTE

going up to her, almost losing her self-control

We're enjoying ourselves enormously and you're an angel, my dear, to bother about us. I haven't said as much as good evening to you yet. You're looking lovelier than ever. (*Kisses her.*) But just leave us and go away again.

HELEN

Am I disturbing you? Then I shall just go away again.

Goes.

SCENE IX

ANTOINETTE

draws her fingers over her face as if to wipe off the kiss

What am I doing? Why should I let her kiss me? That viper, that false creature!

HUBERTA

Do pull yourself together a bit.

SCENE X

Hans Karl has come in right.

Edine, Nanni, and Huberta slip away.

ANTOINETTE

*after standing silent a moment with bent head, goes quickly
up to him, quite close*

I've taken the letters and burnt them. I'm not a sentimental
goose, as my Agathe makes out, to cry my eyes out over old
letters. The only thing that's real to me is what I have at any
one moment, and what I don't have I want to forget. I don't
live in the past, I'm not old enough for that.

HANS KARL

Shall we sit down?

Leads her to the armchairs.

ANTOINETTE

I'm simply not one of the artful kind. If a woman isn't sly and
subtle, she can't hold a man like you. For you're the same sort
as your nephew Stani. Let me tell you that, once and for all.
I know you both. Monsters of selfishness and utterly without
delicacy. (*After a little pause*) Do say something!

HANS KARL

If you would allow me, I should like to remind you of our time
together—

ANTOINETTE

Oh, I'm not going to let myself be ill-used—not even by some-
one who was once not indifferent to me.

HANS KARL

At that time, I mean two years ago, you were temporarily es-
tranged from your husband. You were in great danger of falling
into the wrong hands. Then someone came along—who hap-
pened to be me. I wanted to—to comfort you—that was my sole
intention—to save you from the danger—that I knew—or felt—

to be threatening you. That was a chain of fortuitous events—
or a piece of clumsiness—I don't know which to call it—

ANTOINETTE

These few days at Grünleiten are the only truly precious thing
in all my life. These I won't let you—the memory of them I
won't let anyone degrade for me.

Rises.

HANS KARL *in a low voice*

But it all means so much to me. It was so beautiful. (*Antoinette
sits down, with a troubled glance at him.*) It was so beautiful!

ANTOINETTE

"Who happened to be me." Putting it like that is an insult to
me. You've grown cynical out at the front. A cynic, that's the
right word for you. You've lost all feeling for what's possible and
what impossible. What did you say? It was "a piece of clumsiness"
on your part? You're doing nothing but insult me.

HANS KARL

At the front many things came to look different to me. But I
did not become a cynic. The very opposite, Antoinette. When I
think of what happened between us at the beginning it seems
so delicate, so mysterious, I can hardly trust myself to think of
it. I feel like asking myself: how did I fall heir to that? How did
I have the right? But (*Lowering his voice.*) I regret nothing.

ANTOINETTE

lowering her eyes

All beginnings are beautiful.

HANS KARL

Every beginning holds an eternity.

ANTOINETTE

without looking at him

Au fond you think that everything's possible and everything permissible. You don't want to see how helpless a creature is that you tread underfoot—how utterly at your mercy, for that would perhaps stir up your conscience.

HANS KARL

I have none. (*Antoinette looks at him.*) Not where we are concerned.

ANTOINETTE

I have been this and that to you—and at this moment I know as little how I stand with you as if there had never been anything between us. You are simply frightening!

HANS KARL

Nothing is evil in itself. The moment is not evil, only holding on to it is forbidden. Only the clutching at what may not be held fast—

ANTOINETTE

Oh, we're not simply like those midges that live only from sunrise to sunset. We're still there next day. That doesn't suit you, of course, a man of your kind.

HANS KARL

Everything that happens depends on chance. It doesn't bear thinking of, how much we are creatures of chance, and how chance brings us together and drives us apart, and how anyone could set up house with anyone if chance willed it.

ANTOINETTE

I won't have—

HANS KARL

goes on talking, paying no heed to her protest

And that's so gruesome a thought that men had to find something to haul them out of the morass, by the hair of their own heads. And so they found the institution that binds chance and promiscuity into what is necessary and permanent and valid: the institution of marriage.

ANTOINETTE

I'm aware that you want to palm me off on my husband. There's not a moment since you sat down here that I haven't been aware of it, and haven't let myself be fooled. You really do feel you're entitled to everything, first seduce a woman and then insult her.

HANS KARL

I'm no seducer, Toinette, I don't go chasing women.

ANTOINETTE

Yes, that's your masterpiece, that's what you won me round with, that you're no seducer, no ladies' man, only a friend, but a real friend. You make play with that, as you make play with everything you have and everything you lack. According to you, a woman shouldn't only fall in love with you but love you beyond reason, and for your own sake, and not even just as a man—but—I don't know how to put it, oh my God, why must one and the same man be so charming and at the same time so monstrously vain and selfish and heartless!

HANS KARL

Do you know what a heart is, do you know that? A man who has given his heart to a woman can show it only through one thing, one only thing in the world: through constancy, through permanence. Through that only: that is the proof, the one and only.

ANTOINETTE

You can leave Ado out of it—I can't live with Ado.

HANS KARL

He loves you. Once and for all time. He chose you among all
the women in the world and he has loved you and will love
you forever, do you know what that means? Forever, whatever
happens to you. It means having a friend who loves the whole
of you; for whom you will always be lovely, not only today and
tomorrow, but later on, much later on; for whom the veils that
the years, or whatever comes upon you, may throw over your
face—for his eyes they won't be there, you remain always what
you are, the loveliest, the dearest, the one and only one.

ANTOINETTE

He never chose me like that. He simply married me. I know
nothing about all the rest.

HANS KARL

But he knows about it.

ANTOINETTE

All that fine talk is make-believe, it isn't real. He makes himself
believe it—he makes you believe it—you're all alike, you men,
you and Ado and Stani, you're all cut out of the same block and
that's why you understand each other so well and can play so
well into each other's hands.

HANS KARL

He doesn't make me believe it, this is something I know myself,
Toinette, this is a sacred truth which I know—I must always have
known it, but it was only at the front that it first became clear
to me: there is the accident of chance, which apparently does
with us what it will—but in the middle of being thrown hither
and thither, dazed and in fear of death, we are also aware of,

and we know, that there is also a Necessity which chooses us from one moment to the next, which comes, so quietly, so close to our hearts and yet cuts keen as a sword. Without that there would have been nothing you could call a life at the front but only men dying in heaps like brute beasts. And the same Necessity runs between men and women as well—where that exists, there is a having-to-come-together, and forgiveness and reconciliation and a standing-by-one-another. And here is a place for children, and here is a marriage and a sacrament, in spite of everything—

ANTOINETTE *rises*

And all this means nothing else than that you want to get married and that you're going to marry Helen.

HANS KARL

still sitting, catches hold of her

But I'm not thinking of Helen at all! I'm speaking about you. I swear that it's you I'm speaking about.

ANTOINETTE

But all your thoughts are revolving round Helen.

HANS KARL

I swear to you: I've been charged with a message for Helen. Quite the reverse of what you think. I have to tell her tonight—

ANTOINETTE

What are you going to tell her tonight—a secret?

HANS KARL

Not one that concerns me.

ANTOINETTE

But something that makes a bond between you?

HANS KARL

The very opposite, rather.

ANTOINETTE

The opposite? A farewell—are you to tell her something that comes to a farewell between you and her?

HANS KARL

There's no need of a farewell, for there has never been anything between us. But if it gives you any satisfaction, Toinette, it is almost like a farewell.

ANTOINETTE

A lifelong farewell?

HANS KARL

Yes, lifelong, Toinette.

ANTOINETTE

turning her eyes full upon him

Lifelong? (*Thoughtfully*) Yes, she's a secretive creature and does nothing twice and says nothing twice. She takes back nothing— she has herself well in hand: a single word is decisive for her. If you say farewell to her—then it will be a farewell and forever. For her, it will be. (*After a little pause*) I won't let you talk me into having Ado. I don't like his hands. Nor his face. Nor his ears. (*Very low*) But your hands I love. — What are you, then? Yes, who are you? A cynic, an egoist, a devil, that's what you are! To leave me in the lurch, that's too ordinary for you. To keep me, you're too heartless for that. To hand me over to someone else, you're too subtle for that. So you want to be rid of me and yet keep me in your power, and for that Ado seems to be the right man. — Go and marry Helen, do. Marry whenever you like! I could perhaps have some use for your love, but none at all for your good advice. (*Makes to go away. Hans Karl takes a step towards her.*) Let me go. (*She takes a few steps away from him, then half turns towards him.*) What's to become of me now? Go on and talk me out of Feri Uhlfeldt, then, for Feri has such strength when he wants something. I've told Feri I don't want him, he replied that I can't tell what he's like as a friend, since I've never had him for a friend. These arguments muddle one up so. (*Half in tears, tenderly*) Whatever happens to me will be your fault now.

HANS KARL

You need one thing in the world—a friend. A good friend. (*He kisses her hand.*) Do be good to Ado.

ANTOINETTE

To him I can't be good.

HANS KARL

You can be good to anyone.

ANTOINETTE *gently*

Kari, don't insult me like that.

HANS KARL

Understand it as it is meant.

ANTOINETTE

I usually do understand you well enough.

HANS KARL

Can't you try it?

ANTOINETTE

For your sake I could try. But you'd have to stand by me and help me.

HANS KARL

Now you've given me a half-promise.

SCENE XI

*The Famous Man has come in right and advances towards Hans Karl;
the other two do not notice him.*

ANTOINETTE

You promised me something once.

HANS KARL

To help in the beginning.

ANTOINETTE *close to him*

To be fond of me!

THE FAMOUS MAN

Pardon, I seem to be intruding.

Goes out quickly.

HANS KARL *close to her*

So I am.

ANTOINETTE

Say something sweet to me, just for the moment. The moment
is all that matters. I can live only in the moment. I have such a
bad memory.

HANS KARL

I'm not in love with you, but I'm fond of you.

ANTOINETTE

And what you're going to say to Helen is a farewell?

HANS KARL

A farewell.

ANTOINETTE

So Kari bargains me away and hands me over!

HANS KARL

But you were never so close to me as now.

ANTOINETTE

You will come to me often, to support me? You can persuade me to anything.

Hans Karl kisses her on the brow, almost without being aware of doing so.

ANTOINETTE

Thank you.

She runs off through the middle door.

HANS KARL

discomposed, collects himself

Poor little Antoinette.

SCENE XII

CRESCENCE

comes through the middle door, very quickly

Well, you've done that brilliantly! You're simply first-rate at managing these things.

HANS KARL

What? But you don't know anything about it.

CRESCENCE

What else do I need to know? I know all of it. Antoinette comes rushing along with tears in her eyes and runs right past me, but as soon as she notices who I am she flings her arms round my neck and rushes off again like the wind; that tells me everything. You've roused her conscience, you've appealed to her better self, you've made it clear to her that she has to give up all hopes of Stani, and you've shown her the only way out of her entanglements, that she should go back to her husband and try to lead a quiet, respectable life.

HANS KARL

Yes, well, something like that. But it didn't work out in detail quite like that. I haven't got your purposeful approach. I'm too easily deflected from a line, I must admit.

CRESCENCE

But that doesn't matter. Now that you've made such a brilliant success of this, I can't wait, now that you're in the vein, for you to tackle Helen and Poldo Altenwyl. Please just go and do it now, I'm crossing my fingers for you, only keep in mind that Stani's happiness depends on your persuasions.

HANS KARL

You needn't worry, Crescence, while I was talking to Antoinette Hechingen I suddenly saw the line I must take with Helen. I'm quite in the mood for it. You know, that's my weakness, that I so rarely see a clear issue ahead of me; but this time I do see it.

CRESCENCE

There you are, what a good thing it is to have a program. It pulls everything together so that it makes sense. Come along, then: we'll go and look for Helen, she must be in one of the drawing rooms, and whenever we find her I'll leave you alone with her. And as soon as we know the result, I'll rush to the telephone and summon Stani here.

SCENE XIII

Crescence and Hans Karl go out left. Helen and Neuhoff come in right. One hears faint music from a distant room.

NEUHOFF *behind Helen*

Do stand still for a moment. That trifling empty saccharine music and this half-light set you off wonderfully.

HELEN

has stood still, but now moves on towards the armchairs left

I don't like posing as a model, Baron Neuhoff.

NEUHOFF

Not even if I shut my eyes? (*Helen says nothing, she stands left.*) What a creature you are, Helen! No one ever was what you are. Your simplicity is the result of colossal tension. Motionless as a statue, you are yet vibrating within yourself, no one divines it, but he who does divine it vibrates in sympathy. (*Helen looks at him, sits down. Neuhoff, at a little distance, goes on.*) You are in every way wonderful. And like everything high, almost frighteningly matter-of-course.

HELEN

Do you find what is high a matter-of-course? A noble thought.

NEUHOFF

Perhaps one could marry him—that's what your lips wanted to say, Helen!

HELEN

Are you a lip-reader like deaf and dumb people?

NEUHOFF *a step nearer*

You *will marry me*, because you feel the force of my will in a weak-willed world.

HELEN *to herself*

Must one? Is it a commandment to which a woman must submit: when she is chosen and desired?

NEUHOFF

There are desires that haven't much of a past. These one can well tread under one's fine, aristocratic feet. But mine has a past. It has traveled half round the world. Here it has found its fulfillment. You have been found, Helen Altenwyl, by the most forceful will on the most roundabout journey in the most ineffectual of all worlds.

HELEN

I was born in it and I am not ineffectual.

NEUHOFF

You people have sacrificed everything to fine appearances, your strength too. We, in our northern corner of the world, where the centuries pass over our heads, we have kept our strength. So we meet as equals and yet as less than equal, and out of this inequality has grown my right to you.

HELEN

Your right?

NEUHOFF

The right of the spiritually stronger over the woman he can infuse his spirit into.

HELEN

I don't care for these mystical turns of phrase.

NEUHOFF

There must be a mystical bond between two people who have recognized each other at first sight. Your pride should not deny it.

HELEN *standing up*

It denies it again and again.

NEUHOFF

Helen, you would be my salvation—you would make me whole, draw out my full potentiality!

HELEN

I have no interest in anyone whose life is subject to such conditions!

She takes a few steps past him: her eyes are fixed on the open door right by which she came in.

NEUHOFF

How your expression has changed! What is it, Helen? (*Helen is silent, keeps looking right. Neuhoff has come up behind her, follows her glance with his own.*) Oh! Count Bühl has come into the picture! (*He steps back from the door.*) His nearness draws you like a magnet—why, you incomprehensible creature, can't you feel that you don't exist for him?

HELEN

I do exist for him, somehow I do exist!

NEUHOFF

Spendthrift that you are! You bestow everything upon him, even the strength with which he holds you.

HELEN

The strength with which a man holds one—surely that's bestowed on him by God.

NEUHOFF

You astound me. What is it in a Kari Bühl that can exert this fascination over you? Undeserving, not even making an effort of any kind, without willpower, without dignity—

HELEN

Without dignity!

NEUHOFF

That boneless equivocal creature has no dignity.

HELEN

What words these are to use!

NEUHOFF

My northern style sounds rather harsh in your pretty ears. But I stand by its harshness. Equivocal is what I call a man who half gives himself and half holds back—who keeps a reserve in all things—calculates in all things—

HELEN

Calculation and Kari Bühl! Do you really see such a short way into him? Certainly it's impossible to plumb his words to the bottom, as is so easily done with other people. The awkward diffidence that makes him so amiable, his shy pride, his meeting you on your own level, certainly that's a kind of hide-and-seek he plays, and just as certainly eludes the grasp of coarse hands. — He's never made rigid by vanity, which turns all other people into stiff wooden images—he's never debased by prudence, which makes most people so commonplace—he belongs only to himself—nobody knows him, so it's not to be wondered at if you don't know him!

NEUHOFF

I've never seen you like this before, Helen. I do delight in this unique moment! For once I see you as God made you, body and soul. A spectacle for the gods. I abominate sentimental weakness in men as in women. But severity that relents is glorious! (*Helen is silent.*) You must admit that it shows some superiority in a man when he can appreciate in a woman the way she's admiring another man. But I can do that, since I snap my fingers at your infatuation for Kari Bühl.

HELEN

You mistake your feelings. You're bitter, where bitterness is out of place.

NEUHOFF

How can I be bitter about what I tread underfoot?

HELEN

You don't know him! You've hardly spoken to him.

NEUHOFF

I went to visit him— (*Helen looks at him.*) It's beyond words how cheap this man holds you—you mean nothing to him. It's you he treads underfoot.

HELEN *quietly*

No.

NEUHOFF

It was a duel between me and him, a duel for you—and I was not defeated.

HELEN

No, it was no duel. It deserves no such heroic name. You went there to do exactly what I'm doing now! (*Laughs.*) I take no end of trouble to watch Count Bühl without his seeing me. But I do it with no hidden intent.

NEUHOFF

Helen!

HELEN

I'm not thinking all the time of what I can get out of it!

NEUHOFF

But you're grinding me into the dust, Helen—and I am letting you do it! (*Helen is silent.*) And nothing brings me any nearer?

Nothing.

She takes a step towards the door right.

NEUHOFF

Everything about you is lovely, Helen. When you sit down it is
as if you are reposing after a great sorrow—and when you walk
across a room it is as if you go to meet a momentous decision.

Hans Karl has appeared in the doorway right.

Helen makes no answer to Neuhoff.

She moves slowly and silently towards the door right.

Neuhoff goes out quickly left.

SCENE XIV

HANS KARL

Yes, I have something to say to you.

HELEN

Something very serious?

HANS KARL

That's the assumption with which one is sometimes expected
to comply. For everything in the world is set a-going by words.
(*They sit down.*) It's rather ridiculous, I admit, for a man to imag-
ine that by stringing words together skillfully he can exert God
knows how great an influence in this life of ours, where in the
long run everything depends on what is essentially inexpress-
ible. Speech is based on an indecent excess of self-esteem.

HELEN

If people only knew how little they matter not one of them
would utter a word.

HANS KARL

You have such a clear mind, Helen. You always know at any moment exactly what's in question.

HELEN

Do I?

HANS KARL

You're a wonderfully understanding person. So one has to be very careful.

HELEN

looks at him

To be careful?

HANS KARL

Certainly. Sympathy's a good thing, but to use it as a vehicle, and sit back in it, would be shockingly indiscreet. That's why one must be particularly on guard when one has a feeling of being well understood.

HELEN

You must, of course. That's your nature. Any woman who thought of pinning you down would be lost from the start. Yet anyone who believes that you have said a final farewell might well get a greeting from you another day. — Tonight you found Antoinette charming again.

HANS KARL

You see everything!

HELEN

You use up these poor women in your own way, but you don't really care much for them. One needs to be very self-assured or else a little common to go on being a sweetheart of yours.

HANS KARL

If that's how you see me, you must find me quite repulsive!

HELEN

Not at all. You are charming. In these affairs you behave just like a child.

HANS KARL

Like a child? And yet I'm nearly an old man. But that's monstrous. To be thirty-nine and not to know what one's up to is disgraceful.

HELEN

I've never needed to worry about what I was up to. I'm never really up to anything, there's nothing in me but quiet, respectable good behavior.

HANS KARL

Your good behavior is enchanting!

HELEN

I don't want to be sentimental, that bores me. I'd rather be *terre à terre*, like anybody at all, than sentimental. And I don't want to be moody and I don't want to be a coquette. So there's nothing for me but to be as well-behaved as possible. (*Hans Karl is silent.*) *Au fond*, whatever we women do, singing *sol-fa*, let us say, or going in for politics, we always mean something else by it. — To sing *sol-fa* is more indiscreet, to be well-behaved is discreeter, it expresses the deliberate intention of committing no indiscretions. Neither against oneself nor against anyone else.

HANS KARL

Everything in you is special and lovely. Nothing can ever go wrong with you. Marry anyone at all, marry Neuhoff, no, not Neuhoff, if that can be avoided, but any lively young man, say a man like my nephew Stani, yes, indeed, Helen, you should marry Stani, he so much wants to, and anyhow nothing bad can ever happen to you. For you are indestructible, that is clearly written in your face. I'm always fascinated by a really lovely face, but yours—

HELEN

I'd rather you didn't say such things to me, Count Bühl.

HANS KARL

But no, it isn't your loveliness that strikes one most, it's something quite different: in you one can read Necessity. Of course you don't understand what I mean, I understand myself much worse when I'm talking than when I'm silent. I can't even try to explain it to you, it's simply something I learned when I was at the front: that there is something written in people's faces. You see, even in a face like Antoinette's I can read—

HELEN

with a fleeting smile

But I'm well aware of that.

HANS KARL *earnestly*

Yes, it's a charming, attractive face, but one and the same dumb reproach is stamped on it all the time: Why have you all left me to the frightful accidents of Chance? And that gives her little mask such a helpless, desperate look that one can't help feeling anxious about her.

HELEN

But, all the same, Antoinette is *there*. She is wholly absorbed in the moment, that's what women should be like, since the moment is everything. But what is the world to make of a person like me? For me the moment simply doesn't exist, I stand there and see the lights shining and in me they have already gone out. And I am talking to you, we are quite alone together in a room, but in me that is already over: as if some outside person had come in and interrupted us, Huberta or Theophilus Neuhoff or anyone, and it is all already at an end, that I was ever sitting alone with you, aware of this music that couldn't be more unsuited to either of us—and you already somewhere else among other people. And I too somewhere else among people.

HANS KARL *in a low voice*

Anyone must be happy who is allowed to live with you, and should thank God for it to the end of his life, Helen, to the very end of his life, whoever he may be. Don't take Neuhoff, Helen—rather take a man like Stani, or not even Stani, anyone else as long as he's a fine and noble creature—and a man: all the things that I am not.

He stands up.

HELEN

also stands up, she feels that he is on the point of going away

But you're saying farewell! (*Hans Karl makes no answer.*) And even this is something I have known beforehand. That a moment would come when you'd suddenly bid me farewell and make an end—although there was nothing at all to put an end to. But the others, where there really was something, to them you can never say farewell.

HANS KARL

Helen, there are good reasons.

HELEN

I think I've already gone over in my mind everything in the world that concerns us two. We have already stood together like this, with insipid music in the air, while you bid me farewell like this, once and for all.

HANS KARL

It's not just an impulse of the moment, Helen, that makes me bid you farewell. Oh no, you mustn't think that. For when one has to say farewell to someone there's always something behind it.

HELEN

And what is that?

HANS KARL

One must belong very closely to someone and yet not be allowed to belong completely.

HELEN *flinches*

What do you mean by that?

HANS KARL

Out at the front, there was often a time—my God, who could possibly mention such things!

HELEN

Yes, you, to me. Now.

HANS KARL

There were such hours, towards evening or in the night, at early dawn with the morning star in the sky—Helen, you were very near to me then. And then the trench caved in and buried us, you've heard about that—

HELEN

Yes, I've heard about it.

HANS KARL

It lasted only a moment, thirty seconds, they said, but the inner life has a different measure of time. For me it was a whole lifetime that I lived through, and in that span of time you were my wife. Isn't that amusing?

HELEN

I was your wife?

HANS KARL

Not my future wife. That's the queer thing about it. My wife, quite simply. A fait accompli. The whole thing was more like something in the past than something in the future. (*Helen is silent.*) My God, I'm an impossible person, as I keep telling Crescence! Here I am beside you at a soirée and I start reminiscing like old Millesimo, God bless him, who used to be left sitting alone in the end with his pointless anecdotes and never noticed that he was telling them only to himself.

HELEN

But I'm not leaving you to yourself, Count Kari, I'm listening. You had something to say to me: was that it?

HANS KARL

This was it, a very subtle lecture that some Higher Power read me. I'll tell you, Helen, what the gist of it was. (*Helen has sat down again; he sits down too. The music has stopped playing.*) It had to be impressed on me, at a specially selected moment, just what the happiness looks like that I have thrown away. How I have thrown it away, you know as well as I do.

HELEN

I know as well as you do?

HANS KARL

Simply because I did not recognize, while there was still time, what the one thing necessary consisted in, what really mattered. And I did not recognize it because of the weakness of my own nature. And so I did not stand the test. Later on, in the field hospital, in the many quiet days and nights, I was able to see it all with indescribable clearness and certainty.

HELEN

Was this what you wanted to say to me, just this?

HANS KARL

Convalescence is such a queer state. The whole world came back to me again like something clean and new and yet so natural. I was suddenly able to realize what it is to be human. And what it must be like for two human beings to join their lives together and become *one*. I was able—in imagination at least— to picture to myself—what it implies, how sacred it is and how wonderful. And strangely enough it was not my own marriage that, in a way quite uncalled for, occupied the central place in all this speculation—although it's possible enough that I might marry some day—but it was your marriage.

HELEN

My marriage! My marriage—to whom, then?

HANS KARL

That I don't know. But I was able to imagine to myself in exact detail how it all would be, and how it would run its course, with few people about and everything sacred and ceremonious, and how it would all be as is only fitting for your eyes and your forehead, and your lips which cannot say a superfluous word, and your hands which cannot subscribe to a dishonorable deed— and I even heard your pure, clear voice saying Yes, purely and clearly—all from a distance, since of course I was not there, I was not there at all! — How could an outsider like myself attend such a ceremony? — But it has been a delight to me to tell you for once what I feel for you. — And of course one can do that only in a specific moment, like the present one, in a definitive moment, so to speak— (*Helen nearly breaks down, but controls herself. Hans Karl goes on, with tears in his eyes.*) My God, now I've quite upset you, that's what's so impossible in me, I'm moved to tears as soon as I say or hear anything that isn't utterly banal—it's my nerves since the shell shock, but that of course must infect sensitive people like you—I shouldn't be let out among people—I keep telling Crescence that—I beg your pardon a thousand times, please forget all the nonsense I've been pouring out—there are so many memories that rise up in confusion at a moment of parting— (*Quickly, because he feels that they are no longer alone*) —but anyone in his senses naturally keeps them to himself—adieu, Helen, adieu.

The Famous Man has come in right.

HELEN

hardly able to command herself

Adieu!

They want to clasp hands—neither's hand finds the other's. Hans Karl makes to go out right. The Famous Man intercepts him. Hans Karl looks round left. Crescence is just coming in left.

THE FAMOUS MAN

It has long been my earnest desire, your Lordship—

HANS KARL

quickly makes for the door right

Excuse me, sir.

Pushes past the Famous Man.

Crescence goes up to Helen, who is standing there as pale as death.

The Famous Man has gone away disconcerted.

Hans Karl appears once more in the doorway right,
looks in, as if undecided, and disappears again at once
when he sees Crescence with Helen.

HELEN

to Crescence, almost in a dazed state

Is that you, Crescence? He did come in again. Did he say something else?

She totters, Crescence supports her.

CRESCENCE

But I'm so happy! You're so deeply moved, and that makes me so happy!

HELEN

Excuse me, Crescence, don't be angry with me.

Frees herself and hurries out left.

CRESCENCE

You're much more devoted to each other than you know, Stani and you!

She wipes her eyes.

Curtain

Act III

*Entrance hall in the Altenwyls' house. Right, the outside door
leading into the drive. In the middle a staircase rising to a gallery
from which, left and right, double doors open into the living rooms.
Below, near the staircase, low divans or benches. A conservatory
off the back of the hall, right.*

SCENE I

*The Altenwyls' butler, Wenzel, stands right, beside the exit door.
There are other footmen outside in the porch, visible through the
glass screens of the door. Wenzel calls to the footmen.*

WENZEL

Councillor Professor Brücke!

*The Famous Man comes down the staircase. A footman comes
from right with his fur coat, inside which are hanging two mufflers
and a pair of galoshes. While the Famous Man is being helped
into his coat, Wenzel continues.*

Does the Councillor wish for a car?

THE FAMOUS MAN

Thank you, no. Hasn't his Lordship Count Bühl just gone in
front of me?

WENZEL

Just this very moment.

THE FAMOUS MAN

Did he drive off?

WENZEL

No, his Lordship sent his car away; he saw two gentlemen driving in and stepped into the porter's lodge till they were past. He must be barely out of the gates now.

THE FAMOUS MAN *hurrying*

I'll overtake him.

He goes out; at the same time Stani and Hechingen are visible, entering together.

SCENE II

Stani and Hechingen come in, behind each of them a footman takes his overcoat and hat.

STANI

after nodding to the Famous Man in passing

Good evening, Wenzel, is my mother here?

WENZEL

Yes, her ladyship is in the card room.

He goes out, so do the footmen.

Stani makes for the stairs. Hechingen takes a side-glance at himself in a looking glass; obviously he is nervous.

Another of the Altenwyls' footmen comes down the staircase.

STANI *stopping him*

You know who I am, don't you?

FOOTMAN

Yes indeed, your Lordship.

STANI

Go through the reception rooms and look for Count Bühl until you find him. Then go up to him quietly and tell him I'd like to have a word with him, either in the corner room off the picture gallery or in the Chinese smoking room. Have you got that? Well, what is it you've to say to him?

FOOTMAN

I have to announce that Count Freudenberg wishes to have a private word with his lordship, either in the corner room—

STANI

All right.

Footman returns upstairs.

HECHINGEN

Pst, footman!

The footman does not hear him, goes on his way upstairs. Stani has sat down. Hechingen looks at him.

STANI

Perhaps you'd better go on without me? I've sent up a message and I'll wait here a moment for the answer.

HECHINGEN

I'll keep you company.

STANI

No, don't let me detain you. You were in a great hurry to come here—

HECHINGEN

My dear Stani, you see me in a very strange predicament. Once I cross the threshold of that reception room my fate will be decided.

STANI

irritated by Hechingen's nervous pacing up and down

Hadn't you better sit down? I'm only waiting for the footman, as I told you.

HECHINGEN

I can't sit down, I'm too distracted.

STANI

Perhaps you drank up your champagne a little too fast.

HECHINGEN

At the risk of boring you, my dear Stani, I must confess that something of great importance to me is at stake.

STANI

while Hechingen once more walks away in nervous agitation

But something serious is often at stake. The only thing that matters is not to betray the fact.

HECHINGEN

again coming nearer

Your Uncle Kari, my very good friend, has undertaken to have a talk with Antoinette, with my wife, the outcome of which, as I said—

STANI

Uncle Kari?

HECHINGEN

I must say that I couldn't entrust my fate to the hands of a nobler, a more unselfish friend—

STANI

But of course. — If he has only been able to find the time for it.

HECHINGEN

What?

STANI

He sometimes takes on a little too much, my Uncle Kari. When anyone asks him to do something—he can never say no.

HECHINGEN

We arranged that I should wait in the Club until he telephoned to tell me whether to come here or put off my arrival till a more opportune moment.

STANI

Ah. In your shoes I should certainly have waited.

HECHINGEN

I simply wasn't in a state to wait any longer. Just think what's at stake for me!

STANI

In these critical decisions one should show a certain detachment. — Aha!

Sees the footman coming out above and descending the stairs. Stani goes to meet him, leaving Hechingen standing.

FOOTMAN

No, I think his Lordship must have gone.

STANI

You think? Didn't I tell you to look round till you found him?

FOOTMAN

Several gentlemen have also been asking for him. His Lordship must have slipped out without being noticed.

STANI

Sapristi! Then go to my mother and tell her that I urgently beg her to come to me for a moment in the first anteroom. I must have a word with my uncle or with her before I go in.

FOOTMAN

Very good.

Goes upstairs again.

HECHINGEN

My instinct tells me that Kari will appear in a minute to report the result, and that it will be a good result.

STANI

You have such a reliable instinct, have you? My congratulations.

HECHINGEN

Something has kept him from telephoning, but he has really drawn me to come here. I feel myself continuously in touch with him.

STANI

Wonderful!

HECHINGEN

That works both ways with us. He often puts into words what I've just been thinking.

STANI

You're clearly a marvelous medium.

HECHINGEN

My dear friend, when I was a gay young dog like you I shouldn't have thought these things possible either, but by the time one's thirty-five one's eyes are opened to a great deal. It's as if one had been deaf and blind earlier.

STANI

You don't say so!

HECHINGEN

I have Kari to thank for my second education. I lay great stress on the fact that without him I should simply never have got my feet clear of the entanglements in my life.

STANI

That's saying a lot.

HECHINGEN

A person like Antoinette, even though one is her husband, that doesn't mean a thing, one has no idea of her inner fineness. One should never forget that such a being is a butterfly whose bloom shouldn't be brushed from her wings. If you only knew her, I mean, if you knew her well enough— (*Stani makes a courteous bow.*) I can now see my relationship to her like this, that it's simply my duty to let her have the freedom her bizarre, fantastic nature requires. Her nature is that of a grande dame of the eighteenth century. Only by allowing her full freedom can one attach her to oneself.

STANI

Ah.

HECHINGEN

One must be generous, that's what I owe to Kari. I shouldn't think it at all out of the question to be friendly in a generous way with any admirer of hers.

STANI

I see what you mean.

HECHINGEN

I should try to make him a friend of mine, not out of policy, but quite without forethought. I should meet him warmly more than halfway: that's how Kari has taught me to take people, with a supple wrist.

STANI

But all that Uncle Kari says is not to be taken *au pied de la lettre.*

HECHINGEN

Of course not *au pied de la lettre.* But let me beg you not to forget that I have a fine feeling for what's in question. It all depends on a certain something, an inner grace—I mean to say, it must all be a continuous impromptu.

He paces nervously up and down.

STANI

But first and foremost one must know how to preserve one's *tenue.* For instance, if Uncle Kari had to wait for a decision about anything whatever, no one would be able to guess it from his demeanor.

HECHINGEN

But of course. Behind this statue, or behind the big azalea there, he would stand chatting with the utmost nonchalance— I can just see him! At the risk of boring you, I must tell you that I am aware of what would be going on inside him—down to the finest nuances.

STANI

But since we can't both stand behind the azalea, and this idiot of a footman is apparently never coming back, perhaps we should go up.

HECHINGEN

Yes, let's both go. It's a comfort to me not to be quite alone at such a moment. My dear Stani, I have the greatest sympathy for you!

Takes his arm.

STANI *freeing his arm*

But not arm-in-arm like debutantes in their first year, but perhaps each of us separately.

HECHINGEN

Yes, yes, just as you please.

STANI

Let me suggest that you go first. I'll come close behind you.

Hechingen goes first and disappears above. Stani follows him.

SCENE III

HELEN

comes through a small hidden door in the left wall. She waits until Stani has disappeared. Then she calls to the butler in a low voice

Wenzel, Wenzel, I want to ask you something.

WENZEL

coming quickly out of his room and moving towards her

Yes, my lady?

HELEN

in a very casual voice

Did you notice whether Count Bühl has gone?

WENZEL

Yes, he went five minutes ago.

HELEN

Did he leave anything?

WENZEL

What does my lady mean?

HELEN

A letter, or a verbal message.

WENZEL

Not with me, but I'll ask the others. (*He goes over to the footmen. Helen stands still, waiting. Stani is visible for a moment on the upstairs landing. He tries to see with whom Helen is speaking and then disappears again. Wenzel comes back to Helen.*) No, nothing at all. He sent his car away, lit a cigar and just walked out. (*Helen says nothing. Wenzel, after a little pause*) Is there anything else, my lady?

HELEN

Yes, Wenzel, I'll come back in a few minutes and then I shall be going out.

WENZEL

In the car, so late in the evening?

HELEN

No, I shall go on foot.

WENZEL

Is someone ill?

HELEN

No, there's no one ill. I only want to speak to somebody.

WENZEL

Does my lady want anyone with her as well as the Miss?

HELEN

No, I shall go quite alone, Miss Jekyll won't be with me. I'll slip out here at a moment when none of the guests is about. And I'll give you a letter for Papa.

WENZEL

Am I to give it to him at once?

HELEN

No, give it to Papa when he has seen the last of the guests off.

WENZEL

When everybody's gone?

HELEN

Yes, at the moment when he orders the lights to be turned out.
But then, stay beside him. I'd like you to—

She falters.

WENZEL

What, my lady?

HELEN

How old was I, Wenzel, when you first came here?

WENZEL

A little girl five years old, my lady was.

HELEN

That's all right, Wenzel, thank you. I'll come out by this door
and you'll give me a signal when the hall is clear.

Gives him her hand to kiss.

WENZEL

Yes, my lady.

Kisses her hand.

Helen disappears through the little door.

Wenzel goes out.

SCENE IV

*Antoinette and Neuhoff come from beside the staircase, right,
out of the conservatory.*

ANTOINETTE

That was Helen. Was she alone? Did she see me?

NEUHOFF

I don't think so. But what does it matter? You don't need to be
afraid of meeting her eyes, at least.

ANTOINETTE

But I am afraid of her. Every time I think of her I feel as if
someone has been telling me lies. Let's go somewhere else, we
can't sit about here in the hall.

NEUHOFF

Calm yourself. Kari Bühl has gone. I saw him going away just a
moment ago.

ANTOINETTE

Just at this very moment?

NEUHOFF

understanding her thoughts

He went out all by himself, without anyone else seeing him.

ANTOINETTE

What?

NEUHOFF

A certain person did *not* accompany him here and did *not* ex-
change a single word with him during the last half-hour he was
in the house. I took note of that. You can relax.

They sit down.

ANTOINETTE

He swore to me he was going to bid her farewell forever. If I could see her face, then I should know—

NEUHOFF

That face of hers is hard as stone. Better stay here with me.

ANTOINETTE

I—

NEUHOFF

Your face is enchanting. Other people's faces conceal everything. But yours is a continuous avowal. One could read in your face everything that has ever happened to you.

ANTOINETTE

Could one? Perhaps—if one had only the shadow of a right to do so.

NEUHOFF

That right arises out of the moment and one just takes it. You are a woman, a real, bewitching woman. You belong to no one and to everyone! No, you haven't belonged to anyone yet, you're still waiting.

ANTOINETTE

with a nervous little laugh

Not for you!

NEUHOFF

Yes, precisely for me; that's to say, for a man such as you have never known, a real man, with chivalry and kindness rooted in strength. The Karis of this world have only ill-used you and betrayed you from first to last, the sort of men who have no kindness, no core of strength, no nerve and no loyalty! These playboys, who catch a creature like you again and again in their nets, leave you unrewarded, unthanked, unhappy, humiliated in your tenderest femininity!

Tries to seize her hand.

ANTOINETTE

How you do work yourself up! But I'm safe from you, for your cold cast-iron intellect shows through every word you say. I'm not even afraid of you. I don't want you!

NEUHOFF

As for my intellect, I hate it! I want to be set free from it, I desire only to lose it in you, sweet little Antoinette!

He makes to seize her hand. Hechingen comes into sight upstairs, but at once draws back. Neuhoff has seen him, takes his hand away, alters his attitude and his facial expression.

ANTOINETTE

Ah, now I've seen through and through you! How suddenly your whole face can change! I'll tell you what has happened: you saw Helen passing by upstairs, and at that moment I could read *you* like an open book. Resentment and impotence, anger, shame, and the determination to get me—*faute de mieux*—all that was in your face. Edine scolds me for not being able to read complicated books. But that was complicated enough, and yet I read it all in a flash. Don't waste your time on me. I don't want you.

NEUHOFF *bending over her*
You shall want me, Antoinette!

ANTOINETTE *rises*
No! I don't! I don't! For what shoots out of your eyes is the will to have me in your power, only the will—and it may be very manly—but I don't care for it. And if that's the best you can do,

every single one of us, even the most ordinary of women, has something that's better than your best, and is proof against your best through a touch of fear. But not the kind of fear that turns one's head, only a quite banal, prosaic fear. (*She moves towards the staircase, but pauses again.*) Do you understand? Have I made myself quite clear? I'm afraid of you, but not afraid enough, that's your bad luck. Adieu, Baron Neuhoff.

Neuhoff has gone off quickly to the conservatory.

SCENE V

Hechingen appears upstairs and comes running quickly downstairs. Antoinette is disconcerted and recoils.

HECHINGEN

Toinette!

ANTOINETTE *involuntarily*

The last straw!

HECHINGEN

What did you say?

ANTOINETTE

I'm taken by surprise—you must understand that.

HECHINGEN

And I'm delighted. I thank God, I thank my lucky stars, I thank this moment!

ANTOINETTE

You look somehow different. Your expression is different, I don't know how. Don't you feel well?

HECHINGEN

Isn't it only because these dark eyes of yours haven't looked at me for a long time?

ANTOINETTE

But it's not so long since we saw each other.

HECHINGEN

Seeing and looking at are two different things, Toinette. (*He has come closer to her. Antoinette retreats.*) But perhaps it's something different that's changed me, if I may be so presumptuous as to talk about myself.

ANTOINETTE

What's changed you, then? Has something happened? Have you begun to take an interest in someone?

HECHINGEN

To see your charm and your pride in action, suddenly to see before one's eyes the whole woman one loves, to see her living and breathing!

ANTOINETTE

Oh, so you're speaking of me!

HECHINGEN

Yes, you. I was lucky enough to see you for once as you are, since for once I wasn't there to intimidate you. Oh, what thoughts I had as I stood up there! This wife of mine, desired by all and denying herself to all! My destiny, your destiny, for it's our common destiny. Do sit down here beside me!

He has sat down, stretches a hand out to her.

ANTOINETTE

We can talk just as well standing, since we're such old acquaintances.

HECHINGEN *standing up again*

I've never known you before. I've had to get new eyes for that. The man who comes to you now is a different man, a changed man.

ANTOINETTE

There's a new ring in the kind of things you say. Where have you been learning it?

HECHINGEN

The man speaking to you now is a man you don't know, Toinette, just as he hasn't known you! A man who wishes for nothing else, dreams of nothing else, but to become known to you and to know you.

ANTOINETTE

Ado, I do implore you not to speak to me as if I were someone you'd just picked up in the dining car of an express train.

HECHINGEN

With whom I'd like to travel right to the end of the world!

Wants to kiss her hand, she draws it away from him.

ANTOINETTE

Please do believe that this rubs me up the wrong way. Old married couples are used to taking a certain tone with each other. One doesn't change that all at once, it's enough to make one's head go round.

HECHINGEN

I don't know anything about old married couples, I don't know anything about our situation.

ANTOINETTE

But it's the given situation.

HECHINGEN

Given? There's no such thing. Here you are, and here am I, and everything's starting new from the beginning.

ANTOINETTE

Nonsense, nothing is starting new from the beginning.

HECHINGEN

Life is made up of perpetual new beginnings.

ANTOINETTE

No, no, for goodness' sake get back to your old way of talking.
I can't stand much more of this. Don't be cross with me, I
have a bit of a migraine, I was thinking of going home earlier
on, before I knew I was going to meet you—how could I
possibly tell?

HECHINGEN

You couldn't possibly tell who it would be that would come to
meet you, and that it wouldn't be your husband but a new ar-
dent admirer, as ardent as a boy of twenty! That's what troubles
you, that makes you light-headed.

Tries to clasp her hand.

ANTOINETTE

No, it doesn't make me light-headed at all, it makes me stone-
cold sober. It makes me so *terre à terre* that everything seems flat
and stale, myself included. I've had a miserable evening, I ask
only one favor of you, do let me go home.

HECHINGEN

Oh, Antoinette!

ANTOINETTE

That's to say, if you have something definite to tell me, then tell
me, I'll be glad to listen, but one thing I do implore you! Tell
me in your ordinary style, your usual style.

Hechingen, disconcerted and sobered, is silent.

ANTOINETTE

Well, what is it you want to say to me?

HECHINGEN

I'm upset to see that my presence seems to take you by surprise on the one hand and to be a burden to you on the other. I had allowed myself to hope that a dear friend of mine would have found the opportunity of speaking to you about myself and my unchanging feelings for you. I had persuaded myself that on this basis an improvised explanation between us might possibly find an altered situation in being or could at least produce one. — Let me beg you not to forget that until now you've never given me a chance to speak to you about my own inner life—I regard our relationship as one, Antoinette—am I boring you very much?

ANTOINETTE

But do go on, please. I suppose there's something you want to tell me. I can't think of any other reason for your coming here.

HECHINGEN

I regard our relationship as one that binds me, only me, Antoinette, and lays on me, only on me, a testing time, a trial, the duration of which is for you to determine.

ANTOINETTE

But what's the point of that, what should it lead to?

HECHINGEN

Indeed, if I turn to look inside myself, Toinette—

ANTOINETTE

Well, what's there, when you turn to look?

She puts her hands to her temples.

HECHINGEN

—it seems that the testing time needn't last for long. Over and over again in the sight of the world I shall endeavor to adopt your standpoint, I shall go on defending your charm and your freedom. And if anyone deliberately misrepresents you, I shall refer him in triumph to the experience of the last few minutes, to that eloquent proof of how well you are equipped to keep within bounds the men who admire and besiege you.

ANTOINETTE *nervously*

What do you mean?

HECHINGEN

You are much desired. Your type is the grande dame of the eighteenth century. I see no manner of cause for regret in that. One's judgment should be based on the nuance of behavior, not on the fact. I lay great stress on making it clear that whatever you do, your motives are elevated for me beyond all suspicion.

ANTOINETTE *nearly in tears*

My dear Ado, you mean very well, but my migraine is getting worse with every word you say.

HECHINGEN

Oh, I'm very sorry. All the more as these moments are infinitely precious to me.

ANTOINETTE

Please, have the goodness—

She totters.

HECHINGEN

I understand. A car?

ANTOINETTE

Yes. Edine has offered me hers.

HECHINGEN

At once. (*He goes and gives the order. Comes back with her cloak. While he helps her into it*) Is that all I can do for you?

ANTOINETTE

Yes, that's all.

WENZEL

at the glass door, announces

Her ladyship's car.

Antoinette goes out very quickly. Hechingen makes to follow her, then checks himself.

SCENE VI

STANI

comes from behind out of the conservatory. He seems to be looking for someone

Oh, it's you, have you seen my mother anywhere?

HECHINGEN

No, I haven't been in the drawing rooms. I've just been seeing my wife to her car. It was a situation without parallel.

STANI

preoccupied with his own affairs

I can't understand it. Mamma first sends me a message to meet her in the conservatory, and then another to wait for her here by the stairs—

HECHINGEN

I absolutely must have a good talk with Kari now.

STANI

Then you'll have to go out and look for him.

HECHINGEN

My instinct tells me he went out only to find me at the Club and will soon come back.

Goes upstairs.

STANI

What it is to have an instinct that tells one everything! Oh, here's Mamma!

SCENE VII

CRESCENCE

comes through the hidden little door left at the side of the main staircase

I've come down the service stairs, these footmen do nothing but muddle one up. First he tells me you beg me to come to the conservatory, then he says in the gallery—

STANI

Mamma, this is an evening of general confusion without end. I had really got to the point, if it hadn't been for you, of turning on my heel, going home, taking a shower, and crawling into bed. I can endure much, but to be put in a false position is so odious to me that it jars on my nerves. I implore you urgently to put me au courant in our affairs.

CRESCENCE

But I simply don't understand how your Uncle Kari could go away without giving me so much as a hint. That's his usual absentmindedness, it drives me to despair, my dear boy.

STANI

Please do explain the situation a little. Please tell me in outline what has been happening, never mind the details.

CRESCENCE

But everything went exactly according to program. First your Uncle Kari had a very agitated interview with Antoinette—

STANI

That was the first mistake. I knew it would be, for it was much too complicated. Well, go on, what else?

CRESCENCE

What else can I say? Antoinette comes rushing past me, completely upset, then immediately afterwards your Uncle Kari sits down with Helen—

STANI

It really is too complicated to manage two such conversations in one evening. Then Uncle Kari—

CRESCENCE

His talk with Helen goes on and on for a long time, I come to the door—Helen sinks into my arms, I am in raptures, she runs away in confusion, as one might expect, I rush to the telephone and summon you here!

STANI

Yes, well, I know that, but please explain what has been happening since!

CRESCENCE

I rush full tilt through the rooms looking for Kari and don't find him. I have to go back to my cards, you can imagine what my game was like. Mariette Stradonitz declares hearts, I play diamonds, meanwhile I pray to all the saints in the calendar. On top of that I revoke in clubs. At long last I can get up, I look for Kari again, he's not to be found! I go through the whole flight of half-dark rooms till I come to Helen's door, I hear her sobbing inside. I knock and tell her who I am, she gives me no answer. I slip back to the card table again, Mariette asks me three times if I'm not well, Louis Castaldo looks at me as if I were a ghost—

STANI

Now I understand it all.

CRESCENCE

How? What? I don't understand anything.

STANI

All of it, all of it. The whole thing's clear to me.

CRESCENCE

How can my boy explain that?

STANI

Clear as two and two makes four. Antoinette in her despair must have been telling tales, having understood from Uncle Kari that she's lost me forever. A woman when she's desperate loses all her *tenue,* so she went slinking up to Helen and poured out such scandalous tittle-tattle that Helen, flying up in the air with her colossal sensitivity, decided to give me up even if it should break her heart.

CRESCENCE

And that's why she wouldn't open her door to me!

STANI

And Uncle Kari, when he saw what he'd done, cleared out of the mess as fast as he could.

CRESCENCE

But that would be simply dreadful! My dear boy, what do you say to that?

STANI

My dear Mamma, I say only one thing, the only thing that a gentleman can say to himself in a false position: one remains what one is, and no prospect, good or bad, can make any difference to that.

CRESCENCE

Stani's a dear boy, and I adore the way he's taking it, but still one shouldn't throw up the game at this point.

STANI

But whatever you do, spare me a false position.

CRESCENCE

For a man who carries himself so well as you do, there's no such thing as a false position. I'll go now and look for Helen and ask her just what did happen between a quarter to ten and now.

STANI

I implore you urgently—

CRESCENCE

But my dear boy's a thousand times too precious for me to foist him on any family, even if it were the Emperor of China's. On the other hand, I'm too fond of Helen to let her happiness be sacrificed because of the tittle-tattle of a jealous goose like Antoinette. So let Stani do me the favor of staying here and then taking me home, for he can see how upset I am.

She goes up the staircase. Stani follows her.

SCENE VIII

Helen has come through the hidden little door in the wall left, in her fur cloak, ready to go out. She waits till Crescence and Stani are far enough up the stairs not to see her. At the same moment Hans Karl is visible through the glass door right; he sheds his hat, coat, and stick and comes in. Helen has seen Hans Karl before he has caught sight of her. In a twinkling her expression alters completely. She lets her cloak drop from her shoulders so that it lies behind the staircase and comes forward to meet him.

HANS KARL *discomposed*

Helen, are you still here?

HELEN

now and later in a firm, decided attitude and with a light, almost assured tone

This is where I belong: this is my home.

HANS KARL

You look quite different. Something has happened!

HELEN

Yes, something has happened.

HANS KARL

When, so suddenly?

HELEN

About an hour ago, I think.

HANS KARL *in an uncertain voice*

Something unpleasant?

HELEN

What?

HANS KARL

Something upsetting?

HELEN

Oh yes, that, certainly.

HANS KARL

Something that can't be made good?

HELEN

That remains to be seen. Do you see what's lying there?

HANS KARL

Over there? A fur. A lady's cloak, it looks like.

HELEN

Yes, that's my cloak. I was just on the point of going out.

HANS KARL

Going out?

HELEN

Yes, and I'll tell you why in a minute. But first you'll tell me why you've come back. That's not a usual way of behaving.

HANS KARL *hesitating*

It always makes me rather embarrassed when someone asks me a straight question.

HELEN

But I do ask you a straight question.

HANS KARL

I can't explain it very easily.

HELEN

We can sit down.

They sit down.

HANS KARL

Earlier on, in our conversation—upstairs, in the small drawing room—

HELEN

Ah, upstairs in the small drawing room.

HANS KARL

discomposed by her tone

Yes, indeed, in the small drawing room. I made a great mistake then, a very great mistake.

HELEN

Oh?

HANS KARL

I referred to something out of my past.

HELEN

Something out of your past?

HANS KARL

To certain preposterous, entirely personal notions that ran through my mind out at the front and later in hospital. Purely personal fancies, hallucinations, so to speak. Many things that were absolutely out of place.

HELEN

Yes, I understand. Well?

HANS KARL

That was the wrong thing to do.

HELEN

In what way?

HANS KARL

One can't call the past to witness like the police summoning evidence. What's past is past. No one has the right, in a conversation about present affairs, to bring the past into it. I'm putting it very badly, but I'm quite clear in my mind about it.

HELEN

I hope so.

HANS KARL

It was very painful for me to remember, as soon as I was alone, how little, at my age, I have myself in hand—and so I have come back to give you your full freedom—I beg your pardon, that was a clumsy slip of the tongue—to give you the reassurance that it has nothing to do with you.

HELEN

Nothing to do with me? Reassurance? (*Hans Karl, uncertain, makes to rise. Helen keeps her seat.*) So that's what you wanted to tell me—about why you went away?

HANS KARL

Yes, why I went away and of course also why I came back. The one explains the other.

HELEN

Aha. Thank you very much. And now I'll tell you why you came back.

HANS KARL

You'll tell me?

HELEN

turning her eyes full upon him

You came back because—yes, there is such a thing, praise be to God! (*She laughs.*) Yet it's perhaps a pity that you came back. For this is perhaps not the right place to say what must be said— perhaps it would have been better—but now it simply must be said, here.

HANS KARL

Oh my God, you find me incomprehensible. Say it straight out!

HELEN

I understand everything well enough. I understand what drove you away and what has brought you back again.

HANS KARL

You understand it all? I don't understand it myself.

HELEN

We can speak even more softly, if you like. What drove you away was your lack of confidence, your fear of your own self—you're not offended?

HANS KARL

Fear of my own self?

HELEN

Fear of your own underlying will. Yes, it's inconvenient, that will, it doesn't lead one in the pleasantest paths. But it brought you back here.

HANS KARL

I don't understand you, Helen!

HELEN

without looking at him

Running away like that isn't difficult for you, but you often have difficult moments afterwards when you're alone with yourself.

HANS KARL

You know all that?

HELEN

Because I know all that, I could have had the strength to do the impossible for your sake.

HANS KARL

What impossible thing would you have done for my sake?

HELEN

I should have run after you.

HANS KARL

How "run after"? What do you mean?

HELEN

Run after you here, through that door, into the street. Haven't I shown you my cloak lying over there behind the stair?

HANS KARL

You would have—? But where to?

HELEN

Into the Club, or anywhere—how do I know, simply until I found you.

HANS KARL

Would you have, Helen—? Would you have looked for me? Without thinking about—

HELEN

Yes, without thinking about anything else at all. I am running after you—I want you to—

HANS KARL *his voice faltering*

You, my dear, you want me to—? (*To himself*) These impossible tears again! (*To her*) I can't hear you very well. You speak so low.

HELEN

You hear me quite well. And now you are in tears—but that rather helps me to speak out—

HANS KARL

My dear—what did you say?

HELEN

Your underlying will, your deepest self; do understand me. It turned you right round when you were alone and brought you back to me. And now—

HANS KARL

Now?

HELEN

Now I don't really know whether you can truly love anyone—but I'm in love with you, and I want—but it's monstrous that you leave me to say it!

HANS KARL *faltering*

You want from me—

HELEN

her voice faltering as much as his

My share—of your life, of your soul, of everything—my share!

A short pause

HANS KARL

Helen, all that you are saying agitates me beyond measure, for your own sake, Helen, for your sake, of course. You're mistaken in me, I have an impossible character.

HELEN

You are as you are, and I want to know you as you are.

HANS KARL

It's an unspeakable danger for you. (*Helen shakes her head*) I'm a man who has nothing but misunderstandings on his conscience.

HELEN *smiling*

Yes, so it seems.

HANS KARL

I've hurt so many women.

HELEN

Love isn't a soothing syrup.

HANS KARL

I'm a boundless egoist.

HELEN

Are you? I don't think so.

HANS KARL

I'm so unstable, nothing can hold me firm.

HELEN

Yes, you can—what's the word?—seduce and be seduced. You genuinely loved them all and left them all in the lurch again. Poor women! None of them simply had the strength for both of you.

HANS KARL

How?

HELEN

It's in your nature to desire, to reach out in longing. But not for this—or that—what you long for is everything—from one woman—forever! One of these women should have had the strength to keep you expecting more and more from her. Then you would never have left her.

HANS KARL

How well you know me!

HELEN

After a little while you felt indifferent to all of them, and were wildly sorry for them, but had no great friendship for any of them: that was my comfort.

HANS KARL

How you do know everything!

HELEN

That was my sole interest in life. The only thing I have understood.

HANS KARL

I must feel ashamed before you, my dear.

HELEN

But am I ashamed before you? No, no. Love cuts deep into the living flesh.

HANS KARL

All that you knew and endured—

HELEN

I wouldn't have lifted my little finger to draw one of these women away from you. I couldn't have brought myself to do it.

HANS KARL

What magic there is in you. Not at all like other women. You make one so serene inside oneself.

HELEN

Of course you can't yet realize the friendship I have for you. That will take a long time—if you can give it me.

HANS KARL

How you said that!

HELEN

Now go, so that no one sees you. And come soon again. Come tomorrow, early in the afternoon. It's no business of other people's, but Papa should be told at once—Papa, certainly! — Or don't you think so?

HANS KARL *embarrassed*

It's just this—my good friend Poldo Altenwyl for days past has had an undertaking, a wish—that he wants to foist on me officially: he wants me, quite superfluously, to make a speech in the Upper House—

HELEN

Aha—

HANS KARL

And so for weeks I've been keeping out of his way very carefully—I've avoided being left alone with him—in the Club, on the street, or anywhere—

HELEN

Don't worry—there will be only the one main topic—I guarantee that. — Here's someone coming already: I must go.

HANS KARL

Helen!

HELEN

already on the way out, pauses for a moment

My dear! Good night!

Picks up her cloak and disappears through the hidden door left.

SCENE IX

CRESCENCE *at the top of the stairs*
Kari! (*She comes quickly down the stairs. Hans Karl is standing with his back to the staircase.*) Kari! Have I found you at last! What an evening of confusion this has been!

She comes round and sees his face.

Kari! Something has happened! Tell me, what is it?

HANS KARL

Something has happened to me, but we're not going to pick it to pieces.

CRESCENCE

But, please, won't you explain—

SCENE X

HECHINGEN

comes downstairs, stands still, and calls to Hans Karl in a low voice

Kari, if you could spare me a second—

HANS KARL

I'm at your disposal. (*To Crescence*) I must really be excused.

Stani begins to walk down the stairs.

CRESCENCE *to Hans Karl*

But the boy! What am I to say to the boy? The boy is in a false position!

STANI

comes right down, to Hechingen

Excuse me, I absolutely must speak to Uncle Kari for a minute.

He greets Hans Karl.

HANS KARL

Just a moment, my dear Ado!

Leaves Hechingen standing, turns to Crescence.

Come over here by yourself: I have something to tell you. But we're not going to discuss it at all.

CRESCENCE

But I'm not an indiscreet person!

HANS KARL

You're an angel of goodness. But, listen! Helen has got engaged.

CRESCENCE

To Stani? She's accepted him?

HANS KARL

Not so fast. Don't start wiping your eyes just yet, you don't know yet.

CRESCENCE

It's your goodness that makes me want to cry. The boy owes everything to you.

HANS KARL

Wait, Crescence! — Not to Stani.

CRESCENCE

Not to Stani? Well, to whom, then?

HANS KARL *in great embarrassment*

Congratulate me, Crescence!

CRESCENCE

You?

HANS KARL

But then leave, at once, and don't mention it in conversation. She has—I have—we have got engaged to each other.

CRESCENCE

You have! Oh, I'm in raptures!

HANS KARL

Please, keep in mind above all that you've promised to spare me the odious confusions that a man exposes himself to when he mixes with people.

CRESCENCE

Of course I'll do nothing—

Turns her eyes on Stani.

HANS KARL

As I have said, I won't explain anything to anyone and I beg to be spared the usual misunderstandings!

CRESCENCE

Kari, you shouldn't be so obstinate! When you were a little boy you had exactly that face when anyone crossed you. I never could bear it even then! I'll do exactly as you wish.

HANS KARL

You're the best sister in the world, and now let me be excused, Ado needs to have a talk with me—another talk to be gone through, in God's name.

Kisses her hand.

CRESCENCE

I'll wait!

Crescence and Stani draw to one side, at a distance, but now and then visible.

SCENE XI

HECHINGEN

You have such a serious look! There's reproach in your face!

HANS KARL

Not in the least: I beg you not to start weighing my looks too scrupulously, at least not tonight.

HECHINGEN

Has something happened to alter your opinion of me? Or your opinion of my situation?

HANS KARL *lost in thought*

Your situation?

HECHINGEN

My situation with respect to Antoinette, of course! May I ask you what conclusions you have come to about my wife?

HANS KARL *nervously*

I do beg your pardon, but I'd rather not speak about women tonight. Once one begins analyzing, one falls into the most odious misunderstandings. So I beg you to let me off!

HECHINGEN

I understand. I comprehend entirely. From what you say, or rather from what you are indicating in the most delicate manner, the only conclusion I can draw is that you regard my situation as hopeless.

SCENE XII

Hans Karl says nothing, looks distractedly right.

*Vincent has come in, right, in the same suit as in Act I,
a small bowler hat in his hand.*

Crescence has gone up to Vincent.

HECHINGEN

very cast down by Hans Karl's silence

This is the critical moment of my life, and I did see it coming. Now I need your support, my dear Kari, if my whole world isn't to collapse.

HANS KARL

But my dear Ado— (*To himself, looking at Vincent*) What's going on here?

HECHINGEN

I shall, if you allow me, recapitulate the premises on which I based my hopes—

HANS KARL

Excuse me for one second, I see that something has gone wrong.

He goes over to Crescence and Vincent. Hechingen is left standing alone.
Stani has withdrawn to one side, showing some signs of impatience.

CRESCENCE *to Hans Karl*

Now he tells me you're going off tomorrow morning early—
what does this mean?

HANS KARL

What's this? I've given no such order—

CRESCENCE

Kari, with you one never gets away from shilly-shallying. And
just when I had got myself into the right frame of mind for your
engagement!

HANS KARL

May I remind you—

CRESCENCE

Oh my goodness, it just slipped out!

HANS KARL *to Vincent*

Who sent you here? What does this mean?

VINCENT

Your Lordship gave the order yourself, half an hour ago, by
telephone.

HANS KARL

To you? I gave no order to you.

VINCENT

Your Lordship instructed the porter's lodge that at seven
o'clock tomorrow morning you would be going off to your
hunting lodge at Gebhardtskirchen—or, rather, this morning,
since it's now a quarter past midnight.

CRESCENCE

But, Kari, what does it all mean?

HANS KARL

If people would only stop expecting me to give an account of every breath I draw.

VINCENT *to Crescence*

But it's quite easily explained. The portress ran up to the house with the message, Lukas wasn't anywhere about at the moment, so I took the matter in hand. I warned the chauffeur, I had the suitcases brought down from the box room, I had the secretary Neugebauer stirred up in case he was needed—why should he sleep when the whole house is awake?—and now here I am at your service, ready for further instructions.

HANS KARL

Go back to the house at once, cancel the car, have the suitcases unpacked again, beg Herr Neugebauer to go back to bed, and take yourself off so that I never see your face again! You are no longer in my service. Lukas already knows what is to be done with you. Now go!

VINCENT

I must say, this is a great surprise to me.

Goes out.

SCENE XIII

CRESCENCE

But do let me have only a word or two! Do explain—

HANS KARL

There's nothing to explain. When I left the Club I was quite determined, for various reasons, to go off in the morning early. That was at the corner of the Freyung and the Herrengasse.

There's a café at that corner, and I went in and telephoned home from there; then, when I came out of the café, instead of turning into the Freyung as I had intended, I came down the Herrengasse and arrived in here again—and then Helen—

He draws his hand over his forehead.

CRESCENCE

But you should be left to yourself.

She goes over to Stani, who is hanging about in the background.

HANS KARL

gives himself a shake and returns to Hechingen, very cordially

I do beg you to forgive me for all that has happened, I've done nothing but make mistakes and I ask you to forgive me for all of them. I can't give you any detailed report about this evening's doings. I beg you, all the same, to think kindly of me.

Holds out his hand.

HECHINGEN *overcome*

But now you're taking leave of me, my dear friend! You have tears in your eyes. But I do understand you, Kari. You are a true, good friend; people like me are simply not able to extricate ourselves from the meshes of the destiny prepared for us by the smiles or frowns of women, but you have lifted yourself once for all far above that atmosphere— (*Hans Karl gestures him to stop.*) You can't deny it, you have that aura of superiority around you, and as in the long run life never stands still but must always progress or regress, you simply can't help having round you from day to day the increasing loneliness of the superior man.

HANS KARL

And that's just another colossal misunderstanding!

He looks anxiously right, where Altenwyl with one of his guests
is now visible in the door of the conservatory.

HECHINGEN

How so? How am I to understand your words?

HANS KARL

My dear Ado, please excuse me for the moment from trying to
explain them or anything else. Be so good as to step over here
with me, for there's something approaching from over there
that I don't feel equal to meeting.

HECHINGEN

What is it, what is it?

HANS KARL

There, in the door, behind me.

HECHINGEN

looks over at the door

That's only our host, Poldo Altenwyl—

HANS KARL

—Who thinks that the tail-end of his soirée is the very moment
for swooping down on me with horrid intent; since what does
one go to a soirée for, if not to let every man with something or
other on his mind pounce on one in the most ruthless manner!

HECHINGEN

I don't understand—

HANS KARL

The idea is that I should make my debut as an orator in the
Upper House the day after tomorrow. Our Club has entrusted

him with this charming mission, and since I've been avoiding him everywhere he's lurking here in his own house to catch me when I'm alone and unprotected. Please do fall into lively talk with me, even a little agitated, as if we were settling some important matter.

HECHINGEN

And you're going to refuse again?

HANS KARL

Am I supposed to stand up and make a speech about peace among peoples and the unitedness of nations—I, a man whose sole conviction is that it's impossible to open one's mouth without causing the most ineradicable confusion? I'd rather give up my hereditary seat and crawl into a barrel for the rest of my life. Am I to let loose a flood of words every one of which will seem positively indecent to me?

HECHINGEN

That's putting it a bit strongly.

HANS KARL

with great intensity, but without raising his voice

But everything one utters is indecent. Merely to put anything into words is an indecency. And when one looks at it closely, my dear Ado, except that men never look closely at anything in the world, there's something positively shameless in our daring even to experience some things! To go through some experiences and not consider oneself indecent needs an insane self-complacency and a measure of fatuousness which a grown man may well keep in some hidden corner of himself but can never admit the existence of, even to himself! (*Looks right.*) He's gone.

Makes for the street door. Altenwyl is no longer visible.

CRESCENCE *intercepting Kari*

No making an escape just yet! Kari must explain the whole situation to Stani! (*Hans Karl looks at her.*) But the boy can't simply be left standing! The boy has shown such forbearance, such self-restraint, that I'm struck with admiration. A word can surely be said to him.

She beckons Stani to approach. Stani comes a step nearer.

HANS KARL

All right, one more word. But this is the last soirée I'll ever be seen at. (*To Stani, going up to him*) It was a mistake, my dear Stani, to trust me as an advocate for anything.

Clasps his hand.

CRESCENCE

Kari should at least embrace the boy! The boy has carried himself with the most unexampled self-control throughout. (*Hans Karl stands looking rather absently into the distance.*) Well, if Kari won't embrace the boy, I must at least embrace him because of the way he has carried himself.

HANS KARL

Perhaps you'd be good enough to wait till I'm gone.

Reaches the front door quickly and disappears.

SCENE XIV

CRESCENCE

Well, I don't care, I must embrace somebody! Too much has happened for a woman with a feeling heart like mine simply to go home without more ado and get into bed!

STANI *takes a step back*

Please, Mamma! In my opinion there are two categories of demonstrative behavior. One of them is most strictly reserved for private life: that includes all gestures of tenderness between blood relations. The other has, so to speak, a practical and social function: it is the pantomimic expression of any unusual situation which belongs as it were to family history.

CRESCENCE

Well, that's the situation we're in!

Altenwyl with some guests has come out of the living rooms upstairs and is beginning to descend the stairs.

STANI

And for this kind of situation, the right and proper forms have existed for a thousand years. What we have experienced here tonight was, for good or for ill, if we are to call things by their right names, a betrothal. A betrothal culminates in an embrace between the betrothed parties. — In our case the betrothed couple are too eccentric to recognize these formalities. Mamma, you're the nearest relation to Uncle Kari, and there is Poldo Altenwyl, the father of the bride. Let my Mamma go without saying a word and embrace him, and then the whole affair will have taken on its proper, official aspect.

Altenwyl with his guests has come downstairs. Crescence rushes up to him and embraces him. The guests stand in astonishment.

Curtain

THE TOWER

A Tragedy in Five Acts

CHARACTERS

King Basilius
Sigismund, *his son*
Julian, *Governor of the Tower*
Anton, *his servant*
Brother Ignatius, *formerly the Grand Almoner, Cardinal and Chancellor of the Realm*
Olivier, *a soldier*
A Physician
The Vaivode of Lublin
The Palatine of Krakow
The Lord Chancellor of Lithuania
The Chief Cupbearer
Count Adam, *a Chamberlain*
Starosta of Utarkow
The King's Confessor
Simon, *a Jew*
A Groom
An Officer
A Countrywoman

Aron, *the Tartar*
Jeronim, *a scribe* } *rebels*
Indrik, *the Latvian*
Gervasy } *the King's spies*
Protasy

Courtiers, chamberlains, pages, a man with a wooden leg, a castellan, soldiers, a gatekeeper, a beggar, monks, rebels.

Act I

SCENE I

In front of the tower. Outworks, partly built of stone, partly hewn into the rock. Between the enclosing walls growing dusk while the sky is still light. Olivier, the lance corporal, and a few invalid soldiers, among them Aron, Pankraz, and Andreas, stand in a group.

OLIVIER *calls to the rear*

Recruit! Come here!

A young country lad with flaxen hair rushes up.

Run, fellow, and bring me fire for the pipe!

RECRUIT

Yessir.

Wants to go.

ARON

Very good, sir, my corporal! That's how you say it!

OLIVIER

Get me the fire! Off with you!

RECRUIT

Yessir.

ANDREAS *after a pause*

Is it true, corporal, that you used to be a scholar?

Olivier does not reply. Pause.

PANKRAZ

So you are our new corporal of the guard?

Olivier does not reply.

Recruit brings a glowing torch.

OLIVIER

Which way's the wind?

RECRUIT

Don't know, sir.

OLIVIER

Stand beween the pipe and the wind, you dumb beast.

RECRUIT

Yessir.

OLIVIER *lights his pipe*

This damned rapping noise must stop. Get going, Aron. This is
an order. No woodchopping around here. It bothers me.

PANKRAZ

Nobody's chopping wood. It's him back there: the prisoner.

OLIVIER

The prince who goes naked, with an old wolf's hide round his
body?

PANKRAZ *looks around*

You must say: the prisoner. Don't let that other word slip out of your mouth. Or else you'll be up before the provost.

Olivier laughs noiselessly.

ARON

Not in these times, they can't push a man like him around.

OLIVIER *looks towards the left*

What is the beast up to? Why does he make such a row in his cage?

ARON

He has scraped up a horse bone; he knocks about with it among the rats and the toads, like a madman.

PANKRAZ

They torment him, and so he torments them.

RECRUIT

He has a wolf's body, and out of it has grown a human head. He stretches out five-fingered hands and folds 'em like a man.

OLIVIER

Does it look that rare, the creature? Then I must see him. Recruit, throw a rock and rouse him.

He takes a pike and approaches.

ARON

He cannot hold up under his eyes! Look, how he crawls away, the wolfman.

ANDREAS *steps close to Olivier*

I warn you, corporal. Think of the strict instructions.

OLIVIER

Don't know of any.

ANDREAS

There are ten forbidden points—on those everybody here must take his oath.

ARON

He hoots at those! What, Olivier?

ANDREAS

Not less than ten paces from the prisoner. Not a word to him, not a word about him, on your body and your life.

PANKRAZ

Those the governor issued, and we are all subject to his sovereign rule.

ANDREAS

He has summary rights. He has power over our necks.

ARON

Power! Over thieves and beggars maybe, over such sickly freebooters as you are! Not over a person like this one here!

OLIVIER

Where is the governor? I want to see him!

PANKRAZ

You won't see *him*. When he has an order to give, the bugle calls to attention three times. Then he sends his servant.

ARON

His snotty lackey to this martial personage? Did you hear that?

OLIVIER

Hold your brutish tongue, till the time comes. — Listen, there!

The bagpipes. Now they sound again. And now, silent. Signals, that's what it is. Jews, smugglers.

ARON

We ought to scout them.

OLIVIER

Let them be. Comes in handy, the things they smuggle in.

ARON

What is it?

OLIVIER *in a low voice*

Arms, powder and shot, pikes, cudgels, hatchets. Coming up from Hungary, over from Bohemia, down from Lithuania.

ARON

Accursed Jews!

OLIVIER *in an undertone*

They smell what's going on. Smell it beforehand, the fiery red cock on the roof.

ARON *close by him*

And are *they* all agreed on this, tell me, my valiant captain!

OLIVIER

You will find out when the time comes.

RECRUIT *secretly, fearfully*

A three-legged hare was seen, a lean pig came down the road, a calf with glowing eyes runs through the streets.

OLIVIER *to Aron alone*

All against all. Not a house will be left standing. And what's left of the churches they'll sweep up with brooms.

ARON

And what will become of those who are the masters today?

OLIVIER

They will tumble head over heels into the privy.

ARON

Ah, such words run warm through my belly like a dram of brandy. And there'll be so many of us that we will overpower them?

OLIVIER *in an undertone*

Ten thousand in the houses, ten thousand in the forests, a hundred thousand underground.

THE ONE WITH THE WOODEN LEG

who up to now has been silent

They will draw him out and take him up, and the lowest will come to be the highest, and this one will be the poor man's king and he will ride on a white horse.

ARON

Shut up, Moravian Brother.

THE ONE WITH THE WOODEN LEG

In the moist mountains a kingdom will be founded by him.

ARON

Hold your filthy tongue!

OLIVIER *low, to Aron*

Even such as he we shall need. And the one back there, also. That one I'll train like a dog; he shall jump and retrieve for me.

ARON

I do not understand it, but I know that you will be a commander. For you look upon men as one looks upon stones.

OLIVIER

He will command who has the political fatality on his side.

ARON

Is it so high and mighty, this fatality?

A horn signal. Another. And yet another.

PANKRAZ *softly*

There you are. He has them signal three times to attention. And here comes his footman.

Anton appears on a wooden bridge over the outworks and starts coming down. The soldiers, except Olivier, move away.

ANTON

steps towards Olivier from behind

Delivering an order—*greeting.*

Olivier does not respond.

By order of His Excellency!

Greets again behind Olivier's back. Olivier turns around, measures Anton with a contemptuous look. Anton greets him again, very friendly.

Wishing the commander of the guard a good day. — By general order: He should withdraw his guard from here and occupy the entrances. But his posts must turn their backs and all the same keep their eyes open. Nothing that will take place down here is of any concern to the corporal and the guard—but I am going to tell you: the prisoner will be led out for medical inspection. You understand, sir? I beg you, sir, execute the order.

Olivier spits and goes off. Anton, looking after him

A free-spirited soldier-like young man. Standing here and talking with him for one moment is like discoursing for an hour with another.

OLIVIER *outside*

Mount guard! Right turn!

Short roll of drums.

PHYSICIAN

comes downstage the same way as Anton

Where do I find the sick man?

ANTON

You mean to say, sir: the prisoner. Be patient, sir. I'll bring the creature out to you.

PHYSICIAN

Where is the chamber?

ANTON

What chamber?

PHYSICIAN

Well, the prison, the keep.

ANTON *points towards the back*

There!

PHYSICIAN

What, there? (*Turns in the direction.*) I see a small, open cage, not good enough for a dog kennel. — You do not mean to tell me that in there he—or else an offense has been committed here which cries up to heaven!

Anton shrugs his shoulders.

In there? Day and night?

ANTON

Winter and summer. In the winter, a half load of straw is thrown in.

PHYSICIAN

Since when? How long?

ANTON

Four years ago things became a bit worse. Since then he spends also the nights there in the cage, has no freedom to go about, his feet on the chain, with a heavy ball to it, the stinking hide round his body, summer and winter, sees the sun no more than two hours altogether and only in midsummer.

The dull sound of strokes is again audible as in the beginning.

PHYSICIAN *steps nearer*

My eye is getting accustomed. I see an animal which cowers on the ground.

Steps back.

ANTON

Aye, that is the one in question.

PHYSICIAN

That! — Call him. Lead him out here in front of me.

ANTON *looks around*

I must not speak with him in the presence of a stranger.

PHYSICIAN

I shall take the responsibility.

ANTON

Sigismund! — He doesn't answer. — Take care! He can't bear it if anybody comes near him. Once he locked teeth with a fox which the guards threw over the rail, for the sport of it.

PHYSICIAN

Can you not call to him? Coax him? Is there no human reason in him?

ANTON

He? He knows Latin and runs through a stout book as if it were a flitch o' bacon. (*Approaches the cage calling in softly.*) Come now, Sigismund. Why, who might it be? It's Anton himself is here. (*He opens the gate with a pike which had been leaning against the wall.*) There, now I put down my stick. (*He places the pike on the ground.*) Now I sit down on the ground. Now I sleep. (*Softly to the physician*) Take care, sir. He must not get frightened, or there'll be trouble.

PHYSICIAN

Why, has he a weapon?

ANTON

Always a horse bone. They must have once buried the carcass in the corner. — Deep inside, it is a good creature; if it please, sir, give him something that he may grow gentle again.

PHYSICIAN

When the whole world lies heavy upon him. All things somehow are bound up together.

ANTON

Ssst! He is moving. He is looking at the open gate. That is something unusual!

> *Sigismund steps out of his cage, a large rock in one hand. Anton beckons to him.*

Come and sit down, next to me.

SIGISMUND *echoes the words*

Sit down next to me!

ANTON *sitting on the ground*

A gentleman has come.

> *Sigismund notices the physician, shudders convulsively.*

Don't be afraid. A good gentleman. What will he think of you?
Put the rock down. He thinks you are a child. And you, full
twenty years old.

*Stands up, goes slowly towards him, and gently wrests
the rock out of his hand.*

PHYSICIAN

without taking his eyes off Sigismund

A monstrous offense. Unthinkable, this!

ANTON

Salute the gentleman! Or what will he think? He has come from
far away.

PHYSICIAN *steps nearer*

Would you like to live somewhere else, Sigismund?

*Sigismund looks up to him, then looks away; he speaks
half to himself, rapidly like a child.*

SIGISMUND

Beasts are of many kinds, all rushing at me. I cry: Not too close!
Wood lice, worms, toads, goblins, vipers! All want to fall upon
me. I beat them to death, it sets them free, come the tough
black beetles, bury the lot.

PHYSICIAN

Bring me light, I must look into his eye.

ANTON

I can't leave you alone with him, sir; I am not allowed to do
that! (*Calls to the rear*) A torch there!

*The physician goes towards Sigismund, places a hand on
his forehead. Horn signal outside.*

PHYSICIAN

What is that?

ANTON

It means that nobody must come near, they shoot to kill.

SIGISMUND *very rapidly*

Your hand is good, help me now! Where have they put me? Am I now in the world? Where is the world?

PHYSICIAN *to himself*

The whole world is just enough to fill our mind and heart when we look out at it through the small peephole from the safety of our house. But woe! When the dividing wall breaks down!

A soldier brings a burning pine torch.

ANTON

Here is the torch!

Hands it to the physician.

PHYSICIAN

I must see his eye. (*Presses Sigismund, who leans against his knees, softly towards himself and illuminates his face from above.*) God knows, it is not a murderous eye; only an unfathomable abyss. Soul and anguish without end.

He returns the torch; Anton stamps it out.

SIGISMUND

Light is good. Enters in, makes the blood clean. Stars are such light. Inside me is a star. My soul is holy.

PHYSICIAN

A ray of light must have once touched him which has awakened his innermost life. Then he has been doubly wronged.

*Julian, the governor, accompanied by a soldier who carries
a lantern, appears above on the wooden bridge and looks down.*

ANTON

His Excellency himself is here. They signal up there, so the
examination must come to an end.

PHYSICIAN

I determine that. (*He takes Sigismund's pulse.*) What do you give
him to eat?

ANTON *softly*

It's too mean for a mangy dog. Sir, if you could speak a word
about this!

PHYSICIAN

I have finished.

ANTON

Now Sigismund goes in again.

*Sigismund shudders, kneels on the ground. Anton takes up the
pike, opens wide the gate into the cage. Sigismund remains on his
knees, stretches out his hand.*

PHYSICIAN *covers his eyes*

Oh humankind! Man! Man!

Sigismund expels a sound of lamentation.

ANTON

Shall they come with poles to drive you in?

PHYSICIAN

I beg of you, go for now to your place. I promise you that I shall
do what I can.

Sigismund rises, bows towards the physician.

PHYSICIAN *to himself*

More than dignity in such abasement! This is a princely crea-
ture if ever one walked the earth.

> *Sigismund has returned to the cage. Anton shuts
> the cage from the outside.*

ANTON

With your permission, sir, I'll go before you. Your honor is ex-
pected at once up in the tower.

> *They go up.*

SCENE II

> *A room in the tower, a large and a smaller door. Julian, Anton.*

JULIAN

Has Simon come in? He has been seen. As soon as he shows
himself, report here.

ANTON *points behind him*

The doctor.

JULIAN

Let him enter.

> *Anton opens the small door. The physician enters,
> makes a bow. Anton leaves.*

JULIAN

I am very obliged to you, sir, for your troublesome journey here.

PHYSICIAN

You were pleased to command, your Excellency.

JULIAN *after a short pause*

You have examined this person?

PHYSICIAN

With horror and astonishment.

JULIAN

How do you judge the case?

PHYSICIAN

As a dreadful crime.

JULIAN

I am asking for a medical report.

PHYSICIAN

The outcome will prove whether, among the rest, the physician has not been called too late.

JULIAN

I should hope not! Make use, sir, of your renowned abilities. No expense shall be shunned.

PHYSICIAN

Only quackery would attempt to heal the body through the body alone. More is at stake. The enormous crime has been perpetrated upon all mankind.

JULIAN

How do you, sir, arrive at such irrelevancies? Our concern is with a single private person who is in my keeping.

PHYSICIAN

Not at all. In the spot where this life is plucked out by its roots there rises a turbulence which carries us all along with it.

JULIAN *gazes at him*

You presume a good deal. — You are a famous person, doctor. The medical faculty is ill-disposed towards you, but that has only helped to make you more prominent. You have a great sense of your own worth.

PHYSICIAN

Your Excellency cannot possibly conceive how slight is my regard for myself. My renown is in many ways a misunderstanding. To those who walk in a mist even a torch looks grand like a church portal.

Julian walks up and down, then suddenly stops
in front of the physician.

JULIAN

Speak out, straight from the heart! Who do you suspect is the prisoner? Answer without fear. I ask you as a private person.

PHYSICIAN

Whatever the capacity in which you ask me—I have only one and the same word for it: here is a being of the noblest order held in the most piteous degradation. — Your most noble person alone, who lend yourself to be keeper and jailer of an unknown—

JULIAN

Leave our self out of it. I see you have come here in a singularly prejudiced frame of mind.

PHYSICIAN

I judge by no reports, only by my impression. This living being before whom I stood down there, up to his ankles in filth, is a *quinta essentia* of the highest earthly virtues.

JULIAN

You are pleased to speak in fancy, without insight into circumstances. I remain with realities, insofar as the state secret does not shut my lips. The specimen of young manhood in question

was a victim of coincidences. I have done what I could. Without
me he would be hardly alive.

PHYSICIAN

He would be alive without you as without me, and when his hour
comes, he will go forth. That is the sense of the coincidences.

A knock on the door.

JULIAN *looks at him*

I wish to converse with you further. Above all about what is to
be done. The prisoner, I admit it, has been neglected. You will
propose incisive measures to me.

Physician bows. Anton has entered, with cups on a silver tray.

JULIAN

For the moment I am prevented. In the adjoining room a light
refreshment has been served for you.

Anton responding to a sign comes up with the cups.

JULIAN *takes one cup*

A stirrup cup, I entreat you. My thanks once more for the sacri-
fice of valuable time. I pledge you.

PHYSICIAN *after he has drunk*

But scarcely touching the lips.

JULIAN

It has lately deprived me of sleep. There must be a poison in
this precious drink as well as a balm.

He turns to Anton; they talk privately.

PHYSICIAN

Al-cohol: the most precious substance. It appears inside the body
twenty-four hours after death, at the same moment when the

first breath of decomposition sets in. Out of corruption the vir-
tue of restoration. That is *encheiresin naturae.*

ANTON *reports in an undertone*
The baptized Simon has come, with a letter for your Lordship.

JULIAN
Bring him in, at once.

ANTON
He is right here.

*Lets Simon enter at the larger door. The physician has bowed
and left at the smaller door. Simon hands Julian a letter.*

JULIAN
Received in what way?

SIMON
In the known manner through the known person. I was told
moreover to make haste: a matter of importance for your
Lordship.

*Julian hastily breaks the letter open, signals Simon
to retire. Simon leaves.*

JULIAN *reads the letter*
—The king's nephew killed during the hunt! Thrown into a
wolf's pit with his horse! — It is uncanny. The young prince,
twenty years of age, a robust youth. There is God's visible hand!
(*Walks up and down, and goes on reading.*) The king alone, for
the first time alone, the first time in thirty years abandoned
by his all-powerful adviser. (*Reads.*) The cardinal-minister, your
potent unyielding enemy, into the monastery, without the
king's farewell—he has withdrawn his hand from the public af-
fairs, forever—(*Speaks.*) I am dreaming! It cannot possibly be
that so much stands written on this small scrap of paper! (*Steps*

to the window into the light, reads again.) —Fallen into a wolf's pit—the cardinal-minister into a monastery—divested himself of all temporal honors—under the name: Brother Ignatius—

He rings the handbell. Simon enters.

JULIAN

I have here surprising reports. Great things have happened. — What is new in the world. What do people say?

SIMON

The world, most gracious Burgrave Excellency, the world is one big misery. When it's come to this, that you cannot buy anything with money—can you, with such money? What is money? Money is confidence in the full weight. And where can you find a silver taler? To see a solid coin these days, you have to go on a long journey.

JULIAN *to Anton*

The key!

ANTON

Excellency is holding it in your hand.—

JULIAN

The other one.

ANTON

Here it is, before your eyes.

SIMON

The war began; they paid the soldier, they paid the provisioner with silver talers. The war goes into the second year, and the taler becomes a mixture. In the third year the silver was silver-plated copper. But they took it, people took it. The king finds out he can coin money by printing his face and his arms on tin, on lead, on muck. So the great lords saw it can be done, and the burghers, and the gentry, too. If the king coins money, the lords coin money; who does not coin money? Until everything swims in money.

Julian has fixed his eyes again upon the letter.

However, if you have paid out solid coin, should you take back lightweight money? But how can you not take it? Since the king's own (*He removes his cap.*) sovereign likeness is stamped on it. But for tribute and tax the new money is prohibited! And the soldiers and the miners should take the light coin? So, what is happening? The miners don't go into the mines any more, the bakers don't bake bread any more, the doctor runs away from the sickbed, the student from the school, the soldier from the standard. And the king, his reliability is gone. Then there is in all the world nothing left to trust. (*Noticing Julian's look*) But what do I need to tell your gracious Excellency of all this? When this evening one of the very great lords from the court will ride in on horseback, he will talk over with your gracious Excellency the state affairs and the political—

JULIAN *startled*
Who will come riding here on horseback? What is that you are saying?

SIMON
The great Lord Vaivode of Lublin, with a following of at least fifty, among them noble pages and royal bodyguards, whom I have left behind by two, three hours. — Your gracious Excellency looks at me as if my mouth brought you a message of surprise where your Lordship is holding in your hands the letters in which it must be written down, black on white.

JULIAN
That is all. Let him go.

Simon leaves. Anton comes back in.

Anton! The proudest greatest Vaivode in the whole court! Sent here, to me! From the king himself, sent to me! Anton! They are bringing the corpse back to life! It is to me—me—do you hear? What sort of faces are you pulling?

ANTON

As if I couldn't guess what is going on inside you! This means, after all, no more and no less than this: they are coming to bring you back to court, they are going to press on you the honors, which means—the troubles, the dignities, which means—the burdens, the trusted offices, the sinecures and vexations, all the business you loathe as the child does bitter medicine!

JULIAN

It cannot be true. — Oh God, if it were true!

ANTON

O you my Savior! How do we make our escape now! How do we dodge this? Now good counsel is dear. If your Lordship were to pretend sickness? I am going to make the bed ready!

JULIAN

Stop that nonsense! The paneled room is to be furnished for his Highness the Vaivode. My own bed goes in. My riding coat, have the marten furs ripped out, make a footrug out of them for his Grace, right beside his bed.

ANTON

In God's name, if only he set his foot somewhere else soon enough!

JULIAN

Send the trumpeter up on the outworks!

ANTON

The trumpeter?

JULIAN

The moment he sees the cavalcade, one trumpet signal! One!
Make certain of this: if they are ordinary riders. But if it is a
princely cavalcade—

He must govern his excitement by holding on to the table.

ANTON

Then?

JULIAN

Then three flourishes in succession, as is done for the king! —
Why are you gaping at me? Shall I—

ANTON

I am not going to say a word. (*Looks at him sideways.*) Must be a
glorious feeling, when one knows: I am sure of myself! Come
here, Satan, spread it out before me, the splendor, like a car-
pet—and now take it off quick before I spit on it because such
things I have mastered in myself. (*A knock on the door. Anton an-
swers it.*) The doctor has finished eating and begs permission to
wait on you. — Shall he?

JULIAN

Let him enter. And then off with you to attend to my orders.

*The physician has come in; he has a sheet of paper in his
hand. Anton leaves. The physician stops before Julian, who
stands there lost in thought.*

PHYSICIAN

I find your Excellency much altered.

JULIAN

You are a keen physiognomist. — What is it you see in my
features?

PHYSICIAN

A violent hopeful agitation. Far-reaching arrangements! Great preparations! Encompassing a whole empire. Your lordship is created of heroic stuff.

Julian is obliged to smile, but immediately suppresses his smile.

However—I must pronounce it in the same breath: the source itself is troubled, the deepest root is cankered. In this your imperious countenance Good and Evil wage a fearful coiling battle like serpents.

JULIAN

Give my pulse greater steadiness, that is all I need. I am about to face great excitement. — I need different nights.

Closes his eyes, quickly opens them again.

PHYSICIAN *fixing his eyes upon him*

Your pulse is not steady, and yet—I can answer for it—the heart muscle is powerful. But you deny your heart. — Heart and head must be one. But you have consented to the satanic split; you have suppressed the noble inner organ. Hence these bitterly curling lips, these hands which forbid themselves the touch of wife and child.

JULIAN *nods*

My years have been terribly lonely.

PHYSICIAN

Terrible, but so willed. What you are seeking is a keener desire: sovereignty, absolute power of command.

Julian looks at him.

I see heroic ambition in your carriage and gait, checked in the hips by an impotent will, gigantically warring with itself.

Your nights are raging desire, powerless aspiration. Your days are boredom, self-consuming, doubting what is most high—the soul's wings shackled in chains!

JULIAN

You come close to one's self! Too close!

PHYSICIAN

To point to a malady where I see it, that is my part. The wrong done to this youth, the enormity of the crime, the complicity, the partial consent: all this stands written in your face.

JULIAN

Enough. You talk, sir, without knowledge of the matter. (*Goes to the wall, causes a panel to fly open, takes out a sheet of paper from which hangs a seal.*) I have saved his life, more than once. He was to vanish altogether, to be done away with. I was distrusted. I had handed him over to a good-hearted peasant family, from his eighth to his thirteenth year of life. And I was charged with having ambitious plans in connection with the prisoner's survival. I had to place him again inside the tower.

PHYSICIAN

I understand.

JULIAN

At first I had him kept in a humanly decent prison. — In the first night a shot was fired through the window and grazed his neck, a second one towards morning which went between his arm and his chest. — Without me he would have been murdered. — I wish not to be misjudged by you. (*He holds the paper out to him.*) You see, sir! The very highest seal. In his own handwriting the signature of the most exalted person in the realm. — I go very far with you.

PHYSICIAN *reads from the paper*

"Convicted of a planned attempt on the life of his Sacred Majesty—" — That boy! — This writing is nine years old. At that time he was a child!

JULIAN

The stars had pointed to him before he was born as if with a blood-stained finger. What had been predicted was fulfilled, point by point, horribly to confirm him as the one who stands outside the human community. He was convicted before his lips could form a word.

PHYSICIAN

raises his hands to heaven

Convicted!

JULIAN

Of high treason. — What is there in my power to do!

Locks the sheet away.

PHYSICIAN

takes a scrap of paper from his belt

I wrote down while eating what I hold to be most indispensable. A place of custody worthy of human dignity, facing the sun, pure nourishment, the consolation of a priest.

JULIAN

Give it to me.

PHYSICIAN

No, it is too little; I shall tear it up. (*He does so.*) Only rebirth heals such a shattered life. Let him be brought back into his father's house, not a year from now, nor a month, but tomorrow at night!

JULIAN *up and down*

And if it is a demon and a devil, presumptuous man? A rebel against God and the world! — There!

He listens. Trumpets in the distance. Growing pale,
closes his eyes.

You are accustomed to auscultation, sir; your ear is sharp. May I ask whether I hear rightly?

PHYSICIAN

Three trumpet flourishes at a great distance.

Julian opens his eyes again, draws a deep breath.

At this instant you have given birth to a bold and frightful design. Your face is flaring up.

JULIAN

I see as through a sudden light the possibility of a trial.

PHYSICIAN

Whereby the unfortunate creature could be saved?

JULIAN

I hold it possible that much will be placed in my hands. Sir, as to a sure and effective, powerful sleeping draught, are you capable—?

PHYSICIAN

May I ask—

JULIAN

I would send out a rider for it.

PHYSICIAN

Do I guess correctly? You wish to transport the unconscious body to another place. Bring certain persons before his eyes?

JULIAN

We will not speak one word too much. I am risking my head.

PHYSICIAN

And if he fails the test? — If he dissatisfies. — What becomes of him?

JULIAN

Then it may—perhaps—be possible to spare him and protract the same life which he has led till now.

PHYSICIAN

I will not be an accomplice in this. (*Steps back.*) It would mean driving one of God's creatures into madness.

JULIAN

I give you half a minute's time to reflect. Consider it.

PHYSICIAN *after a few seconds*

Your rider can get the draught from me tomorrow night. — The dose is strictly measured out. Your Excellency, bind yourself solemnly to me that from no other hand shall the prisoner—

JULIAN

From my own hand. Provided that I can effect the trial. That rests with higher persons.

He trembles, rings the handbell.

PHYSICIAN

I am discharged?

JULIAN

With the request that you accept this trifling payment (*Hands him a purse.*) and in addition this ring as a memento. (*Draws the ring off his finger, holds it out; his hand trembles visibly.*)

PHYSICIAN

Your Lordship rewards nobly.

*Makes a bow, and withdraws. Anton enters by the other door, a
rich mantle over his arm, and shoes in his hand. Hurriedly he helps
Julian remove the house robe and put on the rich coat.*

JULIAN

How close are they? I saw a single rider gallop in.

ANTON

Yes, yes.

Fastens the garment.

JULIAN

An outrider, a courier? What?

ANTON

I won't say it, it would annoy you. A puffed-up groom!

JULIAN

What do they want of me?

ANTON

Just because the fellow brings a letter in the King's own hand,
that goes right to his head, common lackey stable boy. Why
shouldn't the King once in a while write a letter by himself? Has
he no hands?

JULIAN

A hand-written letter—to me in person?

He has to sit down.

ANTON *helps put on his shoes*

Did I not know you would be annoyed? — But that it should
touch you so to the quick—

Julian says nothing.

JULIAN *jumps up, out of breath*

Are the men posted?

ANTON

Lined up in formation.

Ties his shoes.

JULIAN

You, out front to the door, with a light.

ANTON

But the torches are up along the stairs. Who wants to tire him-
self out for people that only bring unwelcome trouble into the
house!

JULIAN

A light! You are to kneel on the lowest landing. When his Grace,
the Vaivode, has passed you, run ahead and light him up the
stairs. I will come to meet him, three steps down from the upper
landing, not a step further.

ANTON *lighting a candlestick*

Just so. He shall understand, that court flunkey, that we haven't
been waiting for him these nineteen years.

Curtain

Act II

SCENE I

*Cloisters. In the background, the entrance gate. On the right,
the entrance into the monastery. The Father Superior, before him
the two royal spies Gervasy and Protasy.*

GERVASY

As we report, your Reverence. His exalted Highness in person,
himself.

PROTASY

Yet wishes not to be known.

GERVASY

Known perhaps—but not recognized.

PROTASY

In strictest privacy, most extraordinary secrecy.

Knocking on the gate. The gatekeeper goes to open it.

GERVASY

With humble submission, we shall withdraw.

PROTASY

We will wait outside for his Grace, the Vaivode of Lublin. For
he is summoned here.

*They bow low and disappear in the cloisters. Father Superior
leaves. The gatekeeper opens the gate. King Basilius and courtiers
step in. A beggar enters behind them.*

KING

Is this the place where Brother Ignatius receives those who
come to him with a petition?

GATEKEEPER

Stand here all of you and wait.

YOUNG CHAMBERLAIN

Move on, you, and announce us as I shall tell you.

GATEKEEPER

I may not announce you. That is not my office. My office is to unlock the gate and to lock the gate.

YOUNG CHAMBERLAIN

Do you know in whose presence you are?

GATEKEEPER

I don't know, and I must not know. It is not my office. This one I know. (*Points to the beggar, steps up to him.*) Stand here. He will be joyful because you have come again.

The beggar stands silently to the side.

KING

This is a heavy errand. I will raise my cousins who have gone with me above all Vaivodes, Palatines, and Ordinants.

The courtiers bow. A young monk comes from the right;
graceful, quiet, always smiling.

YOUNG MONK

Speak softly!

KING

Is he asleep so early in the evening that he cannot be disturbed?

YOUNG MONK

Towards morning, when the stars become pale, only then does he fall asleep, and when the birds begin to stir, he is awake again. (*Goes up to the beggar, who is praying, his face in his hands.*) What is your wish?

The beggar does not move.

GATEKEEPER

He is the one without a name who moves about the countryside from one holy place to the next and spends the nights, summer and winter, on stone church steps. He has once before spoken to him.

*The beggar removes his hand from his eyes;
one of his eyes has been put out.*

BEGGAR

Unworthy!

GATEKEEPER

Marauding soldiers, such as you find everywhere nowadays, have struck out one of his eyes. But he has forgiven them and he prays for them.

BEGGAR

Unworthy!

Stands behind the courtiers.

KING

Announce us! Tell him there is someone here, Basilius, and in great need, and his petition is urgent.

YOUNG MONK *bows*

He will soon come. Be patient, gentlemen.

Goes in right; a muffled sound of singing voices becomes audible.

CHOIR *offstage*

"Tu reliquisti me et extendam manum meam et interficiam te!"

KING

takes one step forward, looks upwards

Today is St. Giles' Day: now the stag begins to be in rut. — A beautiful, bright evening: the magpies fly from their nest in pairs without fear for their young, and the fisherman is joyous: the fish will soon spawn, yet still they are eager and leap in the early mist of moonlight, ere night falls. For some time yet it remains light enough to find the mark between river and forest, and great and regal the stag steps out of the copse and parts his lips that it seems as if he laughed, and utters a mighty bellow so that the animals in the underbrush press their shuddering flanks close one against the other, from terror and desire. — We were like him and we relished our days of majesty, before the weather turned, and the knees of beautiful women loosened at the sound of our coming, and where we chose to enter there the silver candelabra or the roseate torch illuminated the marriage of Jupiter with the nymph. (*He supports himself on the young chamberlain.*) And to all this no end seemed to be set, for our strength was royal. — But for a long time now hell has unleashed its powers against us; and there lurks a conspiracy against our fortune beneath our feet and above our hair, which bristles up, and we cannot grasp the rebels. We would go here and go there and strengthen our dominion, and it is as if the ground softened and our thighs sank into emptiness. The walls reel in their foundations, and our path has turned into an impassable bog.

ONE OF THE COURTIERS

The fault lies with the fattened burghers in the towns, these sausage grinders and wool carders and especially the Jews: they have sucked the country's marrow from the bones. They have drawn the silver out of the money and left in our hands stinking red copper, red as the hair on their heads, sons of Judas.

ANOTHER ONE *steps forward from the rear*

They lie bedded down on royal bonds as on goose feathers, their foxholes are papered with mortgage notes of counts and bannerets—and if you grasp ten thousand of them in your harnessed hands till they are crushed, then blood and sweat will flow unto the earth, and out of the ears of corn the gold and the silver will fall upon Polish ground.

THE FIRST ONE

Royal Majesty, let us ride out with our loyal vassals of noble
blood against the Jews and their knaves that sit behind their
palisades, against rebels, escaped monks, runaway school-
masters, and belabor them with as many swords, pikes, maces
as have yet remained in our noble hands—before it is too late.

KING

I cannot seize the filthy rabble. I come riding up; they are
beggars. Out of roofless hovels they come crawling towards me
and stretch emaciated arms out to me. They feed on the barks
of trees and stuff their bellies with clumps of earth. (*He gazes
before him; his head sinks thoughtfully on his breast.*) This also was
in the prophecy. There were horrors in it of which anyone
would have said that they could be meant only as a likeness, and
they begin to be fulfilled in the sense of the word itself. Starva-
tion is in the prophecy; the plague is in the prophecy; darkness,
illuminated by burning villages—the soldier who tears down the
banner and with the halter strikes his commander in the face,
the countryman who runs from his plough and hammers his
scythe into the shape of a bloody pike—all these are in the
prophecy. (*He sighs deeply, forgetting those about him.*) And then
comes the chief part: that the rebellion gets its own banner:
which is a bundle of clanking broken chains fixed to a blood-
stained staff, and he before whom they carry it, he is my own
son—and his face is like a devil's face, and he does not sleep
until he finds me and sets his foot upon my neck. — Thus was
it prophesied! Word for word, written out, as I speak it! (*He
moans and recalls himself, looks back on his train of followers.*) I feel
very ill, my loyal men! I hope you have escorted me to a physi-
cian who can help me.

*Brother Ignatius, the Grand Almoner, is led in from the right. Two
monks support him. The young monk, seen before, walks by his side, an
open book in his hand; a lay brother follows, carrying a folding chair.
They place the chair and let the Grand Almoner sink down on it. He is
ninety years old; his hands and face are yellowish white, like ivory. He*

keeps his eyes for the most part closed, but when he opens them, his look is still capable of spreading fear and respect. He wears the habit of a simple monk. Everyone is silent from the moment he enters. The singing becomes distinctly audible, a single menacing voice.

CHOIR *offstage*

"Ecce ego suscitabo super Babylonem quasi ventum pestilentem. Et mittam in Babyloniam ventilatores et ventilabunt eam et demolientur terram eius."

GRAND ALMONER *with half-closed eyes*

The light of day. A fallow gloom. Read from Guevara. Here is a garden of flowers—jelly, many-colored and stinking.

He closes his eyes.

CHOIR *offstage*

"Et demolientur terram eius! Et cadent interfecti in terra Chaldaeorum."

The Grand Almoner opens his eyes, notices the beggar, beckons to him in a lively manner.

GRAND ALMONER

Look now, what a guest has crossed our threshold!

The King relates this to himself, tries to step forward. The Grand Almoner, without regarding him, contemptuously waves his hand like one who drives off a fly.

COURTIERS *start up*

How! What! How dare he?

The King signals them to restrain themselves.

GRAND ALMONER *to the beggar, with eager interest*

How do you fare, my beloved? And will you now rest with us, at least one day and one night?

The beggar is silent.

GRAND ALMONER

Lead me to him if he will not come to me that I may embrace
him and receive his blessing.

Attempts to rise, supported by the monks.

BEGGAR

Unworthy!

Escapes.

CHOIR *offstage*

"Et demolientur terram eius! Et cadent interfecti in terra
Chaldaeorum."

GRAND ALMONER

Read out of Guevara, as long as the light lasts.

YOUNG MONK *raises the book and reads*

"World, depart from me, in your palaces they serve without
payment, they caress in order to kill, they do honor in order to
disgrace, they punish without forgiveness."

KING *approaching the Grand Almoner*

Cardinal, your king and master wishes you a good evening.

*The Grand Almoner runs his hand through the air as if he were
frightening off a fly. The courtiers grumble among themselves,
turn away as if they meant to leave.*

COURTIERS

Unheard of! Shameful spectacle!

KING *goes towards them*

Remain, my faithful! Do not go from me!

A COURTIER *enraged, but with a subdued voice*
He should be dragged from his chair and his chops pressed in the ground!

KING
I will take from the royal townships their liberties! I will deny my protection to the Jews, and all shall be placed in your hands as it was wont to be in the time of our ancestors. Remain!

The courtiers bend their knees in reverence, kiss his hands and the hem of his garment. The King smiles. The singing has stopped.

GRAND ALMONER
Read out of Guevara. I am weary that it is still day.

YOUNG MONK *reads*
"There the upright are pushed into the corner and the innocent convicted. There credit is given to them that lust after power and to the honest, none."—

KING *to the courtiers*
Leave us, all of you. Turn away. It must be done.

The courtiers go off and remain invisible. Also the monks, except one. The King approaches, falls on his knees in front of the Grand Almoner, and rises again. The Grand Almoner looks at him, long and penetratingly.

GRAND ALMONER
I do not know this man!

Laughs soundlessly.

KING
Cardinal Grand Almoner! Lord Chancellor of the Crown! Lord High Keeper of the Royal Seal! I lift my hands up to you and ask your counsel!

GRAND ALMONER

laughs still more violently, but voiceless

You have lost your war, Basilius. Vain was your war, untimely was
your war, insolent and wicked was your war. And when it was
lost, he who had raised his hands and had cried out against this
war—he was driven from the council table. — For there was
need of self-restraint, only thus was the war to be avoided—and
of wisdom: and difficult is the path of wisdom, for it is full of
thorns. But it was easy to do the deed of vanity, and rush out on
horseback rather than sit and take counsel.

KING

Enough!

GRAND ALMONER *nods*

It is written: the depraved man does not love his punisher. The
word *vain*, note this, Basilius, has a twofold sense. In one way it
means: to boast of one's self, to be one's own spectator, to carry
on a spiritual courtship with one's self. The other way it means:
null and void, for nothing, lost in the mother's womb. — Vain
was your thought, your deed, your begetting, nullified by your-
self in the mother's womb.

KING

You basilisk! Oh that I could wrench the truth out of you, for
you have always concealed the ultimate from me, like the mali-
cious stepmother from the poor orphan.

GRAND ALMONER

The Truth, which is there behind all this show, abides with God.

KING

Is it then God or Satan who speaks through the stars? Answer
me! — Do the stars lie?

GRAND ALMONER

Who are we that they should lie to us?

KING

I have put away my only son where no light shines upon him. For it is prophesied that he will set his foot on my neck in broad daylight and in full view of my people!

GRAND ALMONER

And you will wag your rump before him, like a dog before his master, and you will desire to kiss the butcher knife he takes you off with.

KING

Do you jeer at me? Do you not believe in prophecy? Then answer me! How can they have seen what is not? Where is the mirror that catches what was not there?

GRAND ALMONER

Just so! Hold to that which your eyes can see, and amuse yourself with adulteresses and hounds! — But I tell you: there is an eye beneath which today is like yesterday and tomorrow like today. (*Moves closer to him.*) Therefore the future can be fathomed, and the sibyl stands next to Solomon and the astrologer next to the prophet.

KING *under his breath*

I was sterile, however many virgins and women I have known, and it was said: fertile in the growing season with the queen, and my queen was with child in the month of June. The child was born and he tore the mother's womb, resisting the canny wife and the physician. — He strove to be, naked out of nakedness, deadly out of deadliness, and to fulfill the prophecy with his first cry.—

GRAND ALMONER

And he is your child, got in holy matrimony!

KING

But I have never seen him and I must conceal myself from him with bolts and chains and pikes and bars.

GRAND ALMONER

No one escapes the great ceremony, but the king and the father are placed in the center.

KING

But now that I have rendered the creature harmless in a tower with walls ten feet thick—and the rebellion shall not come to a head—to what end—I demand of you!—to what end has this insurrection come over my kingdom? Shall I be the loser, by day and by night, and cheated of the glory of my empire and of the unspotted mirror of my conscience, of both at once? Are these sham skirmishes? Is God like the Duke of Lithuania who resorts to bluff?

GRAND ALMONER

Wonderfully joined are the tongs, edge to edge, and even the flaccid fruit when it is pressed gives a drop of oil!

KING

Be silent and hear me. I have commanded that the man who guards him shall be brought before me.

GRAND ALMONER

No! You have dared nothing in lifting the veil that was secured by all the terrors of majesty and guarded by tenfold threats of death!

KING

I have commanded that the man be brought who guards him and that he stand in my presence and in yours. And you, you will climb out of your wooden coffin and will preside in a tribunal over this boy whose face we have never seen. — Then it will be revealed whether he is a demon and a rebel out of the mother's womb: his head shall then fall and roll before your feet. Or else: I shall take my child into my arms, and the crown, a triple crown wrought into one, will not be without an heir. — Thereby will I know if God has appointed you my counselor—or Satan.

GRAND ALMONER

God! God! Do you pronounce the word with your dank lips? I shall teach you what that is, God! — You come to me for help and comfort, and you find what gives you no joy. In place of a trusted confidant to whom you show yourself as to a mirror, like the faces of those who cringe before you, you find a countenance unmoved, which fills you with terror. Something there is that speaks through my mouth, but as if it came out of yourself and pointed at yourself; it does not hold you, and it does not release you; you do not proceed from one thing to another, rather one thing after another overtakes you: nothing new, nothing old, living through it but not fully alive, waste, lame and yet turbulent. — You are no longer capable of action and attainment, dissolving but at the same time stone: naked in your need yet not free. But there is something else! You cry out: it is behind your cry, it compels you and bids you hear your own cry, feel your own body, weigh your body's heaviness, observe your body's gesture, like the welter of serpents with lashing tails, inhale your dissolution, smell your stench: ear behind ear, nose behind nose. It despairs behind your despair, horrifies you behind your horror and will not release you to yourself, for it knows you and means to punish you: that is God.

He sinks into himself with closed eyes.

KING *yells*

Advance my loyal men, take him. My chief minister owes me counsel and wants to defraud me of his debt!—

Courtiers rush in, monks appear, raise their hands in defense.
The Grand Almoner lies back like a dead man.

CHOIR *offstage*

"Ecce ego suscitabo super Babylonem quasi ventum pestilentem."

KING *turns away*

Carry him out.

*Monks take the Grand Almoner up and bear him away. A knock on
the gate. The gatekeeper unlocks it, lets in the Vaivode of Lublin and
Julian as well as Gervasy and Protasy, behind them, Anton.*

GERVASY AND PROTASY

approach the King, bend their knee and announce

The Vaivode of Lublin.

VAIVODE

steps before the King, bends his knee

Your Highness forgive the delay. The roads are cut off by rebels.
We had to move through the forests. I have brought the noble
burgrave!

Julian steps up, kneels before the King.

KING

This one? His guardian? (*He steps back suspiciously. Julian remains
on his knees.*) We graciously recall a former meeting. (*Holds out
his hand to be kissed, signals to rise.*) We shall know how to re-
ward. — But we fear that we mark in your eye the reflected
image of a demon.

JULIAN

rising to his feet, but with bent knee

He is a gentle, handsome, well-made youth.

KING

Full of hatred inwardly?

JULIAN

Guileless. A blank white page.

KING

Human? Ah!

JULIAN

Oh that it were your inscrutable will—

The King knits his brow, steps back.

—to subject the youth to a trial—

The King takes another step back.

Should he prove incapable, let him vanish again into the ever-lasting night of imprisonment.

KING

The dream of a night? Bold—and too bold! Who could give me assurance—

JULIAN

I! To your Majesty for everything! With this head!

KING *smiles*

A counselor! At last, a true counselor!— (*With reference to the preceding; he beckons him to come up very close.*) How many years have you performed your difficult office?

JULIAN

Twenty-two years less one month. His age.

KING

Unexampled! Learn, my grandees, learn what devotion is. Twenty-two years!

Julian bends over the proffered hand; he has tears in his eyes.

JULIAN

They are in this instant extinguished.

Anton approaches from behind, unnoticed;
he pricks up his ears.

KING

Meeting you again has moved us deeply. It is your arms that
shield our kin. (*He draws him close, with the gesture of an embrace.*)
How would we bear it, were he himself— (*His face changes, but
only for a moment.*) A loyal man near at hand, what a treasure!
Counselor, comforter! You have given me back my life. (*Beckons
to Julian confidentially.*) You will follow us to court. We have much
to discuss, in confidence.

*Julian bows to the ground. The King signals to the gatekeeper,
who unlocks the gate. Courtiers approach Julian. Anton tries
inconspicuously to get closer to his master.*

A COURTIER *with a slight bow*

We are close relations. Your Lordship's grandmother was my
honored grandfather's sister. I would hope that your Lordship
had not perhaps become unmindful of this during the years in
which your Lordship was not seen at court.

Anton pricks up his ears.

TWO OTHERS *in the same manner*

Sir, grant us your protection. We would die my Lord's ever ready
and most obliged servants!

YOUNG CHAMBERLAIN

stepping up to Julian, with a deep reverence

I kiss your hands, Excellency!

All leave.

SCENE II

*Inside the tower. Pentagonal room with a narrow barred window. In a
back corner, a small iron door. On the wall a large crucifix. A wooden
bench, a pail, a washbasin. In the background Sigismund sits on some*

half-burnt straw. He wears a clean-looking suit made of heavy cotton; his feet are bare, but without chains. The door is being unlocked from the outside.

Anton enters. He takes a broom, which leans next to the door, sprinkles the floor with water from the pail and begins to sweep. Sigismund looks at him, but is silent.

ANTON *while sweeping and sniffing the air*
What's that? You've been kindling fire in the straw? A heap of straw burnt up, and sprigs, everything! — God's mercy, if a guard had caught you. — What have you been doing, and why?

SIGISMUND *quickly*
My father was in the fire.

ANTON
Then what did he look like? A face of fire, a coat of smoke, a bluish-glowing paunch and red hot shoes?

SIGISMUND *turns his head away*
My father has no face!

ANTON
You've got bats in your— (*Sprinkles holy water over him from a small leaden basin which hangs on the wall underneath the crucifix.*) Tidy up now! Aren't you a human creature? Humankind is disgusted when a place looks like the devil's bedchamber.

SIGISMUND *anxiously*
Anton, what is that: human—as I am, humankind?

ANTON *pouring water into the basin for him*
Here now, wash your face, and that will put different thoughts in your head. (*The sound of the door being unlocked from the outside.*)

Here's a towel. (*Throws a gay-colored cotton cloth towards him; Sigismund wipes his face.*) And now! Look there! They're coming for you!

From the outside the iron door has been opened. A countrywoman, Sigismund's foster mother, has entered; she remains standing near the door. Sigismund turns his face to the wall.

COUNTRYWOMAN *comes closer, to Anton*

Is he sick? Does he have his senses about him?

Sigismund hides head and hands in the straw.

Seven years that I have not seen him. Is't true he has grown claws? Burning eyes, like the night fowl?

ANTON

A lie! Show your hands, Sigismund. — There he is, look at him!

SIGISMUND *collects himself*

Mother, have you come to me?

COUNTRYWOMAN *advances*

Your hair is a tangle. Where's your comb? Give it to me so I can comb it.

Anton hands her a leaden comb from a wall shelf. The countrywoman combs Sigismund's hair.

Image of God, watch over yourself. Don't you recall how the countrywomen used to spy through the fence because of your white cheeks and raven-black hair? Used to put milk and honey outside the gate, I had to hide you away, board up the window shutters! Strict was the order!

SIGISMUND

Where is your husband?

COUNTRYWOMAN

Your foster father is dead these four years. Pray with me for his soul.

SIGISMUND

But where is my soul?

COUNTRYWOMAN

How? What is it you are asking?

SIGISMUND

I ask justly. Do you remember still, the pig that father slaughtered—it shrieked so hard, and I shrieked too. Then it hung from the crossbeam, in the hall, close by my door; I could look deep into its inside. Was that the soul which fled out of it when it shrieked so frightfully, and is my soul gone into the dead animal instead?

COUNTRYWOMAN *prays*

Our Father which art in heaven—

SIGISMUND

Where is my own father that he abandoned me! Although he made me!

COUNTRYWOMAN *points to the crucifix*

There is your Father and your Redeemer! Look on him, there! — Imprint his likeness on your heart, stamp it in, like mold and die!

Sigismund looks at it for a long time, mimics the posture, with spread-out arms; then he lets his arms sink.

SIGISMUND

I cannot keep it asunder, myself with him there and then again myself with the animal which was hung up on a crossbeam and black with blood inside. Mother, what is the end of me and the end of that animal?

He closes his eyes.

COUNTRYWOMAN

Open your eyes! Look at him! Forsaken by his Father in heaven! Crowned with thorns, beaten with rods, spit at, in the face, by the soldier-men! Keep your eyes on it. — Look there, obstinate boy!

SIGISMUND *cries out*

Mother, do not make me angry!

He pushes her from him.

COUNTRYWOMAN

folds her hands, in prayer

O you fourteen holy saints and helpers-in-need, you strong warriors and servants of God, glorified and crowned with golden crowns, draw near to help this boy, help him turn his mind from gnashing teeth, clenched fists; better that you caused his hands to drop off, his feet to get lame, his eyes to get blind, his ears to get deaf and defend his soul from the violent deed and from evil. Amen.

She makes the sign of the cross over him.

SIGISMUND *cries fearfully*

Mother!

In the back, the door has again been unlocked, and Julian has entered. In the door another person becomes visible who waits. The countrywoman bows, and kisses Julian's coat. Julian remains standing. — Sigismund flees to his bed of straw.

JULIAN

Is this how you have calmed him? Has the woman not been able to do better? And you— (*Steps closer.*) Sigismund, I have come to visit you. (*Beckons, Anton brings him a low wooden stool on which he sits.*) I have come to bring you joy, Sigismund. Attend to what my lips will now say: you have passed a long, difficult time of trial. Do you understand what I say?

Sigismund conceals his hands under his sleeves.

Are you listening to me?

SIGISMUND

You have supreme power over me. I tremble before you. I know that I cannot escape you. (*Instinctively he conceals his hands.*) I look upon your hands and your mouth that I may rightly understand your will.

JULIAN

Power is given from above. From someone higher than I am, note this well. But I was your rescuer. Secretly I poured oil into the lamp of your life; because of me alone there is still light in you. Remember that. — Do I seem so strange to you, Sigismund? Did I not let you sit next to me at a wooden table and open before you the great book and pointed in it figure after figure to the things of the world and called them by name for you and have I not thereby singled you out from among your equals?

Sigismund remains silent.

Have I not told you of Moses with the tablets and Noah in the ark and Gideon with his sword and David with the harp, of Rome, that great and mighty city and her emperors, and that from them are descended our illustrious kings? Have I not taught you the meaning of master and servant, of distance and nearness, of guilt and punishment, of heavenly and earthly? Answer me!

Sigismund stares fixedly on the ground.

SIGISMUND

Unlike the beast, I understand my ignorance. I have knowledge of what I do not see, I know what is far from me. Therefore I suffer torment like no other creature.

JULIAN

Excellent privilege! Thank me! For thus the lips of man become potent because he endows the letter with spirit, calling and commanding! — Why do you groan?

SIGISMUND

Still there is one fearful word, which outweighs all the others!

JULIAN

What kind of word is that? What is it called, this word? I am eager to hear what magic word it is!

SIGISMUND

Sigismund! (*He runs his fingers over his cheeks and down his body.*) Who is that: I? Where does it end? Who called me so first? Father? Mother? Show them to me!

JULIAN

Your parents have cast you off. You were guilty before them.

SIGISMUND

Loathsome is the animal. It eats its own young still moist from the mother's womb. My eyes have seen it. And yet it is guiltless.

JULIAN

Search not out these things until the veil is rent. Stand firm upon your self! Alone! I have so endowed you! Spirit of light, before whom angels kneel! Son of fire, supreme! Firstborn!

SIGISMUND

Why is your speech so grand? What are you waving in your hand
that sparkles so and glows?

JULIAN

That which stag and eagle and serpent thirst for: that they might
with plants and minerals, with draughts and waters renew their
life: for the chosen one is born twice. Flaming air I wield in my
hand, elixir of a new life, freedom healing like balsam! Drink
this and live!

Sigismund recoils from the vial in Julian's hand.

ANTON

Hurrah! Sigismund! We go on a journey! Large is the world!
Up with you, out of the straw!

SIGISMUND

Must I go back into total darkness! Young as I am! Woe to me!
My blood will then be upon you!

JULIAN

Into the light! So close to the light that only a young eagle would
not go blind. — Drink this.

SIGISMUND

You have taught me yourself that they pardon prisoners with a
draught.

*Julian has stepped to the door, and beckoned. A masked servant,
who holds a cup, has entered. Julian takes the cup, pours from the vial,
and puts it again into his belt pocket. The servant disappears.*

JULIAN

Drink this!

SIGISMUND *falls down before him*

Tell me first who I am?

ANTON

They'll tell you, surely, soon as you arrive, somewhere! Only, don't ask too many questions beforehand, it makes people contrary! Drink it down, quick!

JULIAN *hands Sigismund the draught*

You are you. Hear me: The world is subject to deeds. Do you know what deeds are? Drink and behold.

SIGISMUND

Help me, Anton!

JULIAN

Shall my men lay hold of you with their hands? I will call them—you there, advance!

He is near the door.

ANTON

kneels down next to Sigismund

Let him but live, your Lordship, spare his life only!

SIGISMUND

takes the cup and drinks from it rapidly

While you speak harshly, I have drunk it for your sake.

*He takes a few steps to the rear and sits on the ground
after giving the cup to Anton.*

ANTON *drops the cup*

I must hold up his head, he shall not die leaning against hard rock.

JULIAN *restrains him*

Silence, fool! Who speaks of dying? Now he begins to live.

ANTON

kneels next to Sigismund, strokes his feet

Doesn't your Lordship see, then, he has a halo above his face!
O my saintly blessed martyrized—

JULIAN

Silence and call in the servants!

ANTON

walks towards the iron door which stands ajar

They're already here!

*Two masked servants have quietly entered and
remain standing near the door.*

SIGISMUND

to Julian and Anton, but as if to strangers

I feel very light. All my fear is quite gone. Only my feet are
getting cold. Warm them, Anton.

ANTON *close to him*

You know me then?

SIGISMUND

Raise them into the fiery furnace in which walk the young men,
singing, my brothers: O Lord God, we praise you! Face to face!
Chosen! (*He throws his hands upwards.*) Father—I come—

Falls back senseless. The two masked servants step forward.

JULIAN

The robes made ready? The shoes, the belt, everything? Put on
his garments, with courtesy and respect!

*The servants take Sigismund up. Julian has
spread a cloak over him. To Anton*

The carriage to be ready and harnessed! The escort prepared to mount! The guard stand to arms. Give the signal! Move on!

> *Anton pulls out a kerchief, runs out. The servants carry Sigismund out. Julian follows. Trumpet signal outside. Julian beckons Olivier to him. Olivier removes his cap, which had served as a mask.*

You and your fellow take the nearer road. Wherever we should meet, you do not know me. You will take up quarters on the edge of town and make contacts with malcontents, tax evaders, deserters.

OLIVIER

That's already done. The fellowship of unbelievers and debtors has been notified.

JULIAN

Who gave you permission to act beforehand?

OLIVIER *slyly*

I am a dragon with many tails. One must make use of my person according to its nature.

JULIAN *steps closely up to him*

Must?

ANTON *running in*

He's lying in the carriage. Everything is ready to mount.

JULIAN

In God's name.

> *He goes out. One more trumpet signal outside.*

> *Curtain*

Act III

*The death chamber of the Queen, in the royal castle. A tall window in
the background. In the right wall an alcove with the bed, which can be
screened off by a curtain. On the left in front an oratory from which one
can look down into the church. In the center of the left wall, opposite
the entrance door, a fireplace. From the oratory a secret door leads into
a narrow passageway part of which is just visible in the left wing of the
stage. The window shutters are closed. An eternal light burns in the
alcove. The Castellan unlocks the door from the outside and enters with
two servants; they open only one wing of the main door. The servants
open the wooden shutters of the tall window in the back: outside it is
broad daylight.*

CASTELLAN

clanking the large ring of keys

The death chamber of her late Majesty the Queen! No one has
entered here by this main door in twenty-one years. The rever-
end sisters of the Visitation, two of whom remain here in prayer
from midnight till dawn, they come in by this small door; it
leads down a winding staircase, hidden inside the pillar, right
into the sacristy.

*From below the sound of the organ and the singing voices of nuns become
audible. The Castellan goes to the alcove, sprinkles holy water on the
bed out of a silver basin near the entrance to the alcove, then draws the
curtain reverently. Approaching human voices can be heard outside.
Then three strokes of a halberd against the stone floor. The Castellan
signals, the servants run to the doors and open both wings wide. The
court enters: trabants, mace-bearers, pages with tapers. Then the bearer
of the imperial standard with the silver eagle, followed by a page who
carries upon a crimson cushion the King's prayer book and gloves. The
King, wearing a curved saber and his Polish hat in his hand. Close on
his heels, his confessor. Courtiers in pairs, preceded by Julian walking
alone; behind the courtiers, four chamberlains. Lastly the physician with*

his assistant—a young man with spectacles—behind him Anton who carries a covered silver basin. — The King halts in the center of the room, holds out his hat. A page rushes forward, takes the hat on bent knee. The King takes his gloves off the cushion, which the kneeling page holds up to him, puts on the left glove, tucks the right one in his belt. The trabants and the mace-bearers have moved around the room and out again through the double doors, also the Castellan and the servants. The doors are closed. Two mace-bearers post themselves inside the doors. The gentlemen of the court stand in front of the oratory, Julian farthest to the right. The physician and his assistant stop next to the doors. The King steps towards the alcove. A chamberlain hastens to pull the curtain back. Another chamberlain hands the King the aspergillum. The King sprinkles holy water on the bed, then kneels and remains for a moment in prayer. The confessor kneels down with him. The King rises, steps into the center, the confessor a little to his side and behind him. The singing and the music of the organ have stopped.

KING *to the confessor*

I have prayed before the deathbed of my wife, blessed be her memory, for me and for him. This short prayer has wonderfully refreshed my soul. (*He beckons to the physician.*) You persist in your wish to withdraw?

PHYSICIAN

Your Majesty has granted me this one condition, that I be spared from standing myself in the presence of the prince, should the need arise to administer a drug again. My assistant is completely informed, that is, about the procedures which may be necessary—not about the facts of the case. (*In a lower voice.*) He looks upon the prince as a mentally disordered person in whom your Majesty because of distant kinship takes an interest. May it all turn out—I have prepared a sponge dipped in essence of unfailing strength. The servant there keeps it in a covered dish. He has been close to the prisoner; if necessary, he can be of help. May these preparations prove to be superfluous, I pray God.

KING

That has been our incessant prayer these last nine days and nights. — You have grown very close to us in our esteem in these days. We regard your illustrious person from this moment as our loyal and sworn physician in ordinary.

Holds out his right hand to be kissed; the physician bends over it,
then goes to the door, which is opened by a mace-bearer. The physician
leaves; at the door he bows once again.

Strengthen me continually with your advice, reverend father. — I have allowed my counselors to persuade me. — I have submitted my tender human nature to higher judgment.

CONFESSOR

Even Holy Scripture—

KING

I know, the pagans too. Even the pagans. They did not scruple; their own sons—

CONFESSOR

In one day the consul had the heads of two sons laid before their feet.

KING

Two! In one day! What were his reasons?

CONFESSOR

To render satisfaction to the offended law.

KING

How? To the law? The law? But—

CONFESSOR

The law and the sovereign are one.

KING

Paternal authority—the father is the creator—his power directly derived—

CONFESSOR

From the power of God the creator, the source of all that is.

The King takes one step away from the courtiers,
draws the confessor after him.

KING

And the absolution, if I find myself forced to have him brought back there, again—my own son—there again where the light of the sun does not shine on him—?

CONFESSOR

You have doubts? To prevent incalculable evil!

From the outside a scraping on the door. The chamberlain goes to
the door, speaks with someone through the half-opened wing. He then
approaches the King, and on bent knee whispers to him. The
King makes a sign. Mace-bearer opens the door, lets Gervasy and
Protasy come in. Gervasy and Protasy hasten towards
the King, bend their knee.

KING

inclines his ear to Gervasy who whispers

This youth rides his horse nobly like a cavalier?

He looks at Julian severely.

JULIAN

He has never in his life mounted a horse. I have always been mindful of the strict prohibition.

Protasy meanwhile whispers into the King's other ear.

KING *sternly to Julian*

Those whom we have appointed his followers he does not deign to notice with a single glance! What manner of speech is to be expected when he stands in our presence?

JULIAN

Perhaps the speech that angels speak. His words are the issue of an inward source—as in a blazed tree which discharges even through its wound a balmy sap.

Gervasy and Protasy, bending their knee, withdraw.

KING *to Julian, softly*

Has this boy been impressed with the supreme concept of authority? The concept of absolute obedience?

He looks at him severely.

JULIAN *steady under his eye*

Consider, my King, that the youth does not know this world, nor his position in it. He knows one Supreme Being: he lifts his eyes to the stars and his soul to God.

KING

We will hope that this is enough. (*Very audible.*) For the world is out of hand, and we are determined to quench the spreading flames—and if need be in rivers of blood.

The courtiers who stand in the rear near the window gaze down. The pages crowd around the window and seek with some commotion to look down. The King notices this and turns to look.

CHAMBERLAIN

The prince is dismounting. He turns towards the portal and steps inside the castle.

KING

to Julian, controlling himself with an effort

I do not yet wish to see him. (*He conducts Julian away from the courtiers, to the front.*) A great moment, a terrible decisive moment.

JULIAN *falls on his knees*

His words sound at times violent and rash—consider, your Majesty, in your wisdom and forbearance: the creature has never had a friend.

KING

I too have never had a friend about me.

JULIAN *on his knees*

His youthful foot has never taken one step without a heavy bestial chain!

KING

I too, Count Julian, have never taken a free step.

JULIAN *on his knees*

Show forbearance, great prince, to this sorely tried creature!

KING *looks at him*

Be always his counselor, my wise Julian, gentler to him than mine has been to me. — I hold you in great esteem—I am almost ashamed to show how much! (*He takes the golden chain with the white eagle set with diamonds off his neck and hangs it around Julian's, pronouncing.*) Sic nobis placuit! (*Holds out his hand to be kissed by Julian, and raises him. With an altered expression.*) And this ever restless people? This half-stifled yet ever smoldering insurrection? What do you think of it? You have your connections everywhere, your restless hands reach everywhere—

He looks at him suspiciously.

JULIAN *tries to speak*

My king—

KING

These secret fellowships—these sinister alliances shunning the light? — I am informed.

JULIAN

But *one* princely gesture—with *one* act, my king—

KING

You suppose we will overthrow them easily if we give you full authority?

JULIAN

It is easy for a great king to regain the confidence of his people.

KING

Ah, you mean that I must regain *their* confidence—not they mine?

He stares at him fixedly.

JULIAN

Both, my king, both will come to be in one.

KING

When I have abdicated?

JULIAN

God forbid! — Your mildness towards the one will subdue all hearts. Each will feel himself singly overcome with gratitude— to see such a fount of grace flow forth.

KING

O cause for gratitude—he will have it. And my people too. — If I could discover to you my inmost self.

The organ becomes again audible, but without the singing voices.

KING *beckons to one of the courtiers*
Assemble the court outside.

*The mace-bearers open the door, the pages run out, the mace-bearers
follow. The two young chamberlains and several courtiers withdraw.
— The King joins the group which is left. The Castellan has come
in with the keys and hands them, bowing, to the eldest courtier;
he goes out again.*

KING

You, my most trusted companions, bound to me by sacred
oaths—wait there, inside. The antechamber, even where the in-
timate company of the queen used to gather before mass—stay
in there. What I have to say to the prince is not meant for wit-
nesses. But if I step onto the dais with my young guest and as a
sign of accord place a father's arm around his shoulder, then
let the trumpets sound: because then a great hour has come for
this kingdom.

*The courtiers bow and leave. They can be seen going through the secret
door of the oratory into the small passageway and withdrawing to
the left: all except the confessor. They are followed by the physician's
assistant, and behind him Anton.*

ANTON *in passing, to Julian*
I dreamt of muddy water! It will end badly.

*The King beckons to the confessor to wait, then calls Julian
with a wink of his eye.*

KING

Those words of my late honored great uncle, the Emperor
Charles the Fifth, with which he gave his crown and lands to his
only son, Don Philip, now rise before my soul.

JULIAN *kneels and kisses his hand*
May his soul reveal itself to you. Does not the crystal attain its

noble form under terrible pressure? Thus will he be when your eye discerns him truly.

KING

Perhaps I too will retire into a monastery for the remainder of my days—may a worthy son repay my subjects what he deems owing to me in gratitude.

His face is altered; he beckons to the confessor. Julian steps back.

KING *to the confessor, quickly*

But where runs the borderline that must not be crossed, where transgression would—before God and the world—justify the extremest harshness? Where, my father? — You are silent. If he were to raise his hand against me?

CONFESSOR

God forbid!

KING

Some will say even then: the victim of the reason of state had not been master of his disordered senses.

CONFESSOR

Wise judges, my king, have passed the verdict: a five-year-old boy becomes punishable and can be deprived of life by the sword insofar as he knows how to choose between an apple offered to him and a copper penny.

KING *smiles*

A five-year-old child! Most wisely thought out! A wonderful paradigm! A prince who sits on horseback like a born king and in his pride does not condescend to address his noble followers is at any rate no five-year-old child.

The chamberlain comes quickly through the door on the right.

CHAMBERLAIN *announces kneeling*

They are coming!

KING

Who is with him?

CHAMBERLAIN

The prince with an imperious gesture bade his gentlemen-in-waiting to remain behind. Count Adam alone, bound in duty, has followed him and escorts him up the stairs.

KING

Away with you, in there. To the others. You too, reverend father. (*Confessor and chamberlain leave. To Julian*) You stay!

The confessor, and behind him the chamberlain, can be seen going off through the passageway. Then the King and Julian step into the passage and remain standing, visible. They look through the window into the room. The room remains empty for one second, then the young chamberlain, Count Adam, appears in the opening door: he holds it open from the outside. He lets Sigismund enter, comes in behind him, and closes the door. Sigismund is splendidly attired, but does not carry a weapon in his belt. He enters, looks about him; then steps to the window and looks out: then again to the middle of the room.

KING

visible next to Julian, looks on, outside the room

Noble! Princely in his every gesture!

He supports himself on Julian.

The very image of my wife! Armed against every means of approach with absolute dumb impossibility. (*To Julian.*) Go in and prepare him! Entirely! Tell him everything!

JULIAN *softly*

Everything, even to the last point?

KING *overcome by tears*

Even the last! And then open the door for me and leave me with him, alone. Go!

Julian steps through the secret door into the oratory and from there into the room. The organ sounds for a moment a little louder, thereafter it is now and then softly audible. The chamberlain notices him first, steps back and bows. Upon a sign from Julian he goes to the door, makes a low bow once more in the direction of Sigismund and leaves. Sigismund turns his head, sees Julian, draws himself suddenly up, and turns his back to Julian. He trembles violently. Julian, three paces behind Sigismund, goes down on one knee. He also can barely master his emotion.

JULIAN *softly*

Prince Sigismund!

Sigismund raises his hands in a gesture of defense, as if imploring, but without turning towards Julian, with a low hardly audible sound of terror.

Yes, I. (*Silence*) This was the journey which I promised you. This house is its destination.

Sigismund quickly looks behind, but immediately turns his back to him again.

KING

How he screws his eyes up at him, from below. He hates him obviously. This is manna for my soul!

JULIAN

rises and speaks from the same distance

You have said to yourself that it is your father who thus governs over you. You comprehend that your father's ways had to be inscrutable to you as were your ways to the animals. You would not wish to live unless someone higher were above you, that is the sense of your thinking. — You do not ask: What has happened to me?—

Sigismund shakes his head.

Nor: Why has it happened to me? —

Sigismund shakes his head.

For your heart is not vain. You respect power which is above you; you are ever aware of something higher because you are yourself of the highest. And now, are you ready?

Sigismund hides his hands.

Stay. Do not hide your hands. Show them without dread. Hold this fast in your mind: I am your father's servant. A man recalls with each breath that which is above him.

The King, outside but visible, kneels down and prays

KING

Work a miracle, Lord in heaven! And reconcile him to his fate whose innocent tool I have been. Amen.

His face, as he rises again, streams with tears.

JULIAN *having looked around*

Sigismund, crown prince of Poland, Duke of Gotland, I have to announce to you the visit of your royal father.

Sigismund falls on his knees, covers his face with his hands. Julian hurries to the door, opens it and lets the King enter. The organ music becomes softer. The King stands in the room; Sigismund is still on his knees, his face in his hands, even as his father stands before him. Julian goes out into the passageway, disappears to the left.

The organ now sounds stronger, the music swells mightily; the vox humana *stands out strongly. Sigismund stands as if deprived of his senses, then his eyes search where this sound originates; he looks up, trembles violently. Tears rush to his eyes.*

KING *after a pause*

Speak, my son, let me hear your voice.

Sigismund remains on his knees, his head towards the ground.

My son, we have forgiven you. You have returned home. Our arms are open. Let us see your countenance!

Sigismund trembles, starts convulsively; he turns his head towards the wall; kneels down, there, his face averted. He presses his face against the wall.

No, it rests with us. We humble ourselves before him who has suffered. We bow down.

He bows slightly. Sigismund trembles more violently, conceals his head behind a chair.

Like Saint Martin as he came upon the beggar, naked and shivering with cold—(*He grasps his sword.*) Look up! Shall we divide our royal cloak with you? Or (*He pushes the sword back into the sheath.*) will you come to our heart, into its undivided warmth?

He opens his arms. Sigismund stands up.

Let us hear your voice, young prince! We desire it. We have missed its sound too long.

Sigismund speaks, but no sound issues from his lips.

What do you whisper to yourself? May it be a good spirit that whispers from within you!

Sigismund cannot speak.

Your eye upon ours! Hearken, Poland's Heir, once for all! We can do no wrong, as king to the subject, as father to the son; and if we had placed your head without trial upon the block, then the sacred power was bestowed upon us, and there is no one who could find fault with us. For we were before you—therefore you are delivered into our hand by God Himself.

Sigismund shows by signs that he is afraid of power,
afraid of the King's hands.

SIGISMUND *groans*

From where—so much power?

KING *smiles*

Only the fullness of power profits: in the midst of which we sit, peerless, solitary. Such is the power of the king. All other is borrowed from it and is a semblance.

SIGISMUND

From where, so much power? From where?

KING

From God directly. From the Father whom you know. On the day when it pleased God—did we step into our right as heir. The herald's proclamation resounded into the four winds, the crown touched the anointed head, this cloak was placed around our shoulders. And there was again a king in Poland. What is it? What ails you?

SIGISMUND

Then reveal your secret to me, even now! Uncover your face before me!

His eyes are very close to the face of the King; he steps back.
The King stares at him fixedly.

I have never kissed anyone. Give me the kiss of peace, my father!

KING

Enough. I do not like such words. Come to your senses, Prince of Poland. Remember whence I, your King, have called you and to what heights I have raised you.

SIGISMUND

Raised? Do you raise me now above myself and up to you? Yes? — Uncover your face. Give yourself to me as you have taken me. Mother, father! Take me to you.

KING

The desire for power consumes you. I can read it in your features. — But you were taught to win hearts with words of sentiment. (*With an ironic smile.*) May such talents profit you after my death. — But now sit here at my feet, my son. (*He sits on a high seat, Sigismund at his feet on a low stool.*) In me put your trust and in no one else. — Of one thing kings have need: to learn how to guard themselves against their evil counselors. They are vipers at our breast. Do you hear me, my son? Answer me.

SIGISMUND

I hear, my father.

KING *looks into his face*

Do you hear? I look for childlike devotion in your eyes, and I do not find it. You are withdrawn, my son. You are sly and self-confident. — Good. I see you are equal to any enterprise. — I will entrust you with the first and greatest.

He rises, Sigismund too.

Set us free from the serpent Julian, who has entangled us both.

SIGISMUND

What, father? What says my father?

KING

in the direction of Sigismund's hand

How, my father? What? (*Suddenly, terribly*) Held in chains? The heir to three crowns under his whip and pretended to me you were wild? My days poisoned, my nights made hollow with the horrible tale of a raving boy with murderous eyes! With the ghost of a born rebel! — (*Altering his tone*) And to what end? You sense it, my poor son? To chain you to him joined by the wrong done to me—to make him your lord and master forever—debasing you to become the tool of your own tool—to make a second Basilius of you, and a second Ignatius of himself— (*He gnashes his teeth wildly.*) if you do not prevent him. —

Sigismund looks at him terrified, covers his face with his hands.

Closer to me! (*Softly*) What is this common revolt with the threat of which he now again assails my unsuspecting heart!

SIGISMUND

What revolt! I know of no revolt!

KING *draws him close to himself*

I do not ask you: who has been stirring up this insurrection in my lands for the last year? In whose hand, if not in his, do these threads run together? Quiet! (*He puts his hand over Sigismund's mouth.*) I am not questioning you. I do not wish that you surrender your teacher to me. I surrender him to you.

SIGISMUND

You surrender him to me? My teacher? He has taught me to read in a book. He has taught me everything.

KING

Let his fate be in your hands. Quiet. Take this ring. I place it upon your finger.

SIGISMUND

This ring!

KING

Whoever wears it is lord and master. My guards obey him. My ministers execute his commands. Go forth out of my arms and strike like lightning. Let your first deed be sudden, terrifying, bewildering!

SIGISMUND

My first deed! I imagined it when I swung the horse bone over vermin—do not recall it!

KING *close to his ear*

Arrest this traitor Julian and see whether this plotted rebellion does not wither like a bundle of sprigs!

Sigismund is speechless. The King draws him nearer.

With this look, which you cast at me now, step in front of him. The prerogatives of this ring on your hand are immeasurable. They make you equal to me, my son.

SIGISMUND

Your equal? Your power—is now here?—

He holds the ring in front of him.

KING *softly, confidentially*

They place the grip of the hangman's axe directly in the hand of the trabant who goes with you on a night time errand. There is also from now on only one king in Poland—

SIGISMUND

Only one!

KING

But he appears in two shapes, and one of them is new and terrible. Woe to our enemies! (*He pushes him gently away.*) Go! Go!

SIGISMUND *steps back*

What are you, Satan, who cheats me of father and mother?

He strikes him in the face.

KING

Trabants! In here! On your knees, reckless fool!

SIGISMUND *takes hold of him*

What, do you bare your teeth? Why does your face look so mean? — Once before I have had to strangle an old fox with my hands! He smelled like you.

Thrusts him away.

KING

Down on your knees, rebellious beast! When! Does no one answer! We will chastise you! We will not shrink from dragging you along the ground in front of the people, and up the headman's block!

SIGISMUND

I am here now! — My will! There is nothing of woman in me! My hair is short and it bristles. I show my claws. This moment, to your horror, has born me.

KING

Untouchable! Sovereign Majesty! Help, here!

He turns to the left; Sigismund cuts him off.

PAGE *from the left*

The King calls!

Sigismund presses hard upon the King, pulls his sword out of the sheath, brandishing it.

SIGISMUND

I command! Over there! Down on the ground! I will tread

upon you! — Since I am here, I am king! Else, why did you bring me here?

The King groans under his grip.

Bellow! Make an uproar! Call out! Scream yourself to death! Off with your cloak!

The King tries to escape. Julian appears in the passageway, left, rushes in and out again through the door on the right. Sigismund runs after the king with drawn sword. The King collapses. Sigismund tears the cloak off him and hangs it around his own shoulders. Pages in the passage, left, cry out: "Help!" Several courtiers rush in, make their way through the oratory into the room. The passageway is crowded with courtiers, chamberlains, pages. All cry out in confusion: "Who calls? What has happened? In here! It is forbidden! The King is dead!" — Those who have rushed into the room keep to the left.

Sigismund, his eyes fixed on them

Silence! Not one look at the old corpse! On your knees, all of you! Kiss the ground at the feet of your new master and throw the ancient carcass there into the ditch—move there! The first two in front!

The courtiers remain motionless. Behind them several have moved into the room. The door on the right opens, Julian's head appears. He looks in all directions, then leaps into the room. He holds the royal banner tightly against his body, throws himself down on his knees in front of Sigismund, and handing the banner over, he calls out: "Long live the King." Sigismund grasps the banner with his left hand.

Come in here, you! Here, look on your lord! Prepare yourselves! I shall clean house here like a hawk in the hencoop! My deeds will do justice to my will. Understand me right. My power will reach as far as my will. On your knees! (*He throws the naked sword at their feet.*) There! I do not need that! I am master here!

Several in front kneel down.

COUNT ADAM

among the courtiers cries out

The King lives! Assist his Majesty! (*He tears the standard from Sigismund's hand.*) There is but one King in Poland! *Vivat* Basilius!

Two chamberlains move cautiously along the left wall and get in back of Sigismund. One throws his arms from behind around Sigismund and brings him down. Several others now fall upon him, too. He is half dragged, half carried into the alcove. The elder courtiers and the pages hasten towards the King, and help him rise. Pages bring the cloak from the prince's back and place it around his shoulders. The confessor supports him. At the same time a voice from the alcove: "He is down!" Another voice: "Call the physician!" — The assistant of the physician and Anton with the covered dish next to him are the last to step out of the oratory. The assistant goes to the alcove where he is being called. He looks around for Anton, who clasps the covered dish against his body. Several persons come running, pull the dish out of Anton's hands, carry it quickly towards the alcove. The King has risen to his feet.

KING *trembles*

It has happened as it was prophesied. He set his foot upon me in view of the people. — But we have remained in possession of our crown and can decree his punishment! Ah! Who would have dared to hope for that! I am thirsty.

A COURTIER

A draught for the King!

Several pages run out.

KING

touches his right hand with the left

My ring!

Someone runs to the bed, brings the ring,
hands it over on his knees.

KING

It too must be washed clean in blood. (*Looks at it. He beckons several of them to approach.*) A frenzy must have taken hold of the common people! They lie prostrate in the churches, I hear, and pray for a new king, an innocent boy, who will come in chains and bring on a new kingdom. — We will give them a wholesome spectacle. The scaffold shall go up in the center of the great market square, higher than any that has ever been erected. Three times twenty steps shall he climb till he find the block whereon to lay his head. (*Louder, addressing all of them.*) I wish to see the people of my capital city, each rank and station, ceremoniously invited, and they that are chained in the mines and on the galleys shall be set free. They shall be lined up in clean holiday robes, and he shall also be led past them in order that even the lowest of my subjects will not be left without a diversion on such a festive day.

The door opens.

TWO PAGES

Room for the King's draught!

Three pipers playing. — The goblet, carried by a page.

The chief cupbearer, kneeling, hands the goblet to the King, rises again, and as the King touches his lips to the goblet calls out.

CHIEF CUPBEARER

The King is drinking!

ALL

Hail to your Majesty!

The chief cupbearer on his knees receives the empty goblet, goes out with the pipers and pages.

KING *rises*

The physician! We are in need of his skill. The creature shall atone under the sword, being of sound mind and body!

Pages go out. The King takes a few steps. The courtiers move
aside and reveal to view: Julian against the wall surrounded by
three of them who hold their drawn daggers pointed at him.
Julian, with closed eyes, groans.

ANTON *near him*

Oh my, do you feel so poorly? Does your Lordship need to be
let blood?

The King keeps his eye on him, whispers to a courtier.
Three pages stand nearby.

COURTIER

Pages, do your duty!

The pages fall upon Julian, rip the chain of the order off
him and pull the royal seal from his belt.

JULIAN

Stand, now! Walk upright out of here!

He collapses. The physician enters rapidly and
goes towards the King.

KING

Not here! — We have even now defended ourself alone against
a very serious assault. There you are needed. And his accom-
plice too must soon regain his senses for me. In these next three
days I have yet several questions to ask him. Then they shall
drag him to the gallows on a cowhide, and the hangman shall
do his office a second time.

The physician steps up to the bed where courtiers and trabants
are standing. They make room for him. Gervasy and Protasy enter
noiselessly, steal up to the King, writhing in a deep obeisance,
each holding a piece of paper in his hand.

You come pat, in good time, always in good time, my honest
fellows. — Now I am master in my own house.

*Gervasy and Protasy on bent knees; they leave. The King
scans the papers, puts them away in his belt, looks about him.
The court in a semicircle.*

Zdislaw!

A grandee steps forward.

Last night your son expressed himself before witnesses as fol-
lows: If it should so come about that this mysterious stranger
were really of royal blood, and if this prince should aspire to
the crown, then he would not draw his sword against him. These
are traitorous Ifs and murderous Ands! A tower stands empty
high up in the mountains, there we will give him time to repent
of his words. Rise. Step back. (*To the Starosta of Utarkow, to whom
he beckons to approach.*) You spoke to your wife when you were
alone with her: you said there were such inward congestions
and tainted humors as produced unexpectedly a strangulation
of the overburdened head. With this covert speech you were
alluding to us, the head of this realm.

STAROSTA OF UTARKOW
I know nothing! No one could have heard this!

KING
Step over there, rebel. The guard will carry you off. — You shall
all look at one another and not know which one is not yet be-
trayed. Bohuslaw!

An old courtier steps forward.

Why do you tremble so when I beckon to you graciously? (*Softly*)
Your two maiden nieces are very beautiful. We must, whether
we will or no, make of their twofold beauty the jewel of these
approaching festive days. (*Louder*) Our good people will surely
not wish to go without offering a pleasure-penny. (*To the Chancel-
lor*) See to it that the tax lists will be newly drawn up. From the
Jewish quarter we expect a voluntary gift, worthy of such an
occasion. (*Again to the old courtier*) The beauty of your nieces

is exquisite. (*To the Castellan of Krakow*) Cover the gallows with black cloth. And also the statue of the most Blessed Virgin, opposite the scaffold, envelop it in black tissue. — But he shall wear a blood-red shirt of scarlet, for he who has raised his hand against the sacred majesty ought to be regarded as a parricide—is it not so, (*turning to the confessor*) my father? (*To the old courtier*) Bring us the two maidens tonight, and be yourself the guardian of their honor. Make all arrangements, take to yourself the keys of our hunting lodge, be our master of the ceremonies. Go! go!

> *He grasps his hand before the old man can kiss the King's hand;*
> *he dismisses him, then turns suddenly to Count Adam.*

ADAM

We are greatly indebted to you for your presence of mind. Only do not run up your merits so high that we might become uneasy about being able to repay worthily. Favor that is stretched too far may easily shift about into disfavor. God forbid! Follow me, my courtiers. We will yet today give chase to a warrantable stag.

> *He walks with firm steps through the door on the right;*
> *the court follows him.*

PHYSICIAN *in the alcove*

Bandages on his feet. This light cloth over his face—O rare creature, precious like a single gem, you must not suffer disgrace!

ANTON *comes running*

If you please, sir, come this way; my Lord is in a worse state.

> *Julian lies stretched on the ground, his head leaning against*
> *a chair, breathing with difficulty. The physician goes there, hands*
> *him a small bottle from his pocket.*

PHYSICIAN

Drink from this, sir, it will give you strength enough to take my arm and walk as far as my room where I shall bleed you. (*To the guards who want to seize Julian, holding them off.*) Away with you! Here I command! I am responsible to his Majesty and to no one else. (*Softly to Julian, who with Anton's help has raised himself to his feet.*) Now more than ever this noble youth entrusted to you is entitled to all your strength.

The servants, under the supervision of the physician's assistant, have lifted Sigismund from the bed and carry him slowly out.

JULIAN

What do you want of me? What hope is yet left?

PHYSICIAN

The greatest. For he lives and will live, I promise you. — Such and no other (*He points to him who is being carried out.*) has ever been the narrow bed vouchsafed the saint for his awakening.

JULIAN

And the hangman's clenched fist above the head! Already they are hammering at the scaffold!

The physician leads him one more step towards the front.

PHYSICIAN *in a low voice*

Acheronta movebo. I shall unbar the portals of hell and make of the powers below my instrument: since the day you were born this sentence had been written on the tablet of your soul.

They walk slowly towards the door where the guards have been posted.

JULIAN

How shall I understand you? You know, then—?

PHYSICIAN *stopping*

Violent is the time which endeavors to renew itself through a chosen being. It will break chains like straw, it will blow away granite walls like dust. That I know.

JULIAN

Yes! Powerful man! How bright with knowledge your eye shines. Stay with me. United with you—

PHYSICIAN

To set the forces free is our part, a higher power decides the end. — We must be gone from here!

They go; the guards follow.

Curtain

Act IV

A hall in the castle. On the left side wall a raised throne under a canopy, next to it a concealed door. On the opposite wall, double doors lead out onto a balcony. On the right front and in the center of the rear wall the main doors of the hall. Several old courtiers and several ladies. Pages and footmen, serving refreshments. Part of the company on the balcony, part inside. The passing bell rings persistently.

FIRST OLD COURTIER *emptying his cup*
Is he still being led past the stands? It seems endless.

SECOND OLD COURTIER *looks down*
Now the priest is on the scaffold. High up there. A Paulist.

THIRD OLD COURTIER *coming in from the balcony*
A fan for the countess; the sun is on her face.

FIRST OLD COURTIER
A fan for the Countess Palatine. Bring one, pages.

SECOND OLD COURTIER
And his majesty on the platform, with the sun in his face; it has been two full hours by the clock!

FIRST OLD COURTIER
The sun is soon going down behind the roof of Sancta Maria.

SECOND OLD COURTIER
Thank God.

On the balcony, restless strained attention. A page with a fan goes outside. The three old courtiers also step outside. Count Adam and the Starosta of Utarkow have entered through the door, next to the throne, which is concealed behind an arras. Both are very

*pale. They notice the people on the balcony and do not make
a sound. The passing bell tinkles monotonously.*

ADAM

What does it feel like, Starosta, to witness an execution on the
very day your own was fixed for?

STAROSTA

My nerves are too strained to answer witty questions. Why don't
they fire the signal shot? Something has gone wrong.

ADAM

They will fire the shot as soon as the bell has stopped tolling.
In the same instant the two thousand convicts fling themselves
upon the horseguards.

STAROSTA

Why is the shot not fired? A plot which has five thousand acces-
sories is lost over a minute's delay.

ADAM

The shot will be fired as soon as the bell stops tinkling.

STAROSTA

It is not possible, he must long since have gone up the steps to
the gallows. Something is wrong. We are betrayed, Adam! (*Puts
his hand to his sword.*) Basilius shall not have me alive.

The bell is silent. They listen tensely.

ADAM

Quiet, Starosta. Now we play the great play. In three seconds we
strike the King, or the King strikes us.

*A shot is heard down below, directly followed by more. Shouting.
Commotion on the balcony. A few ladies jump to their feet. A shriek.*

ADAM

We strike the King! Quick, Starosta, to your post.

*The Starosta lifts the arras and disappears. Count Adam
runs to the rear door, opens it and disappears. All the ladies
come in from the balcony.*

THE LADIES

What is it? What has happened!

ONE LADY

They are pulling the dragoons from their horses!

YOUNG LADY

I saw the bannerets around the king draw their sabers! What
does that mean?

AN OLD COURTIER

Insurrection! It is high treason, a conspiracy!

SECOND OLD COURTIER

Then why don't the guards fire?

*One alarm bell begins ringing, then several. Everyone
in the hall running about in confusion.*

FIRST LADY

You cannot make it out clearly. They are shouting something.

SECOND LADY

I am afraid.

SECOND OLD COURTIER

Why don't the guards fire? Help for the King!

*He draws. Ladies run towards the door at the right front
and come back directly. The steward of the table runs to the
concealed door on the left.*

OLD COURTIER

You there, where to?

STEWARD

To secure the gold plate. The world's upside down.

Disappears through the small door.

THE LADIES

The main staircase is cut off. No one is allowed through! —
How, cut off? By the troops?

OLD LADY

We must get out. Who commands the guard?

YOUNG LADY

This way! Through the chapel!

*They try to leave by the door at the back. Count Adam with an
officer of the guard enters the hall through the door at the back.*

COUNT ADAM

No one leaves here. Take everyone here present into custody.

YOUNG LADY

What has happened?

COUNT ADAM

The ladies that way, please. Through the chapel. The staircase
will be shut off. The King is coming directly up here.

Below, shouting. Several shots.

OLD COURTIER

Our King is below there in the hands of rebels.

COUNT ADAM *turning back*

Post the guard! (*To those in front*) His majesty, King Sigismund,
will be here immediately in the midst of his trusted bannerets.
(*To the guard*) Long live the King!

GUARD

Vivat Sigismund!

The ladies leave the hall past the guards.

THE OLD COURTIERS

High treason!

They draw.

COUNT ADAM *very calmly*

Disarm them! Take them away!

The old courtiers are led away. Count Adam and the officer follow them. The door is closed at once. The concealed door opens. Gervasy and Protasy come out, peering anxiously. Gervasy at the door in the back, listens. Protasy sneaks towards the window to peer down, then to the door at the right. Basilius's face looks out behind the arras.

PROTASY *softly to Gervasy*

Locked?

GERVASY

The room is full of men; they are holding their breath, but their weapons are clanking.

PROTASY *noiselessly goes up to him*

There is an eye at the keyhole. They are looking in.

GERVASY

tries to look through the keyhole

Here too.

Basilius steps forward, in a magnificent but damaged cloak, the naked sword in his hand. No one is with him except an old courtier. Protasy and Gervasy signal to him, warning him.

BASILIUS

How did I escape them?

THE OLD COURTIER

They did not dare lay their hands on the anointed king.

BASILIUS *pale with anger*

Not one shall escape with his life. Why do my guards not fire?
Call the officer who commands the palace guard. Bring him to
me right here.

Gervasy and Protasy come closer, their hands on their mouths.

THE OLD COURTIER

Back, my gracious Lord! Back! Through the chapel. You are
lost here.

He lifts the arras. Basilius leaves, the courtier behind him.
Gervasy wants to follow, Protasy behind.

GERVASY *recoils*

The door won't open. It is bolted from outside. Now they
have him.

They listen.

PROTASY

They have caught him in the mousetrap.

GERVASY

And us with him.

*Outside, a fanfare. Gervasy and Protasy hide behind an arras. The
double doors behind them open. Count Adam steps in; guards are visible
behind him. Another fanfare. Sigismund enters from the right, half-led,
half-carried by the Vaivodes. He wears a long white shirt; over it, tattered
remnants of the scarlet robe. Two of them conduct Sigismund to the
throne. The guard offer a military salute.*

*Outside, fanfares. All the Vaivodes kneel in front of the throne. Sigis-
mund gives a faint sign to rise.*

PALATINE OF KRAKOW *remains kneeling*

With raised hands we beg your forgiveness that we could not spare your exalted person this procession across the market-place. We needed the revolt of the lowest classes in order to sweep along all and to overwhelm the troop.

SIGISMUND

I pray you, rise, gentlemen. (*Somewhat stronger*) I wish to see no one kneel! — I should have been kneeling this minute to lay my head upon the block.

PALATINE OF KRAKOW *kneeling*

Even now, before the crown has been lowered on your Majesty's head, the golden glory of a saint and martyr encircles it for all time to come.

He rises. All the others with him. They stand facing Sigismund. The Vaivode of Lublin and the Chancellor of Lithuania approach Sigismund, who sits; they remain standing on the lowest step on both sides of the throne.

VAIVODE OF LUBLIN

Is your Highness able now to grant us your attention?

CHANCELLOR *calling towards the back*

The physician! His Highness needs a tonic!

PALATINE OF KRAKOW *calling to the back*

Chamberlains! Provide us clothes for his Majesty.

ANTON

at the door in the back, to the soldiers lined up on both sides

Let me in, I must go to my master.

He is let through.

SIGISMUND

looks at Anton, who is coming closer

Anton!

ANTON

Is my master not here? (*Looks about him, frightened.*) Your Highness! Your Majesty! Where is his Lordship, my gracious master?

Sigismund says something that is inaudible. Vaivode of Lublin and Chancellor of Lithuania step up closer to him.

SIGISMUND

Find him! My teacher!

CHANCELLOR

Whom does your Highness wish to be found?

SIGISMUND

The one who was imprisoned with me! The one they dragged on the cowhide.

ANTON

Shall I go?

Sigismund nods to him.

VAIVODE OF LUBLIN

The count is uninjured, I can answer for it. He was informed about everything. He will be brought here later. But now your Highness needs all your strength for the state affairs that cannot be postponed.

Commotion at the door in front. Calls from among the Vaivodes: "The clerks, let the clerks through! No one else!" The Chancellor goes to the door, lets two public scribes enter.

CHANCELLOR

From now on no one enters here who is not a banneret.

VAIVODE OF LUBLIN

calls over the heads of the guards

Push them down the stairs, the gentry. The country delegates into the courtyard. Close it off!

PALATINE

The Supreme Court of Law is now in session, and no one is to come into this hall.

OFFICER

Guard, about face!

The guard turns, facing outward.

SIGISMUND

Let some go and bring the one they dragged on the cowhide.

ANTON

tears the scarlet shreds off Sigismund

Some of them have gone, your Majesty!

SEVERAL

Bring in Basilius. There is no time to be lost!

CHANCELLOR

Captain of the guard!

Officer steps forward.

You are commissioned, sir, with six officers to seize the person of the former king in the Carabiniers' Hall and to present him here.

OFFICER

At once, your Grace.

Sigismund whispers meanwhile to Anton.

ANTON

goes to the line of soldiers in the back

I must get clothes for the King.

They let him through.

SIGISMUND

about to descend from the throne

I wish to go with him and find the one whom they dragged on the cowhide.

The Vaivode of Lublin and the Chancellor of Lithuania gently urge him back on the throne.

VAIVODE OF LUBLIN

We beg you humbly to submit. A most important act of state demands of your Highness self-possession and presence of mind.

CHANCELLOR

It is necessary, my gracious Lord! It is necessary.

Drumbeat, slow, muffled, on the outside. The guard clears the door at the right front, and forms in line for the procession coming in. The courtiers step back and make room. Basilius bareheaded, without weapons, in a magnificent but damaged cloak, between the halberds of two bodyguards. Four more behind, the officer with drawn sword in front. Officer salutes with the sword. The Chancellor signals him to step aside with the guards, then takes a scroll from the hand of one clerk.

Basilius, you have been called before us to read in a loud voice the manifesto of your abdication and to sign it before all our eyes.

BASILIUS

My abdication is to be deliberated here? — I demand legal counsel for the crown. Who represents my rights here? What kind of court is this?

SEVERAL VOICES *very sharply*

Enough!

CHANCELLOR

handing him the document, in a low but emphatic voice

Read and sign it!

BASILIUS

unfolds the document and looks in, then

I have come here after I was given solemn assurance of my life in the other hall. Where are the courtiers? Why did they not accompany me?

VAIVODE OF LUBLIN

Read out the manifesto; there is nothing to discuss!

BASILIUS

*looks at Sigismund, who does not seem to take notice of him,
unfolds the document and reads*

"I, Basilius, heretofore King of Poland . . ." The rest of the titles are missing here!

CHANCELLOR

They will be inserted later. Make haste!

BASILIUS *reads*

". . . King of Poland, at the height of my sins illuminated by God's punishing bolt of lightning, have recognized my unworthiness and, thrown from the summit of my pride, have sought the advice of my ever loyal and true cousins, the Vaivodes, Palatines, and bannerets—"

VAIVODE OF LUBLIN

Bow down at this point!

BASILIUS

looks at him, then makes an exaggerated bow,
and continues reading

"—to which I submit, absolutely and without complaint."

He sighs.

PALATINE OF KRAKOW

Continue!

BASILIUS *reads*

"Recognized as a tyrant and thief, traitor to the land and my own crown"—recognized, how? — Oh, recognized by you!—

SEVERAL VOICES

Continue!

BASILIUS *reads*

"—I resign this crown, relinquish the seal, lay down the War Lord's staff and the standard"—the standard also? — "—waive my prerogatives and dignities, renounce my rank"—that? How so? That I cannot!

VAIVODE OF LUBLIN

Stand still, Basilius!

VOICES

Finish it! Let the Chancellor read!

PALATINE OF KRAKOW

standing in front, to the Chancellor

If it please your Grace to read the document aloud to the end so that we may come to the signature!

The Chancellor takes the document from Basilius's hand.

CHANCELLOR *reads*

"—renounce my rank and shall be from this hour no longer King and Lord over the lands of the Polish crown, but the most culpable subject of the aforesaid crown and await, submitting to such custody as will be appointed—"

BASILIUS

But my life is assured! Will it say so anywhere in this paper?

CHANCELLOR *with raised voice*

"—await the decrees which the Council of State in its wisdom will adopt."

BASILIUS

More decrees? But not concerning me! I shall retire with a small household to a manor house which will be assigned to me.

CHANCELLOR *raising his voice*

"Issued in my royal castle of former times, on the last day—"

BASILIUS

The last? How, the last? This could be misinterpreted!—

CHANCELLOR

"—on the last day of my abode therein, under the seal of my successor, upon whom may descend the blessing of the Almighty."

BASILIUS

Not, of my son? Your Highness's reversion is still in abeyance? (*He bows exaggeratedly around the circle, but not to Sigismund.*) May God bless your collective Majesty!

CHANCELLOR

Hand him a pen.

Clerk does so.

BASILIUS *looks in the document*

That is all? Such few words? So plain? (*He takes the pen mechanically from the hand of the clerk.*) The most important point is left out. The sum for my maintenance is not named. There is no table.

Vaivode of Lublin points to the lowest step in front of the throne.

The King beckons to me. He seems to want to speak with me.

VAIVODE OF LUBLIN

Here, sign!

*Basilius kneels down and signs; then he rises
and speaks to Sigismund.*

BASILIUS

Son, you have made of me a poor, helpless earthworm—I am going. (*To the courtiers*) My life and my maintenance are assured to me! (*Again turning around to Sigismund*) Our cousins are cleverer at overthrowing than at supporting kings. I warn your Highness.

VAIVODE OF LUBLIN

Silence, Basilius. Bow before his Highness and these gentlemen, your judges, and retire. (*To the officer who steps forward*) Escort him there.

BASILIUS

There? Does that mean: to the tower? I will not let myself be taken there! I have never sent an old man to that tower. A child can be alone—an old man cannot be alone. Let me go! (*He leaps to the side.*) I have not committed a crime deserving death. I did not kill him. It rested with me yet in the last moment to grant his pardon. Who can know whether I was not determined to wave the white kerchief!

CHANCELLOR

Trabants! Put an end to this!

Trabants stand undecided, look at their officer.

BASILIUS

Wait! I could be taken to a monastery. That is permissible. I have clerical prerogatives. The king is the supreme pastor of souls. Bring the cardinal; he is responsible for my soul! I want no court about me, but give me books I can devote myself to— I want edifying books—plainly printed—

OFFICER

Take him, trabants!

BASILIUS

runs from them, holds on to one leg of the throne

—plainly printed with intelligible pictures, for my heart is still the heart of a child—only the world has corrupted me. I appeal! I hold you accountable!

Trabants have taken hold of him and brought him to his feet.

You will witness an edifying miracle if I am treated gently—but if I am locked in a solitary tower, you will have a desperate person on your hands!

Trabants take him away. It has grown half-dark. At the back
door servants enter with candelabra, others, among them Anton,
with clothing and a cloak; the physician in front.

ANTON

The clothes for the King, captain, sir!

The line of soldiers lets them pass.

VAIVODE OF LUBLIN

Before in fealty on our knees we salute your Highness as our
Majesty and Lord, you will take an oath with hand and lips upon
the Constitutum which (*He beckons to the second clerk.*) I here hold
in my hands.

Sigismund recognizes Julian, who has entered, muffled in
disguise, among the servants; he rises.

PALATINE OF KRAKOW

Is your Majesty giving us your attention? It is necessary.

SIGISMUND

May my household servants come to me? You gentlemen are
fully dressed, and I am wearing only a shirt.

He goes down the steps. The servants approach him, also those
carrying the candles, and conceal Sigismund from view. Shots are heard
in the distance. Several of the Vaivodes look out of the balcony door.

FIRST SERVANT

Shooting in the outskirts of the town. There's no help for it—
the rabble that has been let loose must be put back on the chain
again, and with bloody force.

SECOND SERVANT

The devil sows his seeds between the grain; that's the way it goes.

Sigismund steps forward, Julian next to him.

SIGISMUND *softly to him*

Stay close to me now, my teacher.

CHANCELLOR *steps before Sigismund*

It appears necessary that the several powers of the Council of State be fixed by a solemn constitution. The point being that your Highness will be bound by oath—

Sigismund holds his hand out to the physician, who kisses it. Then he seats himself on the throne.

VAIVODE

If it please your Highness to grant the Chancellor audience. It is essential. This fundamental act of state for which we are assembled here should not be delayed.

SIGISMUND

steps down, goes up to the Vaivodes

Down there I was carried past all of you—I saw your face— yours—yours! You hid your face in your hands. You looked at me firmly and I understood that you wished to give me comfort. You gave me a sign pointing up to heaven. (*They bow reverently and kiss his hand.*) But now go, my cousins, and leave me alone with this man, (*He points to Julian.*) for he will be my minister, and I wish to take counsel with him.

VAIVODE OF LUBLIN

goes up to Julian with vigorous steps

Count Julian, begone from this hall which no one has author- ized you to enter.

PALATINE OF KRAKOW

The Constitution contains the names of those noble persons with whom alone the king may take counsel.

CHANCELLOR

The royal seal remains to hand, jointly of the Council and the King.

JULIAN

The seal is in my hands. In the king's name: my lords, you are given leave to depart. When there is need of your counsel, we shall know how to find you.

THE VAIVODES *menacing*

We shall know how to find you! We shall know how to strike! We shall know how to punish!

JULIAN

Officer! In the name of the King. These gentlemen will leave us. Clear the doorway for them.

THE VAIVODES

put their hands to their swords

Oho! We shall see about that.

JULIAN *very strong*

Guards! Who is king in Poland?

OFFICER

takes his stand somewhat near Sigismund

Standard to me!

Standard-bearer steps behind the officer. Fanfare outside. Guards, holding their pikes crosswise, move between Sigismund and the Vaivodes so that they must yield one step.

JULIAN

Your lordships are cleverer at unseating a king than at setting him on the throne; you shall be treated accordingly.

Guards, holding their pikes crosswise, take one step forward;
the Vaivodes take one step back towards the exit.

PALATINE OF KRAKOW

A royal decree without our consent is null and void!

THE VAIVODES

That is so!

Guards take a step forward.

JULIAN

We shall know how to preserve the royal seal from misuse.

VAIVODE OF LUBLIN

Traitor, you stole the seals! That is a capital crime!

Guards take one step forward.

JULIAN

Retire, my lords, to your houses without delay! Each by himself!
Any banding together will be dealt with as high treason.

Guards take one step forward.

THE VAIVODES

already quite near the door, shake their fists

We have not yet done with you!

JULIAN

To this end, your lordships, are kings empowered by God, that
they create order out of disorder.

The Vaivodes are being forced out. Guards at both doors
withdraw. Anton pushes an armchair up for Sigismund, then
for Julian. The physician steps into the background. Julian steps
in front of Sigismund, bending his knee, then rising at once.

O my King! My son!—for you come from me who molded you, not from him who furnished merely the clump of earth, nor from her who gave birth to you, howling, before she departed this world! I have shaped you for this hour! Now do not let me down! — I understand your look. Your soul has had to suffer in order to rise—and all else was vain.

SIGISMUND

You have taught me to comprehend it. All is vain except the discourse between spirit and spirit. — But now I, the begotten son, am above the begetter. Now when I lie alone, my spirit goes out where yours does not reach.

JULIAN

Yes? Are you filled with a foreboding? A glorious foreboding of your Self? A prodigious future?

SIGISMUND

Future and present at one and the same time.

JULIAN

Exalted being, the royal mantle can raise you no higher. I have led you out of your tower, dressed you in princely robes, but what was that compared with the road which I have now opened before you!

SIGISMUND *smiling*

True! For now I shall never run the danger that the phantom will prove to be a phantom.

JULIAN

You speak true, my King. For this time you are secure.

SIGISMUND

Yes, that I am, Lord and King forever in this solid tower.

He strikes himself on his breast.

JULIAN

We are now the fortune-tellers and the fortune-makers.

SIGISMUND

Yes, we are. Fortunate to have been taught by experience!

He sits down.

JULIAN

To do the deeds, that is henceforth our part.

SIGISMUND

That is our part.

JULIAN

And now to horse and ride with me where you will look upon
legions of your loyal men as the moon on Judgment Day will
look upon them that have risen, and her eye will not be large
enough to encompass the multitude. — Hear me! Understand
me right! My deeds, concealed from you, were fulfillment; a
plan, a tremendous plan, underneath it all. Even on the cow-
hide I was stronger than all of them together. Do you hear me?
These swaggering grandees were the hunting dogs. Now that
the stag is down, you drive them off with the whip. An enormous
uprising, unsuspected by them, moves this night with gaping
jaws across the whole land like the bear climbing over the roof
of a sheepfold. I have pushed on to the limit, the earth itself I
have tickled to life and what dwells inside it, the peasant, the
clod of earth, with his fearful strength—I have blown breath
into his nostrils—his swinish snout and his wolfish maw utter
your name, and with earthy hands he strangles the beadles and
the bailiffs that obstruct his way. — In your name I have called
up the *szlachta*—ten thousand of them, Polish gentry, will ride
and take you into their midst; fifty thousand peasants are up
and have forged their scythes into pikes.

Opens the balcony door; the sky is flaming red.

ANTON

The fire bells are ringing out from all the churches on the outskirts of the town, the wind brings with it a strong burning smell. And the heavy cannon can be heard. Now, what might that be?

A servant carrying a riding habit over his arm has entered from the left and stands waiting.

JULIAN

Living proof of what I have done. — That is my cannon and those who fire it are my men. The mines have yielded their living entrails; with burning stakes naked men advance on a square of muskets—the last judgment has come for all who have not understood the signs of the time. — The great lords stand now on their palace balconies and piss for fear. — Do you hear the shouts? There is no one who does not march this night and shout your name. — But I shall hold them together for you: I subdue force with force, the soldier with the peasant, the flat lands with the fortified towns, the great lords with a levy of the barons, and them with the Switzer regiments that I have put on oath for you, and thus the reins will remain in your hands. — There, take up, my King! Clothe yourself! We will ride out. Why do you look at me like that?

SIGISMUND

I understand what you will, but I will not.

JULIAN

You will not? (*Fails to understand this.*) Ah, but yes! Quick! His riding habit! The belt!

SIGISMUND

I stand firm, and you cannot move me from this spot. I have nothing to do with your schemes.

The physician approaches Sigismund.

JULIAN

My King! Do not fail me now, for now or never your hour has come.

SIGISMUND

What do you know of me? Do you have access to me? I who am inaccessible as if surrounded by a thousand trabants.

JULIAN

Just put on the dress! And buckle on your sword! Horses are ready! They must see you now. Then I will answer for the outcome.

SIGISMUND

Farewell, Julian.

He turns away.

JULIAN

My King! What are you doing to me?

SIGISMUND

You have put me in the straw like an apple, and I have become ripe, and now I know my place. But it is not where you would have me.

They look into one another's eyes.

PHYSICIAN

Consider, your Excellency, what a day the King has lived through.

SIGISMUND

No, my friend. It is simply that I will not. But when I say: I will, then you shall see how gloriously I go out of this house.

ANTON *softly to Julian*

Let be, my Lord. He's grown deep over the things they have done to him.

The door on the right opens a little. Simon shuffles in.

PHYSICIAN

A bedchamber has been made ready here below this hall. I shall watch with the servants.

JULIAN *notices Simon, goes up to him*

How did you come in? How did the guard let you pass?

SIMON

There are no guards anywhere. Not a soul in the anteroom. Not a soul on the stairs.

SIGISMUND

I shall sleep. Much will happen tomorrow, and then I must not stand aside. Farewell, Julian.

He goes; Anton goes before him, opens the door at the back; the physician follows him.

JULIAN

You come from the suburbs, on the other side?

SIMON

It was easy to get there, but coming back was difficult enough.

JULIAN

I see a strong glare of fire. But the shooting has stopped.

SIMON

They that have property have crept into a mousehole. The common rabble is hopping and dancing. Who is there to shoot at?

JULIAN

The Switzers hold the bridge from the outskirts?

SIMON

The Switzers are gone.

JULIAN

Gone?

SIMON

By order of the Council, they say.

JULIAN *calls*

Jerzy!

A groom enters from the right with Julian's hat and sword.

My horses are below by the castle guard?

GROOM

The horses are down below—but there's no guard any more.
They've all quietly left.

JULIAN

The castle guard left?

SIMON

That is the whole point. They have changed the watchword. In
fact, everything is completely changed. Not a word about our
new King, his Highness. No mention of your Excellency. The
one without a name, he is now in complete power over there.

JULIAN

The nameless one is called Olivier and acts on my command.

The groom steps nearer.

SIMON

Very good. He is in power now. He has the artillery and the
men. But it does not look as if he were one to take commands.

GROOM

Your Excellency did send an officer to him: he should stop his
shooting and burning. That is what he charged him with. And
he answered: he was just beginning. And as for his coming here
and reporting to you, he would come in time, but with twenty
thousand behind him. And without more ado shoots the officer
down from his horse. His groom escaped and has reported it.

JULIAN

Before dawn the levy of nobles will be to their rear. Where are
the squadrons now? Is it known?

SIMON

The gentlemen are all gone into the great forests—over there.
But they don't come out.

JULIAN

How? They don't come out?

SIMON

Their feet are up in the air. — The rebels have overrun them
and hung them all from the trees.

JULIAN

I have opened the gates of hell, and now all hell has broken
loose. Then I must look it in the face.

Buckles on his sword, puts his hat on, and goes out rapidly.
The groom follows him. Simon sneaks out.

Curtain

Act V

An antechamber in the castle; on the right an iron grating, with a door inside it leading to a further antechamber. On the left, two doors. It is nighttime, close to morning. On the left wall not far from the second door is a low bedstead. Anton, dressed, cowers on the bed; he rises, goes to the grating, and peeks through.

ANTON

Officer! Sir! Are you there? Nobody there? Nobody at all? (*He takes a tinderbox, kindles a light, and holds it through the grating.*) Where are the guards? Where is the sentinel? Doctor! This is sickening—I am scared! (*Goes to the nearer door on the left.*) Can you hear me, doctor?

PHYSICIAN *comes out*

What is it, Anton?

ANTON

The sentinel is gone—there's nobody left. What is going on, doctor?

PHYSICIAN

Is the King asleep?

Listens at the farther door.

ANTON

in the background at the window

Some people are running down there with lanterns. They are bringing someone! I don't like it at all.

JULIAN'S GROOM *appears at the grating*

Disaster! My Lord is dead!

PHYSICIAN *runs to him*

Quiet, don't shout—the King is asleep.

GROOM

Shot him down from his horse. Stabbed him with pikes as he lay on the ground. They are bringing him.

ANTON

Who is bringing him?

GROOM

Our men. But ours are not alone. With them such bareheaded, barefoot rabble.

Sigismund steps softly out of his door; they do not notice him.

ANTON

Now it's life or death. Holy Mother of Jesus!

The physician exits with the groom through the door behind the grating.

SIGISMUND

Why does Anton clench his fists?

ANTON

Quick, hide yourself! They shoot at anything that smacks of lordship.

Sigismund steps calmly to the window, looks down.
Anton trips with fright.

If only these things did not happen so fast! For twenty years it all went along so slowly!

Men are approaching on the right, outside the grating. Torchlight.

Now it's coming: hand round the throat, the knee on the chest! — How did I ever come into this confounded country. I can't keep my wits straight any more!

VOICES *very close*

Sigismund! Sigismund!

ANTON

Now these hot devils bellow your name! Hide yourself, for the love of—hide yourself inside!

SIGISMUND

Here I am. Go and meet them, point to me and shout loudly: Here he stands, the man you are looking for. Then they will not harm you.

The physician, the groom and Anton carry in Julian. His eyes are closed and he looks like a dead man. At the same time rebels enter the room, partly armed, partly unarmed. Among them are several with stern faces and long hair, holding torches in their hands; some are half naked, still wearing severed chains around their feet and iron rings around the neck. Most of them stay outside and look in through the iron grating. Julian is placed on the low bedstead which Anton had occupied before.

ONE IN FRONT

Look on him, naked brethren, firstborn sons of Adam! Behold: the King's son underneath the earth, chained to the streaming vaults! This is the one!

ONE WITH A WOODEN LEG

pushes his way forward

This one is the poor man's King, and they will carry before him the sword and the scales.

Sigismund looks motionless on Julian.

ANTON *softly to the physician*

Must our master die?

ONE OF THEM

Speak to us!

ANOTHER

Call him by his name!

A THIRD

Those that have called him by name, their tongue has grown dumb in their mouths.

Julian opens his eyes, raises himself partly and looks about.
Two with torches stand near his bed.

JULIAN

Where am I? (*He looks around in a circle, with difficulty.*) You—face of a rat! You—front of a swine with eyes that squint upwards! You snout of a dog! Clods, all of you, shuffling about! By the light of this torch, I will laugh at you without being tickled! (*He raises himself completely.*) Take your pikes away! (*They make room.*) Ha, Nothingness growing a thousand heads, stand up beneath my look. As long as I subdue you with my eyes I shall not be deprived of the sense of my self!

ONE WITH A TORCH

The flock has no shepherd. But they who hold staffs and swords in their hands are devils. We make short shrift of them. So you are condemned.

JULIAN

You have condemned me? You are the sweepings that I have alone swept together!

SIGISMUND *takes one step nearer to Julian*

My teacher, why do you speak to them? The tongue is too thick to say what is worth the trouble of saying.

JULIAN *turns towards him*

You are also here, creature of mine? — He is, as he stands there, my work and it is wretched.

THE ONE WITH THE TORCH

We are the light-bearers, the anabaptists in the fire. You are our light, and now we will choke the prince of darkness with our naked hands.

ONE IN RAGS

We stand at your side! Speak to us, our King!

SIGISMUND *nearer to Julian*

My teacher, I am near you.

JULIAN

Turn away from me, you lump of clay, under whose tongue I have put the wrong word. I do not wish to see you.

SIGISMUND

You have put the right word under my tongue, the word of comfort in the desert of this life—and I give it you again in this hour.

Julian lies down again; he shuts his eyes.

I smile to you in your solitude. — Your prayer is not without virtue even though you clench your fists instead of folding your hands.

JULIAN

opens his eyes and closes them again

I have brought the lowest up above. But it has not borne fruit.

SIGISMUND

You torment yourself that a vein may break open inside you from which you might drink. But inside me it flows without hindrance, and that is your work.

Julian opens his eyes once more as if he were about to speak;
then he shuts his eyes and sinks back with one word.

JULIAN

Nothing!

SIGISMUND *looks at him*

He is dead.

THE ONE WITH THE TORCH

Do not heed the dead man; for you will remain with us forever.

AN OLD MAN *makes his way forward*

Look on him, on our King, how he stands here. Like one bathed
in the living waters of the river, he gleams from head to foot.

ONE OF THEM

Speak to us!

ANOTHER

Do not wake him. If he were to cry out, our soul would burst in
us like a sack.

ONE ALMOST NAKED

with a chain on his foot

We know you well. You were carried past us, you Lamb of God,
and to each one of us you gave greeting with your dying eyes!

He bends down and kisses Sigismund's garment.

ANOTHER

Remain with us! Endure with us!

SIGISMUND *in an undertone, as if to himself*

Yes, I will go out with you.

ONE OF THEM

He speaks to us. He says he will go out with us.

ANOTHER *kneeling down*

That we may not die, O Lord!

ONE OF THEM

Form a lane so that all who stand outside can see him.

SIGISMUND

I feel a broad open land. It smells of earth and salt. I will go there.

ONE OF THEM

We will fit out a cart and yoke twelve pair of oxen to it. You shall ride on it before us, and a bell shall ring on your cart as if you were a church riding on wheels.

VOICES *inside and outside*

Remain with us! Endure with us!

ONE OF THE NAKED

with an iron ring around his neck

We are uncovered—but may we clothe you? Will our King consent that we clothe him with a robe of gold?

ANOTHER

We took it down from the altar and we would put it on you with reverence.

SIGISMUND *views the naked figures*

These are untrimmed people. We will live together under the sky; I dislike those who live in houses.

THE ONE WITH THE TORCH

Therefore we shall not leave one stone upon another in the churches; for God does not hide himself in a house.

SEVERAL

Let us lift you and carry you out that all may see you.

OTHERS *further back*

Lord, protect us! Endure with us!

> *They sigh. A sharp roll of drums outside, quite nearby.*
> *Sigismund starts in alarm.*

THE ONE WITH THE TORCH

Fear not, for you are a torch, and no one can extinguish you.

SIGISMUND

Who is this who now wants to come to me? I hear his footsteps
on the stairs.

ANOTHER OF THE TORCH-BEARERS

The hairs on your head are numbered, and there is no one who
would lift his hand against you.

SIGISMUND *very anxious*

But who are they that are coming now?

ONE OF THE NAKED

They are those without a name who until now have commanded
us. But we set you above them. Come then on our shoulders
and speak to them from above.

SIGISMUND

No, there is someone coming now whom I must face.

> *A short drum roll outside. Olivier steps in, covered with iron*
> *and leather, pistols in his belt, a battle helmet on his head, a short*
> *iron club in his hand. Behind him Jeronim, the scribe, and the*
> *Latvian Indrik; they too are armed with short pikes. The people*
> *make room. Olivier steps up to Sigismund, contemplates him.*

ONE OF THE PEOPLE

This is the chosen one! He shall ride before us on a cart with bells.

ANOTHER

All that has happened has happened for his sake.

A THIRD ONE

At his feet all will kiss one another, and the wolf will embrace the lamb. Therefore he must ride before us on a cart.

OLIVIER

Good. It shall be so ordered. (*He notices Julian's dead body, approaches it; the people make room.*) I know him. He was your jailer. He kept you worse than a dog, and now he is repaid.

SIGISMUND

You are mistaken. He did not keep me as he was commanded to, but he kept me as he had planned in the fulfillment of his mind's work.

OLIVIER

Get rid of the dead Jesuit.

SIGISMUND

No, carry him in there and lay him on my bed.

Several men raise Julian up and carry him into the next room.

THE ONE WITH THE TORCH

going up to Sigismund

We are always at your side! We will stay around this house to answer your call.

OLIVIER

Off with you, make room.

A SECOND ONE WITH A TORCH

turning to Olivier

We know no ruling power. Should you nameless ones try to set yourselves up—you will be condemned.

OLIVIER

You are deceived! There is no governing power—but there are those whom you charged with doing what must be done. — Now leave me alone with this person.

Aron, Jeronim, and Indrik hold their pikes crosswise and force the people out of the hall. Drum roll outside. The people give way silently, all eyes on Sigismund.

SIGISMUND *points to Anton*

This one shall remain with me. Anton, I am thirsty. Bring me something to drink, Anton.

The physician is one of the last to leave the room; not with the others, but alone by the door at the front, right. Anton places a candlestick on the table.

OLIVIER

in an undertone to his three followers

You will stay within calling distance, my adjutants, all three of you. (*To Aron still more softly*) Those incendiaries with the torches, isolate them in the courtyard. Have them surrounded with reliable people; attract no attention.

Aron, Jeronim, and Indrik go off.

I have to speak with you, and you will answer me.

Sigismund looks at him, looks away again.

Do you know before whom you are standing?

Sigismund remains silent.

We are your helpers. We snatched you from under the axe when it whistled through the air.

SIGISMUND

Yes, they had already disposed of my head, removed it to some other place. But thereby, as when one places an iron finger under the hinge, they have lifted out a door in front of me, and I have stepped behind a wall where I can hear all that you speak, but none of you can come to me, and I am safe from your hands. (*He sits down.*) Anton, look outside, where are those with whom I had made friends just now? Is the doctor also with them?

ANTON

Better mind this man here; his word counts for a great deal now.

OLIVIER

Sigismund! The time has come to make amends for what you have suffered. You shall have an important office.

ANTON *in a low voice*

Thank him kindly.

OLIVIER

As we start on our march now, you will ride on a cart and they will come by the thousands and hail you, because you have driven your father from the throne. In this way the ignorant, tongue-tied people will be taught by us to read emblems with their eyes, and the lords will plunge head over heels into the earth. But you will be well content; instead of an earthen jug you will have full silver bowls to swill from, and women will take you to your bath and wait upon you.

SIGISMUND *to Anton*

Let all those that are friendly to me hold together and come for me.

ANTON

Heed this man; he has great power.

OLIVIER

You do not answer me? You are a sly rogue, son of Basilius. You've smelled it: now is the time to exercise power; you would have power then and not the mere show of it. You are right! We shall draw the shrewd men to us, but the stupid ones we shall ride. Come now, and we will see of what use you can be among those that command.

SIGISMUND *with contempt*

Who is it that gave you power to hand out to others?

OLIVIER

Do you see this iron tool in my hand? The hand grips it and strikes with it; just so I am myself in the hand of fatality. What you are facing now you have never known before. What you have known up to now was jesuitical machinations and hocus-pocus. But now you are face to face with reality.

SIGISMUND

I understand you well. I know that the Here and Now fetters many men as with a chain. But not me, for I am here and I am not here! So you may not command me.

OLIVIER

That is what I have you for, you and your kind, in order to put you to good use.

SIGISMUND

You do not have me. For I am alone unto myself. You do not even see me: for you are incapable of looking, because your eyes are walled up with that which is not.

OLIVIER

Is that all you have to answer me? Epileptic creature, can you not see who stands before you?

SIGISMUND

I see you have the neck of an ox and the eyes of a dog. So you
are fit for the task that has been set you.

OLIVIER

That is all?

Anton, afraid, folds his hands.

SIGISMUND

I have always had people like you sitting about me in my
pigsty.

*He gets up, turns his back on Olivier, and goes slowly out of the
back door, on the left. Anton follows him.*

OLIVIER

tosses his head three times in a dreadful threat

It is enough. It is enough. It is enough. — Come in, adjutants,
all three!

Aron, Jeronim, Indrik enter.

Have you done away with Basilius?

JERONIM

We have. On the stroke of seven. Against a cellar wall, a sack
over his head, and buried right there.

OLIVIER

Clear the courtyards gradually. (*He looks at his pocket watch.*) At
nine o'clock they must be cleared. The outer doors will be left
ajar, a cannon behind, loaded with case shot. — But mean-
while—(*He steps to the window.*) three picked sharpshooters over
there. They must keep their eye on these windows. At once.

Jeronim goes.

Look in there. What do you see?

ARON *softly*

Sigismund, Basilius's son. He stands by the bed and bends over the one who lies in it.

OLIVIER

Imprint his face on your memory. Take careful note of his measurements, how he is built, the color of his hair, every last thing.

ARON

His likeness goes around the countryside, a bad print, and they light candles before it as before an ikon.

OLIVIER

That's why. I need a fellow so like him that you could mistake him for the other, and one who suits me like the glove on my hand.

ARON

Why do you need his counterfeit, too, when you have him in person?

OLIVIER

He himself is not usable. — Let us go. I will personally give instructions to the three sharpshooters. Go.

*Aron and Indrik leave. The physician quietly opens the
small door at the left front, enters hurriedly. Olivier sees him,
points his pistol at him.*

Who goes there?

PHYSICIAN *raises his hands*

Give me one minute's hearing, sir! I am the King's physician.

OLIVIER

The man Sigismund is not sick, so far. Do you suppose he will need a physician in the near future? Are you a fortune-teller? —

I know of you. We will find employment for you elsewhere. Report to the town command. Say I have sent you.

PHYSICIAN

I am at my proper post here. I have heard all that you have spoken. (*Folds his hands.*) O Sir! Sir! Do you have any notion who it is you are going to kill!

OLIVIER

None of your playacting. This cleric and comedian style is abolished. A sober day has dawned over the world.

PHYSICIAN

Have you no idea in whose presence you were standing? Have you no sense to perceive the nobleness of this being?

OLIVIER

He is a man who stood before his judge just now. That is the sober fact.

PHYSICIAN

Who is the judge over purity? Where has innocence its judge?

OLIVIER

I had thought, sir, you were a doctor, but I see you are a parson. The concepts with which you operate, sir, are done with and lie in the carrion pit. — The man stands here before me: "Basilius and the Jesuit in there, that impostor, they have made you, the one your body, the other your mind—therefore you are guilty, you are marked so by fatality, and you shall be punished bodily, for we have nothing to take hold of except your body." That is the ruling of our court.

PHYSICIAN

Look over the whole world: it has nothing nobler than what confronts us in this human being.

OLIVIER

I look on the world which produces the like of him as on a juggler's booth at the fair.

PHYSICIAN

And the people feel it! Far and wide it makes them go down on their knees!

OLIVIER

These very same creeping exhibitions will all be abolished.

PHYSICIAN

The world is not ruled by iron clubs, but by the spirit that is in him. He is a powerful man. Take care!

OLIVIER

Now you have pronounced his sentence. For this he must be quashed, annulled, obliterated. To that end I stand here. — For I and some others, we have sacrificed ourselves and we take the burden of government off the people lest they become giddy.

PHYSICIAN

And you have come here for that?

He throws himself down before him.

OLIVIER

Indeed! People should rightly lie at our feet for what we have taken upon us, but we scorn that; nor shall they idolize our names, therefore we keep them secret. — Let go, sir, or I will free myself in a different manner.

He pushes the physician away and goes out.
The physician raises himself. Gradually the day breaks.

SIGISMUND *steps in through his door*

Is that fellow gone? I saw him once before in another place, but now I have seen him for the last time.

A N T O N *has entered behind Sigismund*

Shall we be off? Down this way? Should I call somebody? Make signals?

Sigismund remains standing and looks on the wall next to the door of his room; it reflects faintly the light of the morning sun.

S I G I S M U N D

The peasant had slaughtered a pig which was hung next to the door of my room, and the morning sun struck its inside which was dark, for its soul had been called away and had flown elsewhere. They are all joyful signs, but in what way I cannot explain to you.

He sits down.

V O I C E S *from outside*

Sigismund!

A N T O N *at the window*

Now a great many of them are coming into the courtyard. They are looking up here.

He has opened the window, steps back.

S I G I S M U N D *sitting*

They will come for me, won't they? And I shall go forward and never again look back.

V O I C E S *outside*

Sigismund! Remain with us! Endure with us! Do not abandon us!

S I G I S M U N D

I am alone and I long to be united.

He rises.

V O I C E S

Sigismund! Do not abandon us!

ANTON

They behave just like the players at the comedy. These are not honest people.

SIGISMUND

I will go to the window and speak with my new-made friends; they are calling me.

He goes slowly towards the window.

ANTON *anxious*

Better not, sir, not to the window!

PHYSICIAN *to himself*

Avert it, all-prevailing God!—or let my heart break and, sinking down, let me see the heaven in which I will be with him!

VOICES

Come to us, Sigismund!

Sigismund steps to the open window. A shot is fired from the outside. The physician and Anton see that Sigismund has been hit; they catch him in their arms and bring him into the interior of the room where they set him down on the chair.

ANTON *clenching his teeth*

Shot from down below! Doctor! These murderers! These vile assassins!

SIGISMUND *opens his eyes*

Quiet, Anton, I shall die shortly.

ANTON

As long as there is life, there is hope. I have heard this often. Do say something, doctor!

The physician feels Sigismund's pulse.

SIGISMUND

I feel far too well to hope.

He is silent.

ANTON

And has our King nothing to say to us?

SIGISMUND

looks at the physician

Bear witness, I was here, though no one has known me.

The physician and Anton kneel. Sigismund falls back, draws a deep breath and is dead.

Curtain

NOTES

In Memory of the Actor Mitterwurzer

Friedrich Mitterwurzer (1844–1897), the Austrian actor who pioneered a more naturalistic acting style, was a leading figure at Vienna's Burgtheater in such roles as Faust and Mephisto.

The Tale of Night Six Hundred and Seventy-Two

This pastiche of the Indian, Persian, and Arab folktales gathered in *The Thousand and One Nights*, which first became known in Western translations during the eighteenth century, was written a decade before Hofmannsthal wrote his essay "The Thousand and One Nights," which appeared in *Der Tag* in 1906, and was subsequently used as the introduction to Felix Paul Greve's twelve-volume translation, based on Richard Burton's English edition.

A Tale of the Cavalry

56 *July 22, 1848* In 1848, fifty years before this story was written, Venice and Lombardy were ruled by Austria in the face of local patriotic resistance. In March, 1848, the so-called Five Days' revolution broke out, followed by a more general uprising that expelled the Austrian garrisons. By June, after a series of fiercely contested battles, Austrian forces recaptured most of what they

had lost. After the decisive battle of Custoza on July 23–25, the Austrians were ready to retake Milan, and the cause of Italian unification was set back.

Rofrano Twelve years after this story was written, Hofmannsthal used the name again as the surname of Octavian in *Der Rosenkavalier.*

THE LETTER OF LORD CHANDOS

Written in August, 1902, it was published as *"Ein Brief"* that October in the Berlin newspaper *Der Tag,* and in book form three years later. Grey Brydges, the fifth Baron Chandos (and no relation to either the Earl of Bath or the Duke of Exeter), on whom Hofmannsthal partly based his character Philip, lived from c.1580 until 1621 and was known as the "king of the Cotswolds" because of the grand style of life at his residence, Sudeley Castle. Francis Bacon (1561–1626), the English philosopher, essayist, and statesman, knighted in 1603, created Baron Verulam in 1618 and Viscount St. Albans in 1621, once described himself as "fitted for nothing so well as for the study of truth; as having a mind nimble and versatile enough to catch the resemblances of things (which is the chief point), and at the same time steady enough to fix and distinguish their subtler differences." His most celebrated work, the *Novum Organum,* appeared in 1620. His work invigorated his era's notions of science and moral philosophy, and influenced later thinkers.

70 *Palladio and Sansovino* Andrea Palladio (1508–1580), architect born in Padua, whose buildings in the Veneto became a model for classical revivalism; his name became that of a style that has influenced the history of architecture ever since. Jacopo Sansovino (1486–1570), Florentine architect and sculptor, most famous for his works in Venice's Piazza San Marco, particularly his Biblioteca Marciana, said by Palladio to be the finest building erected since antiquity.

Sallust Gaius Sallustius Crispus (86–34 BC), Roman historian.

71 *Apophthegmata* Grk.: A collection of sayings.

Nosce te ipsum Lat.: Know thyself.

75 *Alba Longa* The legendary birthplace of Romulus and Remus, located in central Italy, the city was said to have been founded by Ascanius, son of Aeneus. Its power was eventually rivaled by

Rome's and, in the seventh century BC, Rome attacked and destroyed the city, an episode recounted in Book I of the famous history of Rome, *Ab Urbe Condita*, by Titus Livius (59 BC–17 AD).

78 *Crassus* Lucius Licinius Crassus (140–91 BC), the most renowned Roman orator of his era. Cf. Bacon, *Apophthegms*, no. 157.

MOMENTS IN GREECE

Part I was written and published in 1908, following his travels in Greece with his friend, the art patron and writer Count Harry Kessler (1868–1937), and the French sculptor Aristide Maillol (1861–1944). Part II was written in 1912 and published in 1917. It is not known when Part III was written, but it was also first published in 1917.

A MEMORY OF BEAUTIFUL DAYS

Though this essay—more a fantasia—was written and published in 1908, it seems to refer to the time ten years earlier when Hofmannsthal was staying in Venice and wrote his play *Der Abenteurer und die Sängerin* (*The Adventurer and the Singer*).

SHAKESPEARE'S KINGS AND NOBLEMEN

110 *quoting Karl Werder* The famous German critic (1806–1893) delivered a comprehensive series of lectures on Shakespeare, some of which appeared in English as *The Heart of Hamlet's Mystery* (1907).
a paragraph from Otto Ludwig's essays Otto Ludwig (1813–1865), the German dramatist, novelist and critic, published his *Shakespeare Studien* in 1891.

116 *the performance of* Twelfth Night *by Beerbohm Tree* Sir Herbert Beerbohm Tree (1853–1917), the English actor, starred in a production of the play at Her Majesty's Theatre in London in 1901. Its ending reminded Hofmannsthal of the Dance of Death, one of his own principal motifs.

BALZAC

This essay first appeared as the introduction to the twelve-volume edition of Balzac's work published by Insel Verlag in 1908.

134   *the one famous book we have on the same subject*   Stendhal's *De l'amour* (1822).

136   *infinitis modis*   Lat.: The medieval notion of the infinite layers that separate things from divinity.

137   *the ancient wisdom of* Panta rei   At the heart of Heraclitus's writings is his notion that everything flows or changes.

138   *the hand which created the* Massacre of Chios *and* Dante's Barque   The hand was Eugène Delacroix's. There is no portrait of Balzac by Delacroix but—unknown to Hofmannsthal—there exists a drawing of him by Daumier.

140   *Taine in his great essay*   Hippolyte Taine (1828–1893), the French critic and historian, wrote his influential essay on Balzac in 1858. *Robert Mayer*   The German physicist (1814–1878) whose early crucial studies of heat and energy led to his grandly synthetic writings on celestial dynamics and organic motion.

SEBASTIAN MELMOTH

143   *C33*   Prisoners in Reading Gaol were addressed by their cell numbers, and Oscar Wilde's was C.3.3. "Sebastian Melmoth" was the alias he adopted when he expatriated to France after his release from prison.

FROM THE *BOOK OF FRIENDS*

The *Book of Friends*, first published in 1922, is a compilation of aphorisms drawn from Hofmannsthal's notebooks of 1917–1922 and from quotations. A supplementary volume, *Ad me ipsum*, was posthumously published in 1930.

THE CAVALIER OF THE ROSE

Soon after their successful collaboration on *Elektra* (1909), Hofmannsthal and Richard Strauss discussed ideas for further operas. It was Hofmannsthal who convinced the composer that a farcical romance would be best, and outlined for him a libretto that was at first called *Ochs auf Lerchenau*. For his material he had drawn on Jean-Baptiste Louvet de Couvray's novel *Les amours du chevalier de Faublas* (1786–1791), Molière's comedy *Monsieur de Pourceaugnac* (1669), and conversations with Count Kessler. Over the course of their collaboration, Hofmannsthal enlarged the role of the Marschallin, shifting the balance of the opera towards a *drame des sentiments*. In a sumptuous production designed by Alfred Roller, *Der Rosenkavalier* was given its premiere in Dresden, at the Königliches Opernhaus, on Januray 26, 1911, starring Margarethe Siems as the Marschallin, Eva von der Osten as Octavian, and Karl Perron as Baron Ochs. It was an instant triumph. In 1925 Hofmannsthal revised the libretto into a scenario for Robert Wiene's silent film version of the opera.

166   *the Wieden . . . the Platz am Hof*   Fashionable neighborhoods in Vienna.

180   *Le chapeau Paméla . . . Gioconde*   Fr.: Hats by Pamela. Queen of Golconda Powder. Golconda was an old city in India famous for its diamonds.

181   *C'est la merveille du monde!*   Fr.: A wonder of the world!

183   *Di rigori armato il seno . . .*   The Italian Singer's two verses—until broken off—are:

> Armored in steel was my heart,
> I had rebelled against Love.
> Then her eyes played their part
> Like lightning bolts from above.
> Alas! no heart of ice entire
> Can resist those arrows of fire.
>
> So precious is my plight,
> So sweet the wound to me
> That my agony is my delight
> And to be healed a tyranny.
> Alas! no heart of ice entire—

187   *Come statua di Giove*   It.: Like a statue of Jove.
      Per esempio   It.: For instance.
      dico per dire!   It.: To take an example!
      Affare nostro!   It.: That's our line of work!

188   *Sai tu, cosa vuole? . . . Niente!*   It.: Know what he wants to know? . . . Not a thing!

THE DIFFICULT MAN

In 1916, Hoffmansthal's *Die Lästingen,* "a comedy in one act after Molière," was performed in Berlin in a production by Max Reinhardt. It was an adaptation of Molière's rather one-dimensional 1661 comedy *Les Fâcheux* (*The Pests*), in which the troublesome friends of Erastus are constantly interrupting his efforts to woo the fair Orphisa. It is thought to have planted the seed for what became *Der Schwierige,* though the first drafts of his comedy were actually jotted down on the flyleaves of books by Søren Kirkegaard, which Hofmannsthal was studying. The play was completed in 1918, and premiered at the Residenztheater in Munich on November 8, 1921. Gustav Waldau starred as Hans Karl Bühl and Elisabeth Bergner played Helen Altenwyl.

208   *pour revenir à nos moutons*   Fr.: To return to the matter at hand.

211   *the* Gotha   The *Almanach de Gotha,* first published in 1763, was an annual directory of the European aristocracy.

215   *sappers*   A term for combat engineers, those who undermine, or sap, the enemy's fortifications.

230   *Riesener*   Jean-Henri Riesener (1734–1806), the renowned cabinet maker at the court of Louis XVI.

232   *Ça va sans dire*   Fr.: That goes without saying.
        hors ligne   Fr.: Outstanding.

243   *that man is my* guignon   Fr.: Bad luck.

260   *au fond*   Fr. Basically.

285   *raffinement*   Fr.: Refinement.

288   *every sort of* bassesse   Fr.: Baseness.

291   *terre à terre*   Fr.: Prosaic.

323   *Sapristi!*   Fr.: Heavens!

326   *au pied de la lettre*   Fr.: Literally.
        tenue   Fr.: Demeanor.

332   *faute de mieux*   Fr.: For lack of anything better.

THE TOWER

As early as 1902 Hofmannsthal began working on an adaptation of *La vida es sueño* by Pedro Calderón de la Barca (1600–1681), a project that ultimately consumed him for the rest of his life. In 1918 he returned to his work on the play and, after resolving his difficulties with completing the last act, Hofmannsthal published his first version of *Der Turm* between 1923 and 1925. Encouraged by Max Reinhardt to change the last two acts to shorten the play and make it more dramatically convincing, he published a revised version in 1927, altogether a much darker tragedy. Both versions were first performed on February 4, 1928. The 1925 version played at Munich's Prinzregententheater, and the 1927 version at Hamburg's Schauspielhaus. It is the revised version that is printed in this volume.

383 *Al-cohol* The physician is referring to the word's Arabic origins: *al-kuḥul.*

384 *encheiresin naturae* An eighteenth-century hybrid term (part Greek, part Latin) meaning "Nature's handhold" and referring to the elusive factor that binds biological components together into a living organism. The phrase is used by Mephistopheles in Goethe's *Faust.*

398 *"Tu reliquisti me . . ."* Lat.: "Thou hast forsaken me, saith the Lord, thou art gone backward: and I will stretch out my hand against thee, and I will destroy thee." Jeremiah 15:6.

401 *Guevara* Antoñio de Guevara (*c.*1480–1545), Spanish moralist, author of a popular didactic novel *Libro llamado Relox de Principes, en el qual va encorporado el muy famoso libro de Marco Aurelio* (1529).
"Ecce ego suscitabo super Babylonem . . . et demolientur terram eius." Lat.: "Behold I will raise up as it were a pestilential wind against Babylon and against the inhabitants thereof. And I will send to Babylon fanners, and they shall fan her, and shall destroy her land." Jeremiah 51:2.
"Et demolientur terram eius! Et cadent interfecti in terra Chaldaeorum." Lat.: "And shall destroy her land. And the slain shall fall in the land of the Chaldeans." Jeremiah 51:4.

421 *Trabants* I.e., footmen.

426 *Sic nobis placuit!* Lat.: Thus it pleases us!

445 *Acheronta movebo* Lat.: I will move Acheron.

FOR FURTHER READING

Hugo von Hofmannsthal, *Selected Prose*, translated by Mary Hottinger, Tania Stern, and James Stern; introduction by Hermann Broch. (Bollingen Series XXXIII, Pantheon Books, 1952)

Hugo von Hofmannsthal, *Poems and Verse Plays*, edited and introduced by Michael Hamburger; preface by T. S. Eliot. (Bollingen Series XXXIII–2, Pantheon Books, 1961)

Hugo von Hofmannsthal, *Selected Plays and Libretti*, edited and introduced by Michael Hamburger. (Bollingen Series XXXIII–3, Pantheon Books, 1963)

Hugo von Hofmannsthal, *The Lord Chandos Letter and Other Writings*, selected and translated by Joel Rotenberg; introduction by John Banville. (New York Review Books, 2005)

A Working Friendship: The Correspondence between Richard Strauss and Hugo von Hofmannsthal, translated by Hanns Hammelmann and Ewald Osers; edited by Franz Strauss, Alice Strauss, and Willi Schuh; introduction by Edward Sackville-West. (Random House, 1961)

The Poet and the Countess: Hugo von Hofmannsthal's Correspondence with Countess Ottonie Degenfeld, edited by Marie-Therese Miller-Degenfeld. (Camden House, 2000)

• • •

Benjamin Bennett, ed., *Hugo von Hofmannsthal: The Theatres of Consciousness.* (Cambridge University Press, 1988)

Hermann Broch, *Hugo von Hofmannsthal and His Times: The European Imagination, 1860-1920*, translated, edited, and introduced by Michael P. Steinberg. (University of Chicago Press, 1984)

Adrian Del Caro, *Hugo von Hofmannsthal: Poets and the Language of Life.* (Louisiana State University Press, 1993)

Arthur R. Evans, Jr., ed., *On Four Modern Humanists: Hofmannsthal, Gundolf, Curtius, Kantorowicz.* (Princeton University Press, 1970)

Hanns Hammelmann, *Hofmannsthal: A Study of the Austrian Poet, Dramatist and Librettist of "Rosenkavalier."* (Yale University Press, 1957)

Thomas A. Kovach, ed., *A Companion to the Works of Hugo von Hofmannsthal.* (Camden House, 2002)

David H. Miles, *Hofmannsthal's Novel* Andreas: *Memory and Self.* (Princeton University Press, 1972)

Ronald Peacock, *The Poet in the Theater.* (Harcourt, Brace, 1946)

Carl E. Schorske, *Fin-de-Siècle Vienna: Politics and Culture.* (Alfred A. Knopf, 1980)

Robert Vilain, *The Poetry of Hugo von Hofmannsthal and French Symbolism.* (Oxford University Press, 2000)